BONDAGE
Human Rights & Development

LAKSHMIDHAR MISHRA
IAS (RETD)

Vitasta
LET KNOWLEDGE SPREAD

SATYARTHI
KAILASH SATYARTHI CHILDREN'S FOUNDATION

Published by
Renu Kaul Verma
Vitasta Publishing Pvt Ltd
2/15, Ansari Road, Daryaganj
New Delhi-110 002
info@vitastapublishing.com

ISBN 978-93-86473-91-2

First Edition 2020

MRP ₹750

Editor: Manjula Lal

Cover and layout: Somesh Kumar Mishra

Printer: Vikas Computer and Printers, New Delhi

*To the 'exiles of civilisation',
condemned to bondage for generations*

Freedom Song

The sweetest
and best
of all symphonies
is not
the song of mehfils
nor the murmurs
of streams
flowing through the hills
and into the sea
nor the plaint
of the cuckoo.
It is the sound
of laughter
anywhere, of everyone.
It is the sound
of a chain breaking.

—Ajit Siralkar

Contents

Foreword

The great contribution of Dr Lakshmidhar Mishra to the cause of the harrowing conditions of the poor, deprived and exploited sections of our society deserves grateful national recognition. His brilliant mind, great scholarship and unparalleled devotion to the cause of the underprivileged have earned him an enduring place in the nation's efforts to mitigate the lot of the unfortunate and exploited, whose only sin is that they were born in an unjust and uncaring society. His long, continuing and dedicated battle against injustice has had its own impact on his sensitive personality. Anyone else with this exposure to and proximity with the grim and tragic predicament of his fellow men would have become a cynic and bitter critic of India's pretensions of being a just and caring society. But Dr Mishra has endeavoured to retain a cautious optimism that someday, sometime, somehow, something will come through to brighten the present miserable plight of a large section of our unfortunate fellow men condemned by an uncaring society and its official machinery to a life of indignity, servitude and more than anything else—irrelevance. Only a sage like him has the will to continue his untiring efforts.

The present masterly work exposes the shortcomings, weaknesses and quite often collaboration of the official machinery that enables the pernicious and inhuman practice of Bonded Labour and all the indignities that go with it. The book brings out the grim details of the situation and the individual aberrations, institutional infirmities and the bane of a corrupt and insensitive governing process.

Dr Mishra's earlier writings *Burden of Bondage*, *Child Labour in India*, *Human Bondage—Tracing its Roots in India* and *Discovery of Truth: Memoirs of a Civil Servant* are pioneering documents.

Bonded Labour continues to be a tragic reality even today. Dr Mishra's persistence in addressing this issue over a long period of time indicates both his optimism and a deep sense of disappointment at the way both societal and governmental systems respond to this pathetic human predicament.

The present work is of exceptional merit in presenting the problem and indicating ameliorative mechanisms, both national and international, in its Question & Answer format. The information provided by way of answers is comprehensive and educative. The painstaking way in which the questions and answers are structured indicate the masterly and comprehensive understanding of the issues by the author and his anxiety and concern for a proper understanding of the potential remedies.

The book bears testimony to the deep concerns of a committed scholar to draw attention to a serious human situation. A large number of studies, reports and analysis bear testimony to this social philosopher's deep understanding of the problem. Dr Mishra refers to the great and benevolent judicial activism. Between 1981 and 2012, the Supreme Court of India pronounced twenty-six judgments on various aspects of the law bearing on the issue of Bonded Labour. However, Dr Mishra laments:

> That was the time when DMs and SPs of the districts used to raid households and establishments to release victims of BLS while apprehending and putting the Bonded Labour keepers and their accomplices behind bars. Not any more. The gusto and tempo with which the States proceeded to wipe out this social scourge are rarely visible. Today it is virtually a non-issue or a non-priority issue which seldom figures in any public policy statement or discourse.

One hopes that the relentless endeavour of the scholar-author will one day result in the realisation that India's progress is inextricably interlinked with the way in which we respond to this call.

Bengaluru
October 2019

M N Venkatachaliah

Acknowledgements

The bureaucracy has very limited option and discretion to get a posting of choice; this is mostly a matter of administrative and political expediency or coincidence. The author is no exception. In the Indian Administration Service (IAS), for which he was selected in April 1964, he was made to rotate from revenue and land reforms to labour at a nascent stage of his career and from the latter to industrial and rural development, education, health, provident fund, voluntary social action to Panchayati Raj and development of backward areas before being brought back to labour at the pinnacle of his civil services career.

It was, therefore, no surprise when he was posted as Director General (Labour Welfare) in the Ministry of Labour and Employment in August 1982 in the eighteen year of his service.

As Charles Dickens writes in the first paragraph of his epic work, *A Tale of Two Cities*: 'It was the best of times; it was the worst of times.'

On the one hand, a state of National Emergency had been proclaimed in the early hours of morning of 26 June 1975 under Article 352 of the Constitution by then President of India, late Fakhruddin Ali Ahmed, suspending the right to life, liberty, freedom of expression and association and many other rights for the time being. Large numbers of political and trade union leaders were detained and there was an unusual psychosis of fear, anxiety, uncertainty and insecurity.

On the other hand, a Twenty Point Economic Programme was announced which listed goals like elimination of bonded labour, liquidation of rural indebtedness, imposition of agricultural land ceiling, review and revision of minimum wage for agricultural workers, workers' participation in management of industry, supply of textbooks free of cost to poor students and programmes for training and rehabilitation of the disabled. These were a beacon of light and hope for the poor, landless, assetless, resourceless and disabled. They brought a breath of fresh air after years of deprivation and disadvantage.

In the wake of the announcement, Ministries and Departments of the Government of India (GoI) and State Governments moved with lightning speed to enact new laws and introduce new programmes. There was a new wave of excitement all around. Those were indeed memorable years (1975-77) as far as deliverance from bondage, indebtedness, landlessness and deprivation are concerned.

On 14 January 1982, two years after Mrs Indira Gandhi had returned to power after a landslide victory in the elections to Seventh Lok Sabha held in December 1979, yet another Twenty Point Economic Programme was announced in which some of the old points like elimination of bonded labour through effective rehabilitation continued to figure. For about two and a half years (until 31 October 1984 when she was assassinated) the same gusto and tempo as in the mid-1970s prevailed, giving a fresh lease of life to the poor, deprived and disadvantaged.

As a nodal officer, the author was required to report to (late) Arjun Sengupta, Additional Secretary in the Prime Minister's Office (PMO) and (late) JC Pande, Principal Adviser, Planning Commission on the pace and progress of rehabilitation of freed Bonded Labourers in all States and Union Territories. This necessitated extensive field visits. During this period, the author was also appointed as a socio-legal investigating Commissioner of the Supreme Court on two occasions, which took him to the stone quarries of Vijayawada and Faridabad for conducting social investigations.

Even though in his childhood days in the household of his adoptive parents, the author had interacted with landless agricultural labourers working as *bhagchasis* (share-croppers) who are members of the Scheduled Caste (SC) community and the worst victims of caste system, untouchability and dire poverty, he never had the opportunity to come face to face with victims of the Bonded Labour System as during 1982-85. Many of them belonged to SC and Scheduled Tribe (ST) communities and were 'dumb, mute and expressionless' victims of an age-old culture of silence and dependence.

Spending hours with them for interface in a natural and spontaneous manner, the following questions began to agitate the author's mind:

I. Why is it that in the same human society, there are members who are affluent, resourceful and influential with all the resources at their command and other denizens who toil from morning till midnight for sheer biological survival and yet who have very little or nothing to fall back upon, who seldom receive a just and fair price for their labour or product of labour, who are willy-nilly resigned to their inexorable destiny and who have eyes to see, ears to hear, but no tongue to speak?

II. Why is it that the instinct of one person for making quick bucks at the cost of others and attempting to rob another of his/her freedom, dignity, decency and equality is so pervasive? In this culture of impunity, people commit crimes without qualms and escape unscathed.

III. Why is it that society by and large remains indifferent or apathetic to the wall of artificial difference or discrimination erected by human beings as also insensitive to the story of unspeakable misery and suffering of mute millions?

Such questions have continued to agitate his mind in all the subsequent positions he held in civil service and the positions he held after retirement, both nationally and internationally. The English translation of Rabindranath Tagore's *Prabhater Sesha Surya,* reads: 'Years have rolled by, I have raised the same questions again and again but did not get any response to my queries'.

There is indeed no straight and simple answer to these enigmas.

A French philosopher has expressed the same anguish in a slightly different vein: 'The same things will have to be told and re-told, again and again, as nobody seems to listen'.

Engaged in this eternal quest of human mind and conscience, the author adopted a dialectical approach to this book, where as many as seventy questions have been raised and answered. They may or may not fully satisfy many other similar inquisitive minds but an honest, sincere and candid effort has been made in that direction. It has been the author's endeavour to present facts as clear as daylight and analyse facts in an objective and dispassionate manner. The author would beg the forgiveness of his readers if he has gone wrong anywhere or has hurt anyone's feelings unwittingly.

A dialectical approach to social analysis has certain distinct advantages. It opens up a debate. It makes a probing mind think, reflect, analyse and introspect: 'Where have we gone wrong? Is there a way out? Is there light at the end of the tunnel?' Such reflection and analysis eventually helps to find practical solutions to myriad problems engulfing and afflicting human lives.

The primary inspiration and motivation for this work came from International Justice Mission (IJM), an NGO founded by Gary A Haugen, a human rights activist, with which the author has had a memorable association for more than half a decade. IJM has scores of functionaries who are working unremittingly for the cause of the elimination of child labour, Bonded Labour and trafficking for two decades. They have encountered State Governments in denial mode, the apathy and insensitivity of local administration, the callousness and cruelty of those who keep Bonded Labour and the fatalism of hapless victims but have not given up. Like Rabindranath Tagore, they have moved on and on with rare grit, courage and determination 'with truth as the pole star, being unafraid of death'.

While Ajoy Varghese and Shamira Manwar have provided the logistic support and secretarial assistance to make this monograph possible, Sam John, an ex-employee of IJM and Katja Heesterman, an international intern (attached to IJM for a year), Abigail Samyuktha Rabindran, intern (attached to IJM for a month), VS Chauhan and Kamlesh Kumar took pains to put the volume in black and white and assisted in editing and bringing out the final draft. The author owes a deep debt of gratitude to all of them.

This volume would not have seen the light of the day but for the patronage of Nobel Peace Laureate Kailash Satyarthi and Sarad Chandra Sinha, a former Director General of Police posted with the National Investigation Agency, former Member, National Human Rights Commission and currently head of Kailash Satyarthi Educational Foundation at New Delhi. The author owes a deep debt of gratitude to both of them for their ungrudging encouragement and timely support which he considers as a very noble gesture.

Ever since Justice PC Pant joined as Member, NHRC in charge of Bonded Labour and became Chairperson of the Core Group on Bonded Labour, he has been taking keen personal interest in all matters relating to elimination of BLS. For the author, he has been a source of great inspiration and motivation. The author is deeply beholden to him for his constructive guidance and support to this cause.

The author had also the opportunity of interacting with Jaideep Govind, Secretary General of the Commission on matters relating to elimination of Bonded Labour system from time to time. He always found him to be positive, pro-active and sensitive to issues of Bonded Labour, which is one of the worst violations of human rights. The author is grateful to him for lending his valuable time to discuss this issue and for his active encouragement and support to carry it forward.

Sanjay Dube, Director and DM Tripathy, Under Secretary (Coordination) of the Commission have been dear friends and colleagues ever since the days (2006-11) when the author was Special Rapporteur of the Commission. The author is deeply obliged to both of them for ungrudgingly making available necessary secretarial support and all relevant inputs relating to the role of the Commission on elimination of BLS which were immensely helpful.

Swami Agnivesh, President, Bandhua Mukti Morcha, Bhuvan Rivu of Bachpan Bachao Andolan, Dr Narendra Gupta of Prayas (Chittorgarh, Rajasthan), Kiran Kamal Prasad of Jeevika/Vimukti Trust (Bengaluru, Karnataka), Bagambar Patnaik of Goti Mukti Andolan (Bhubaneswar, Odisha), Vivek Pandit and Vidyutlata Pandit of Vidhyak Sansad and Sramajeebi Sangathan (Thane, Maharashtra), Dr Sunita Krishnan of Prajwala (Hyderabad, Telangana), Colin Gonsalves and Nirmal Goirala of Human Rights Law Network (Delhi), Dr K Krishnan of Foundation for Sustainable Development (Chennai), Dr Sreenivasan of Vivekananda Girijan Kalyan Kendra (Mysuru), Tulsi Das Raj of Jan Bhim Vikas Shikshan Sansthan (Jodhpur, Rajasthan) Asif Sheikh of Jan Sahas (Madhya Pradesh) Priti and Pravin Patkar of Prerana (Mumbai), Chandan Kumar of Pune and last but not the least, late AV Swami, former Rajya Sabha MP of Viswas and Achyut and Vidya Das of Agragamee (Rayagada, Odisha) have been living legends in their fight against bonded labour and trafficking and the author would like to recall with gratitude their formidable individual and organisational contribution in this field which remains alive and inspiring despite heavy odds.

Last, but not the least, the author is immensely grateful to Justice MN Venkatachaliah for having most ungrudgingly agreed to write the Foreword to this book. He has been the author's mentor and guide for more than two decades. He has written the Foreword despite his advanced age and failing health as he did earlier for three of the author's works in succession: *Child Labour in India* (1999), *Human Bondage–Tracing its Roots in India* (2011) and *Discovery of Truth—Nothing but Truth—Memoirs of a*

Civil Servant (2017). The author does not have adequate words to express his deep debt of gratitude to him for his kindness, affection and encouragement which has sustained him through numerous trials and tribulations.

October 2019 Dr Lakshmidhar Mishra

Preface

There was a time when every Indian State was vying with the other to boast of its achievements in elimination of Bonded Labour System (BLS) figuring as the fourth of the Twenty Points announced by then Prime Minister Indira Gandhi to the nation on 1 July 1975. That was the time when DMs and SPs of the districts used to raid households and establishments to release victims of BLS while apprehending and putting the bonded labour keepers and their accomplices behind the bars.

Not any more. The gusto and tempo with which the States proceeded to wipe out this social scourge are now rare. Today it is virtually a non-issue which seldom figures in any public policy statement or discourse.

And yet BLS is a tragic reality even today. Far from disappearing, it has assumed new incarnations: trafficking for forced/bonded labour, commercial sexual exploitation, forced transfer of organs, forced adoption, forced marriage, domestic help or bondage related to inter-State migration. Forty-three years after enactment of the law, the malady is acquiring a new intensity. BLS will remain alive as long as there is poverty, landlessness, migration and indebtedness on the one hand and illimitable greed and rapacity on the other. As an old adage in Sanskrit says, "One who has one hundred, lusts for one thousand, one who has one thousand, lusts for one lakh, one who has one lakh lusts for more; human appetite goes on getting younger day by day". Human appetite is indeed insatiable.

International treaty provisions, Constitutional and statutory provisions, judgments of courts, collective wisdom of human rights institutions and defenders of human rights pale into insignificance before the aberrations of human mind which contribute to injustice, tyranny and oppression. It is indeed ironic that all the advancements in science and technology, all the innovations in rocketry and spacecraft and all the manifestations of human imagination, innovation, ingenuity and creativity have not made human beings more kind, compassionate and considerate, more humane, empathetic and sensitive towards their fellow beings, the 'hewers of wood and drawers of water' on account of whose unceasing labour man is what he is and human civilisation is what it is.

I quote from Edwin Markham's poem '*The Man with the Hoe*' to prove my point:

Bowed by the weight of centuries
He leans upon his hoe
And gazes on the ground the emptiness of ages on his face
And on his back the burden of the world.

India ratified ILO Conventions 29 (of 1930) and 105 (of 1957) and put the BLS (A) Act on the statute book w.e.f. 9 March 1976. Between 1981 and 2012, twenty-six judgments of the Supreme Court with a broad, liberal and expansive interpretation of the law came like breaths of fresh air. The National Human

Rights Commission (NHRC) was mandated by the apex court w.e.f. 11 November 1997 to monitor the pace and progress of implementation of BLS (A) Act. The Commission has not spared itself to live up to the expectations of the latter through painstaking efforts over the last two decades. We, however, still have miles to go before the social scourge of BLS gets fully eliminated. Since freedom is the most cherished object of all human beings, this dialectical exercise has been undertaken with a view to infusing new hope, faith and conviction among stakeholders to end the abhorrent practice.

Section I

AN OVERVIEW

Introduction

UNLIKE CONTRACT LABOUR (Regulation and Abolition) Act, the thrust in the BLS (A) Act is on total abolition. BLS is an offence punishable in accordance with law; it is unbecoming of civilised human beings and repugnant to civilised human conscience.

When the said law was enacted in 1976, the country was under Emergency. A Twenty Point Economic Programme was announced on 1 July 1975 by then Prime Minister Indira Gandhi. Between July and October 1975, a flurry of activities took place in quick succession culminating in promulgation of BLS (A) Ordinance by the President of India on 25 October 1975. Three State Labour Ministers' conferences took place in quick succession in July '75, October '75 and January '76 to discuss abolition of BLS as one of the items on the agenda. All these conferences were addressed by the PM.

In the Ministry of Labour of Employment (which is the nodal Ministry in GoI for this purpose) while late K V Ragunath Reddy, then Union Labour Minister provided the leadership and overall direction, he was ably assisted in drafting the BLS (A) Ordinance and later the law by two of his very capable and dedicated lieutenants—late T S Sankaran and Debabrat Bandyopadhyay, then Additional and Joint Secretary, respectively.

A slightly different version of elimination of BLS through rehabilitation of freed bonded labourers figured as item 5 in the second Twenty Point Economic Programme announced on 14 January 1982 by Indira Gandhi after she returned to power for the second time in January 1980.

At the State level, States were vying with each other in terms of rescue/release of bonded labourers with a lot of gusto and tempo. There are reports that DMs and SPs in a number of States conducted joint raids on the establishments of bonded labour keepers to rescue/release the victims and to put the offenders of the law behind bars. Among the States, Karnataka with late Devraj Urs as CM (1975-78) had the unique distinction of identifying 62,000 plus victims of BLS between 1975 and 1978. With a view to promoting awareness and imparting a sense of urgency to abolition of the social evil, a number of seminars, symposia and workshops were conducted both at the Central and State level.

Lal Bahadur Shastri National Academy of Administration (LBSAA), Mussoorie under the dynamic leadership of late BN Yugandhar, the Director, played a lead role in these efforts by (a) Opening a cell to exclusively coordinate activities at various levels for abolition of BLS. (b) Engaging IAS probationers to conduct surveys for identification of victims of BLS in their district, block, *tehsil* and village attachments (c) Bringing out five compendia on various aspects of the law and its enforcement.

The law was amended in April 1985 (Act 73 of 1985) and an explanation was added to Section 2(g) of BLS (A) Act according to which a contract labourer or inter-State migrant workman may as well come within the purview of BLS if he/she meets the ingredients of the definition of BLS.

Between 1981 and 2012, the Supreme Court pronounced as many as twenty-six judgments on various aspects of the law and its enforcement such as concept and definition, role of the Central and State Governments, that of DMs, representatives of people, NGOs, survey for identification of victims, procedure for release, issue of release certificate, handling all the cases of rescue/release and rehabilitation with a sense of immediacy and procedural simultaneity, provision of adequate funds for rehabilitation of all released bonded labourers, procedure for summary trial of offenders of the law, giving freedom to the inter-State migrant workmen who have been found to be working under bonded conditions and have been rescued/released therefrom to exercise their option and discretion about the place of their rehabilitation, the need for ensuring that the quantum of punishment to be awarded to all offenders of the law is proportional to the severity of the crime, impressing on the State Governments to view existence of BLS not as a slur on their image nor as a discredit on the district administration but as a rare opportunity which comes but once in one's lifetime to bring a little cheer to the faces of the oppressed and marginalised, need for close involvement of good and reliable NGOs (who are committed to social action) with all-out efforts related to identification, rescue/release of victims and measures for their rehabilitation.

All these judgments and directions contained therein have

come like breaths of fresh air. The apex court has not changed the law but has given a very broad, liberal and expansive interpretation of the provisions of the law which is victim-centric and is fully in tandem with the spirit of the law as highlighted in the 'Statements of Objects and Reason'.[1] While dealing with *Peoples Union for Civil Liberties (PUCL) Vs State of Tamil Nadu and Others*, the court pronounced an interim order dated 11 November 1997 (the writ petition was finally disposed of on 15 October 2012) entrusting the NHRC with the responsibility to monitor progress of enforcement of the law.

In pursuance of this direction, the Chairperson, the Member of the Commission in charge of bonded labour and special rapporteurs have been visiting various States/Union Territories for an on-the-spot review of the measures taken for enforcement of the law. Over one hundred State-level review reports have been submitted and the recommendations contained in these reports have been forwarded to State Governments for implementation.

The pace and progress of compliance with the recommendations are being reviewed through Action Taken Reports (ATR) submitted by the State Governments to the Commission from time to time and further review visits are being undertaken till such time the process of compliance with the recommendations is complete. Additionally, a bonded labour cell is functioning in the Commission to coordinate various activities in relation to identification, rescue/release and rehabilitation of victims. A core group under the chairmanship of the Member of the Commission in-charge of the subject has been constituted and the same has been meeting from time to time to take stock of

1 WP No. 3922/85

the developments in the domain of policy, programme of action, success stories, grey areas, extent of compliance with the law by the States/Union Territories and other stakeholders.

The Commission has taken the initiative to organise a number of orientation, familiarisation and sensitisation workshops at the national, State, divisional and district levels with involvement of all the stakeholders. In all, fifty such workshops have been held since 2001 at the State, divisional and districts levels and three workshops at the national level.

Additionally, the Commission receives a large number of complaints relating to exploitation arising out of the existence of BLS. These complaints are either referred to DMs or enquired into by deputing investigation teams from the Commission either under the leadership of the DG (Investigation) or the Special Rapporteur in charge of bonded labour or any other senior officer of the Commission.

In a multi-lingual situation (where there are inter-State migrant workmen from different States speaking different languages) it is ensured that members of the Commission's team have the relevant linguistic skills.

One such team under the leadership of the author who was then Special Rapporteur was deputed to Vijayawada in June-July 2009. After a week of marathon field visits and inquiry, he submitted a comprehensive fact-finding report which was fully approved by the Commission and necessary recommendations were made to the State Government of Andhra Pradesh for compliance in a time-bound manner.

Sometimes on more serious issues (like prevalence of *bartan* system in Odisha) with multiple sociological (caste related) ramifications, the full Commission meets at the headquarters of the concerned State, conducts hearing of the case by involving all stakeholders before making necessary recommendations.

Regretfully, despite all these progressive measures, a large number of glaring pitfalls have surfaced in enforcement of the law characterised by (a) individual aberrations (b) institutional infirmities and (c) systemic failures as would be evident from the following:

- When the issue figured in the two Twenty Point Economic Programmes, this demonstrated a tremendous amount of political will, commitment and determination at the highest level of the government;
- The issue never figured thereafter in any important policy statement or announcement relating to BLS being an infringement of human dignity and decency;

In other words, the political will, commitment and determination which was associated with the enforcement of the law in the 1970s and '80s were no longer visible in '90s and after.

Instead, most of the States/Union Territories on whose shoulders rested the vital responsibility for enforcement of the law were found to be in denial mode as would be evident from the following mindsets:

- BLS was a one-time problem;
- Today it is a thing of the past;
- With enactment of a central law, the pernicious system is deemed to have been abolished lock, stock and barrel;
- All that was required to be done has been done;
- Acknowledging the existence of the system would be a slur on the image of the government; it will bring discredit to the district administration;

- The workmen concerned may be rendering forced labour but are not bonded labourers;
- They may be contract and inter-State migrant workmen but they are not bonded labourers.

Even after amendment of the law in April '85, it continues to be maintained that contract labour and inter-State migrant workmen are not bonded labourers.

Individual aberrations

- Individual aberrations are worse than the mindsets of State Governments and institutions functioning therein; these aberrations would be evident from the following;
- Victims of BLS were bonded to us (bonded labour keepers) in the past, they continue to be bonded even today and will remain bonded forever;
- All the international treaties, Constitutional and legal provisions, policies and programmes of government will be of no avail to put an end to the age-old system;
- They (released bonded labourers) have received so much of rehabilitation assistance from government; they would never have received them had they not been bonded. They should, therefore, out of sheer gratitude render their labour or service free even after being released from bondage and not demand payment of minimum wage.
- Those who continue to be landless, assetless, resourceless and defenceless when bonded were at least getting a morsel of food to eat; but after release from bondage, they will have no semblance of security and no means for biological survival.

Institutional infirmities

Institutional infirmities which inhibit enforcement of the law would be evident from the following:

- Vigilance Committees (VCs) are not being constituted at the district and sub-divisional level in time; the apex court had to remind the State Governments from time to time about their statutory obligation in this regard;
- Some of the State Governments denied the existence of BLS even without constituting VCs and without conducting surveys; this amounts to putting the cart before the horse.
- Besides, the VCs are not constituted in conformity with the requirements of the law as under S13 of BLS (A) Act;
- They are not re-constituted even after expiry of two years as required under Rule 3 of BLS (A) Rules, 1976;
- Instead of comprising women and men of character, integrity and dedication to the cause of elimination of BLS, the VCs sometimes comprise persons who are out to promote the vested interests of bonded labour keepers and not those of victims;
- The members of VCs, wherever they have been constituted, do not go to the field to conduct surveys as required under S14(e) of BLS (A) Act and for investigation into complaints;
- They meet and disperse at the district and sub-divisional headquarters and their transactions are mostly of a ceremonial character;
- They seldom collect, compile and analyse field level intelligence about areas and establishments where BLS is likely to be prevalent;
- They don't maintain any register as required under Rule 7 of BLS (A) Rules on the name, address, avocation/occupation, livelihood and earnings of all victims of BLS who are being rehabilitated;
- Similarly they don't maintain a register containing details of the

benefits and concessions which are the entitlements of a freed bonded labourer.[2]

- The VCs have not been provided with a Secretariat or any logistic support (vehicle, computer, data entry operator, etc.) to enable them to discharge their statutory functions. In the absence of a computer and activity-wise software, they have not been able to maintain a computerised database incorporating all relevant details about rescued/released bonded labourers which would have been useful in tracking the whereabouts of the victims who were found missing or who migrated to a worksite at a destination point.

Sections 10, 11 and 12 of BLS (A) Act have conferred wide powers on the DM of every district. These powers need to be exercised with due diligence and discretion either by the DM or an officer sub-ordinate to the DM who has been so authorised.

The powers and functions are to be exercised/discharged primarily with the following three objectives such as:

- Provisions of the Act are properly carried out;
- Promoting the welfare of the freed bonded labourers by securing and protecting their economic interests so that they may not have any occasion or reason to contract and further bonded debt.
- Taking stringent and deterrent action against those who are perpetuating BLS.

The net outcome or essence of all the three objectives as spelt out above is to prevent the occurrence and recurrence of BLS. Regretfully, due to heavy pre-occupations and a number of

2 Under Section 6(6), u/s 8(2) and u/s 9(2) as also the details of the prosecutions filed u/s 16,17,18,19 and 20 of BLS (A) Act

competing claims continuously engaging the time, energy and resources of the DMs, elimination of BLS has not received the same prioritised attention of district administration as it deserves. This is evident from the following:

- Intelligence about prevalence of BLS in a particular area or establishment(s) is not being collected;
- Wherever such intelligence has been collected, it is not being used for conducting surveys for identification of victims of BLS as required under S14(e) of BLS (A) Act and as repeatedly emphasised by the Supreme Court;
- Wherever surveys have been conducted (as in Tamil Nadu in 1996-97 and Malkangiri in South Odisha in 2001-02) and survey reports have been placed before the Magistrate concerned u/s 21(1) of the BLS (A) Act, orders have been passed by the latter by way of rejection of findings contained in the survey reports without a speaking order, without an elementary understanding of the provisions of the law vis-a-vis Supreme Court judgments and without proper application of mind;
- NGOs and Voluntary Social Action Groups are not being involved in identification of victims, their rescue/release, formulation and implementation of rehabilitation schemes, monitoring and evaluation of the pace and progress of measures taken for enforcement of the provisions of the law as emphasised in *Neerja Chaudhary Vs State of MP*;[3]
- As a matter of fact, there is a lot of reluctance in the district administration on the need for and rationale of involving NGOs in activities which they consider to be their legitimate and exclusive domain.

---

3 WP (crl.) 1263 on 8 May 1984

- All these have contributed to a number of consequences which are not conducive to fulfilment of the central objectives of the law such as:

- The principles of simultaneity and immediacy as emphasised by the Supreme Court are not being observed;
- Even after surveys have been conducted with involvement of good NGOs (though such instances are few and far between) and findings have been presented to the Magistrate concerned, expeditious and well-reasoned decisions to determine the status of the person(s) as to whether the victim is bonded or not are not being taken;
- Even where such decisions are being taken that the person comes within the purview of S2(g) of BLS (A) Act, release certificates in the prescribed form are not being issued;
- Such certificates, apart from establishing the identity of the victim, provide a protective shield to the victim in as much as he/she cannot be coerced to work for the same person from whose captivity he has been rescued/released;
- Such a certificate also constitutes a vital document for formulation of a rehabilitation scheme concerning that person;
- Absence of release certificates and other reasons (such as absence of budget provision) cause delay in formulation of rehabilitation schemes;
- Delay in formulation of rehabilitation schemes keeps the released bonded labourers waiting for rehabilitation, sometimes up to two years and beyond;
- Since the released bonded labourer cannot wait indefinitely for the rehabilitation assistance, he may decide of his own volition either to return to the fold of the erstwhile master (bonded labour keeper) or migrate to the worksite of a destination State;

- Either of the above two contingencies is full of grave occupational risks, hazards and uncertainties; this defeats the laudable objectives with which the framers of the law had set it in motion;
- State-level monitoring committees have invariably not been constituted to keep a tap on these contingencies; the committee additionally is required to oversee the performance of DMs, SDMs and VCs vis-a-vis their statutorily mandated responsibility;
- There could be contingencies where the first dose of rehabilitation assistance has not produced the desired result by way of making the person assisted self -reliant; in that contingency, he/she may look to the old creditor for a fresh loan/debt/advance;
- Tight monitoring must be done so that the second dose of rehabilitation assistance may be provided in time.

Of late, a few other challenges seem to have inhibited smooth and expeditious enforcement of the law in a manner which was never visualised by the framers of the law.

In every interpretation of the law, the intent of the legislature is an important principle which has to be fully respected. The intent of the legislature as far as BLS (A) Act is concerned is evident from the 'Statement of Objects and Reason' such as:

- BLS requires to be fully abolished as it is an infringement of the dignity of human labour;
- Anyone who robs another person of his/her human dignity commits an act of sacrilege; it is an egregious and un-pardonable crime against humanity.

To ensure fulfilment of this intent, the Act has prescribed amongst a host of measures, summary trial as in section 21(2) of BLS (A) Act being one of them.

When we speak of summary trial as in Section 21(2) of BLS (A) Act, we have in mind trial of the offender of the law and not trial of the victim.

The framers of the law were clear and conscious in their perception to provide for a summary trial on account of the following reasons:

- A regular trial will be protracted and expensive;
- It tends to get stretched beyond the normal time limit;
- The cost of waiting will be too heavy for the victim;
- The victim who has already undergone the trauma of un-freedom and loss of dignity will be further traumatised by the tyranny and rigidity of a soul-less judicial process.

The above perception of the framers of the law has been reiterated by late Justice P N Bhagwati when he has re-emphasised the importance of summary trial by observance of an unorthodox and unconventional trial procedure.

Regretfully, a judgment of the High Court of Madhya Pradesh (Jabalpur branch)[4] in *Hanumatsingh Kubersingh Vs State of MP and Another*, has held that Section 21 of the Act violates Articles 21, 14 and 50 of the Constitution and the trial for offences under the Act by the Sub-divisional Magistrate cannot proceed.

Since summary trial comes under Section 21(2) of the BLS (A) Act, by necessary implication of the judgment, summary trial cannot proceed further unless specifically stated to the contrary.

Once the cases stand transferred to the Court of the concerned Judicial Magistrate, first class and summary trial as under S21(2) stands barred, the trial court will proceed to take up trial by

4 Miscellaneous petition (MP) 2522 of 1984

adopting the warrant procedure as under Chapter XIX of CrPC[5] which will be time-consuming and expensive as also detrimental to the interests of the victim.

In two other subsequent judgments,[6] S21 of BLS (A) Act has been struck down on the following grounds:

- Principle of separation of powers as in Article 50 of the Constitution has been violated;
- Justice and fair trial cannot be ensured by Executive Magistrates as they are not legally qualified and trained persons and are required to perform various functions in actual practice;
- The procedure prescribed for trial by Executive Magistrates cannot inspire confidence and has to be held invalid.

On an objective and dispassionate scrutiny of the grounds used to strike down S21 of BLS (A) Act and with full respect to the observations of the High Court(s), the whole issue may be looked at from a slightly different angle such as:

- An Executive Magistrate is vested with powers of a Judicial Magistrate, First or Second Class, for a specific purpose for a specific period;
- He/she ceases to be as such after the specific mandate has been discharged and the notification vesting him/her with the powers is withdrawn;
- He/she does not get converted to a Judicial Magistrate on a permanent basis;

5 S238 to S247 of CrPC

6 Delivered by the High Court of Judicature, Bombay in (Criminal) WP 406 of 1988 in *Govind Sanwar Ghatal vs Dattatray Waman Bhanushali* and Another and High Court of Judicature, Madras in WP 7650 of 2013 and MP 1and 2 of 2013 in *Gajendran* vs CS, *Government of Tamil Nadu, Collector and DM, Thiruvallur,* RDO, *Thiruvallur and Tahsildar Thiruvallur*

- The existing arrangement was made primarily with a view to ensuring expeditious disposal of the cases;
- Executive Magistrates are required to function under the overall administrative control of DMs;
- Sweeping powers have been conferred on the DMs by Section 10, 11 and 12 of BLS (A) Act;
- These powers can also be exercised by an officer who is subordinate to the DM and who has been authorised to exercise all or any of the powers and perform all or any of the duties of DM;
- An Executive Magistrate is an officer subordinate to the DM and he/she can be authorised to exercise all or any of the powers of DM and discharge all or any of the duties of the DM;
- Thus there is a causal and integral link between the DM exercising powers u/s 10, 11 and 12 of BLS (A) Act and an Executive Magistrate who is subordinate to the DM and accountable for discharging his/her statutory functions u/s 21 of the Act;
- Executive Magistrates are also qualified, experienced and trained to try all such cases as judiciously and effectively as any Judicial Magistrate;
- The ability to inspire confidence varies from person to person. To illustrate this point, Executive Magistrates have, during normal as well as emergency situations, functioned with a sense of judicious discretion and circumspection, have given a very good account of themselves, inspiring the trust and confidence of government and people at large.

Supreme Court was absolutely clear and categorical that filing prosecution and securing conviction in an offence committed under BLS (A) Act should be delinked from release and rehabilitation of the victims; the latter should be effected fully independent of the former.

In other words, the trial of the offender which should be by summary procedure should not be mixed up with rescue/release and rehabilitation of the victim which is to be accorded the highest priority.

Under Article 141 of the Constitution, the judgment/direction of the Supreme Court is binding on all subordinate courts including the High Court(s).

However, till an alternative judicial remedy has been made available by taking recourse to the procedure established by law and, if necessary, by amendment of the existing law (S21), there is an element of uncertainty which is bound to adversely affect disposal of all cases u/s 21(2) of BLS (A) Act.

Systemic failures

The author would like to throw some light on systematic failures which prevented elimination of BLS. Creation of institutional mechanism(s) for rehabilitation and redressal of grievances of the aggrieved and victimised persons, getting them manned by individuals of character and integrity who have empathy and sensitivity for the plight and predicament of human beings in general and those who are deprived, oppressed and marginalised in particular is the first *sine qua non* of good governance. The victims of BLS come from a low strata of society, they have none to look up to or fall back upon. They themselves are not in a position to ventilate any grievance and seek redressal thereof. Since members of the VCs, SDMs and DMs heading them at the sub-divisional and district level do not go out to make on-the-spot visits and conduct inquiries, the grievance of the aggrieved victims will never come to the surface. We may have to think of alternative strategies by which such grievances can be timely ventilated and positively redressed. NGOs which are active in the field in this area of social action can play a very useful role provided they are taken into confidence by the district administration and asked to periodically report such grievances to the competent authority after meeting the aggrieved victims. This has not happened so far.

The scenario at the ground level does not inspire confidence. A lot more is required to be done in terms of policy, programme of action, strategy and methodology for eradication of the social scourge of BLS.

India's rating

At the international level, within the UN and the specialised agencies of the UN like the ILO, India's overall rating in terms of prevalence of BLS as also its track record in regard to measures taken for prevention/elimination of BLS including trafficking and forced child labour have not been very encouraging. This is a matter of deep concern as India is one of the founding members of the ILO, its membership in the governing body of ILO being non-elective and permanent. Since inception of ILO, India's voice of sanity and reason has been heard with respect at various fora including UN and its specialised agencies. Regretfully, India as a member state continues to be grilled by the ILO's tripartite committee on observance of ILO standards which is an important supervisory mechanism of the ILO. This is because India has ratified both the ILO Conventions on elimination of forced/bonded labour.[7]

Such ratification brings in its trail an obligation to enact a law, formulate a policy and programme of action and show some positive outcomes in terms of their implementation.

7 ILO's Convention No. 29 of 1930 (ratified on 30 November 1954) and ILO's Convention No. 105 of 1957 (ratified in May 2000)

This obligation does not appear to have been fulfilled in a substantial measure. In the Global Slavery Index and Global Freedom Network, India accounts for forty per cent of the total number of victims of forced/bonded labour or slavery (fourteen out of thirty-five million) which is also a matter of anxiety and concern.

Nationally, existence of BLS is an antidote to various measures taken for removal of poverty, illiteracy, unemployment and under-employment.

Even if a person is lifted above the poverty line, is made literate and numerate and is provided with some avenues of employment, howsoever fragile, these measures will not have much meaning and significance until and unless the person concerned, i.e. the beneficiary of anti-poverty and employment promotion programmes has both freedom and security and has been enabled and facilitated to take informed, judicious and autonomous decisions which are in his/her best interest after considering various alternative options open.

A person who is both free and secure in the true sense of the term will be able to contribute much more significantly to the family, community, society and nation as a whole than a person who is both unfree and insecure. The former will be far more agile, aware, responsible, responsive and hence productive than a person who is both unfree and insecure.

Apart from the inability to articulate the concerns, an unfree and insecure person would lack courage, confidence and resilience and will not be able to effectively participate in the affairs of the family, community, society, and nation. He/she will continue to be a victim of the culture of silence, helpless dependence and diffidence.

The author has already worked on two previous publications i.e. *Burden of Bondage* (1997) and *Human Bondage – Tracing its Roots in India* (2011) encompassing his experience as a socio-legal investigating Commissioner of the Supreme Court and linking issues of poverty, unemployment, denial of minimum wage, hunger, starvation, malnutrition, illiteracy, migration, indebtedness and globalisation with bondage.

Subsequently as Senior Adviser, ILO (2000-03), Special Rapporteur, NHRC (2006-11), Special Adviser, NCPCR (2011-12) and Senior Independent Adviser, IJM (2013 till date) he has undertaken extensive field visits in the context of inquiry into, study and review of current status of BLS. He has been a regular guest speaker at LBSNAA, Mussoorie, VV Giri NLI, NHRC and other human rights bodies and has written extensively on the subject with the following objects:

- remove doubts, disputes and misgivings;
- place the entire issue in a holistic perspective;
- sensitise cynics and sceptics who are consistently in denial mode about existence of BLS;
- carry hope, faith and conviction to all stakeholders that elimination of bonded labour system is possible, feasible and achievable;
- secure positive and pro-active collaboration and cooperation among all Ministries/Departments/Agencies (including NGOs) to achieve the desired object.

In achieving the desired object, a dialectical approach to issues has been adopted as issues are raised and respondents think, reflect, critically analyse and introspect in responding to these issues. Such an approach leads to churning of critical consciousness and helps in taking informed and judicious decisions.

Substantial portions of the book have been presented in bullet form (instead of long narratives) with a view to making the presentation clear and focused on the one hand and maintaining a logical and coherent link between paragraphs on the other.

The author hopes that this work will be of interest and relevance to all the stakeholders in diagnosis, prevention and treatment of this social malady.

What is Development?

BOTH CONCEPTUALLY AND by definition, development has many dimensions and connotations such as physical, development in relation to mind and spirit, development in relation to access to facilities and opportunities, development in relation to treatment of citizens and last but not the least development in relation to human freedom.

Physical development relates to human body (health, nutrition, hygiene, environmental sanitation, an environment free from dust, heat, fume, noise, pollution, accidents, etc.); it also refers to infrastructural development.

Development of human mind and spirit relates to acquiring certain attributes such as kindness, compassion, commiseration, love, self-abnegation, tolerance of dissent, abjuring mindless hatred, cruelty, discrimination and violence.

There is a positive and negative correlation between development and freedom. Positively stated, human beings, if treated with dignity, decency, equality and freedom would be inspired and motivated to contribute their very best to whatever they do at home, at the workplace, profession and calling and anything which is creative, innovative and reformative. The best of human imagination, ingenuity, creativity and capacity for innovation would be unleashed. Freedom as an attribute and prerequisite of human development would enable and facilitate access to a number of facilities and opportunities on the one hand and would contribute to achievement of other goals such as security, self-reliance and social integration.

Negatively stated, loss of freedom would lead to many other undesirable consequences such as:

- Poverty;
- Hunger;
- Starvation;
- Malnutrition;
- Disease.

Development to be true and meaningful must be pro-people, pro-Nature, pro-gender and pro-children. If not, it becomes the very antithesis of development.

This is so as people are not a homogeneous entity but largely heterogeneous. They are born differently, they think differently, they grow and evolve differently. Their thought process, livelihood, lifestyles, opportunities for growth and advancement are quite different. These differences in traits and attributes of human beings which are partly genetic and partly induced by the environment in which they work, live and grow cannot be wiped out; they need to be harmonised. They can be harmonised to some extent by provision of equitable access to a variety of facilities and opportunities and outlet for development such as by providing access to:

- Information, knowledge and wisdom;
- Literacy and education;
- Health and nutrition;
- Skills (life skills, communication skills, survival skills, vocational skills, leadership skills, entrepreneurial, managerial and supervisory skills);
- Creating a climate and enabling mechanism conducive to formation of human capabilities i.e. making human beings more aware, agile, alert, conscious, responsible, responsive and sensitive;
- Making people optimally use their acquired capabilities for productive purposes;

  Such harmonisation becomes a primary responsibility of the State as the agent of society.

The poor in the Indian context would broadly include small and marginal farmers, rural artisans, landless agricultural labourers, fisher women and men, collectors of raw hides and skins, tanners and flayers, handloom weavers, handicrafts, rural artisans and craft women and men (carpenters, cobblers, blacksmiths etc.), salt workers, *beedi* workers (rollers, labellers and packers), carpet weavers, garment makers, workers in brick kilns and stone quarries/crushers, scavengers, sewer workers/*beldars* (mostly belonging to the SC community), collectors of minor agricultural and forest products (mostly members of the ST community), head load carriers, loaders and unloaders, handcart drivers, hawkers, vendors, numerous categories and sub-categories of contract, casual and migrant workers, victims of BLS and working children who also often work under bonded conditions.

Through their 'blood, sweat and tears' they contribute substantially to the growth of the economy and prosperity of the enterprise in which they are placed for work. They by all accounts and reasonable expectations are meant to be the first beneficiaries of development as also participants in the development process but for reasons and circumstances which are often inexplicable, beyond their control and for which they are not responsible, they remain deprived of the fruits of progress which they grow but cannot reap. Additionally, they remain for no fault of theirs victims of social exclusion.

There are both internal and external impediments to the process of social inclusion. Pervasive ignorance and illiteracy, lack of awareness and exposure to a fast changing, modern and fiercely competitive world, consequential lack of bargaining power, absence of viable social and economic organisations to promote, protect and safeguard the interests of the poor, absence of a socially powerful countervailing force are some of the internal impediments.

An effete, unresponsive and non-performing delivery mechanism, encumbered by a rigid bureaucratic and soulless procedure which is time consuming and expensive, prevalence of middle-men, rack renting and absentee landlordism, usury, bondage and social backwardness are some of the external impediments to evolution and growth of the poor. Both the constraints need to be holistically addressed if development has to be pro-poor.

Pro-Nature development basically refers to the positive manner in which human beings interact with land, air, water and other natural resources (forest, sand, minerals).

Development undoubtedly requires the use of natural resources to our benefit. At the same time, conservation requires the sustainability of such use (as opposed to indiscriminate use). There is, therefore, an urgent and imperative need of establishing a balance between environment and development or between Nature and human species.

Irresponsible and insensitive human action and conduct manifests itself in a number of ways and has contributed to degradation of environment in multiple forms such as:

- Unplanned, unregulated and unbridled urbanisation with the attendant evil of congestion, overcrowding and pollution of air, earth and water;
- Huge disparity in consumption of non-renewed resources between relatively well-off people and the poor;
- Substantial acceleration in flow of carbon dioxide and emission of other greenhouse gases;
- Decline in forest and vegetal cover results in loss of biodiversity and wildlife;
- Melting of glaciers, rise in sea levels, rivers drying up contributing to low water table and scarcity of potable water;
- Eventual disappearance of coastal belts;
- With rise in global temperature, cataclysmic climate change, plant, animal and human life is becoming unsustainable with imminent possibility of extinction of mother earth.

The pro-gender dimension of development implies.

- Equal treatment of boys and girls, women and men under all circumstances and dismantling walls of unequal division or discrimination between them;

- Recognising the disastrous consequences of discrimination on the individual, family, community, society and the nation;
- Recognising that a girl child to be able to grow up to an active, skilled, productive, aware, agile, acutely conscious and confident adult woman, should be cared for and nurtured in an environment of love, care, affection, attention, consideration, facilitation and encouragement;
- Putting an end to abominable practices like sex determination test (amniocentesis), foeticide, female infanticide, early child marriage, domestic violence against women and sexual harassment of women at their workplaces;
- Providing easy and hassle-free access to all women to full, freely chosen, productive and remunerative employment with equal wages for work of equal value payable to both women and men.

The pro-children dimension of development implies:

- Recognising that children are the finest and best human resource, that they represent simplicity, pristine purity, innocence, nobility, intrepidity and incorruptibility, that childhood represents the most tender, formative and impressionable stage of development and requires to be promoted, protected and preserved by adopting checks and safeguards against various risks and hazards which inhibit development and growth of childhood;
- Recognising that once childhood is damaged, mutilated and destroyed, it is lost forever and cannot be regained; the excitement and joy associated with childhood will also disappear along with loss of childhood;
- Neither parents/guardians nor employers, contractors or any custodian of children in a controlled environment (Children's Homes) have any moral or ethical right to push children

involuntarily to work regardless of any extenuating circumstances;

- Children have a fundamental right guaranteed by Article 21A of the Constitution to free and compulsory primary and elementary education and this right cannot be compromised; it is non-negotiable;
- Exposing children to harsh drudgery and hazardous work through which they have to expose themselves to dust, heat, fume, noise, smoke, poisonous and toxic substances (as in ragpicking) shatters their health, *elan-vital*, motivation for education and creativity, reduces them to physical and emotional wrecks. As they cross the threshold of childhood and adolescence and enter adulthood, they cannot be responsible, responsive, mature, sensible, sensitive and productive adults;
- Children who are orphaned, destitute, abandoned and street children, victims of autism, cerebral palsy, spasticity, mental illness, retardation, learning disability, physical, sexual and substance abuse and HIV/AIDS, bonded and trafficked children deserve special care and attention of parents, teachers and all sections of the civil society so that they are enabled to grow, evolve and eventually establish themselves in mainstream society as decent and dignified human beings.

What are Human Rights?

THE SIMPLEST WAY of defining human rights is that they are about balancing the inalienable rights of us all as human beings within the community, society or body politic regardless of differences in birth, social origin, caste, class, clan, sect, gender, physical differences, faith and belief, political ideology, nationality and so on.

The essence of this perception is that rights of one human being will have to be seen in tandem with those of another and not to their exclusion.

In essence, it further implies that despite differences in birth, social origin, faith/belief and ideology, human beings can co-exist in this beautiful planet like flowers fluttering gently in breeze in a multi-coloured garden of freshness, greenery and fragrance. The yearning of mankind to live with dignity and decency and to lead a clean, safe, secure and congenial existence has found expression for generations through creative works of poets, playwrights, novelists, painters and sculptors. The crowning glory of this yearning manifested itself in Rabindranath Tagore's poem 'Pran' in the anthology of poems *Kadi and Komal*:

I do not wish to die
In this beautiful planet
I want to live
Amidst the company of human beings
I want to live
In the midst of the rays of the rising and setting sun
Amidst the verdant green
Of this multi-coloured garden of beauty and fragrance
How fervently I wish
I could secure a place
Amidst the hearts of living beings

As the author perceives it, there are six dimensions of human rights which he would like to enumerate seriatim as under:

The first dimension

Human rights connote certain basic entitlements of human beings which go to make human life meaningful. Right to live is the most basic or primordial of these entitlements. Right to live does not mean an animal-like existence resting on the instinct to kill or rob others of their life--the most precious of all mundane possessions.

The true measure of human existence is to live a life of dignity and decency, honour and freedom and do certain things in a decent and dignified manner without impinging on the rights of others as also without causing any injury or harm to them such as:

- Physical;
- Mental;
- Emotional.

This essentially connotes the time-honoured principle, 'Live and let others live'.

The second dimension

It is well known that human life, the finest and best in creation once damaged, mutilated or destroyed cannot be restored to its original form. But such loss of life—witting or unwitting, accidental or motivated—must be compensated by the State which is morally and ethically responsible for promoting, protecting and preserving the sanctity of life. This act of compensation is known as reparation which may take multiple forms such as:

- Monetary compensation to make good some of the losses of life and property suffered by the survivors (of those who are killed in war or communal riot or civil unrest or insurgency or extremist violence or natural calamities);
- Innocent victims of violence (survivors) are assisted by the State to reclaim as close a level of decent livelihood as they had before the onset of violence, which is free from fear and trepidation and a sense of psychological insecurity as at the time of violence;
- The State or authorities guaranteeing non-recurrence of violence by taking stringent and deterrent action against the perpetrators of the acts of violence so that all the denizens can lead a normal life of peace, serenity, security and freedom from unwarranted interference by outside elements.

The third dimension

Every individual is endowed with reason and intellect in varying degrees. Every individual has also in varying degrees certain attributes such as:

- Imagination;

- Ingenuity;
- Creativity;
- Capacity for innovation;
- Resourcefulness;
- Survival instincts;

Every individual has the right in his/her own way to

- Grow;
- Evolve;
- Advance in the ladder of life;
- Expand/enlarge the ambit of his/her vision/perception;
- Diversify in multiple directions by harnessing the attributes/endowments as above.

He/she has, however, no right to do so at the cost of or disadvantage to others.

He/she has no right to rob somebody else who is comparatively weak and helpless of the latter's freedom so that he/she can achieve his/her selfish interests.

He/she has no right to use another person as his/her property which amounts to slavery which is banned both by international and national law.

He/she has no right to coerce or regiment another to submit to his/her ways.

He/she cannot force another to choose an alternative out of a batch of alternatives which is against the interest of that person.

All these acts constitute violation of human rights of the victim who is coerced/regimented, forced to do certain things against his/her wishes or who becomes the property of another person by deceit, fraud, manipulation and compulsion.

The fourth dimension

Right to live has certain essential and integral components such as:

I Right to food which should be wholesome and nutritious, which should be a balanced combination of carbohydrate, protein, oil/fat, trace minerals and vitamins with a prescribed nutritive value measurable in kilo calorie different for children, adolescents and adults.

II Right to potable water which is essential for absorption of food, which should be chemically and bacteriologically free from all impurities and free from excess of iron, sulphur, sodium, calcium, potassium, magnesium and flouride and which should be available in prescribed quantities according to the norm prescribed by WHO.

III Right to decent living accommodation which should be commodious, well-lit and ventilated with the number of rooms corresponding to the size of the family with space for study and play of children, with a chimney attached to the kitchen to make it smokeless and space for kitchen garden for growing fruits and vegetables, consumption of which contributes to the desired levels of nutrition.

IV Right to personal hygiene and environmental sanitation which should include a sanitary latrine (as opposed to a dry latrine) with arrangement for flushing sufficient quantity of water available for the same, existence of drainage and sewerage for discharge of effluents into city/town sewers and arrangements for washing of hands and feet on every conceivable occasion including before and after food.

V A. Right to work/employment which is full, freely chosen, productive and remunerative.

B. Right to enjoy a brief period of rest (spread over) after the prescribed working hours

C. Right to work in an environment which is free from dust, heat, fume, noise, toxic and poisonous substances, pollution (air, water, earth) and accidents.

D. Right to payment of compensation to the legal heirs of a deceased workman who dies in course of and arising out of employment or who gets incapacitated fully or partially, permanently and temporarily.

E. Right to treatment of occupational diseases both communicable and non-communicable, including specialised treatment by admission to hospitals.

VI A. Right to a living and need-based wage in time by a prescribed wage period (between seventh to tenth day of the month following the month to which the wages relate) without any deduction except those authorised by the law.

B. Representatives of the principal employer are required to remain present and certify the payment of prescribed wage without any deduction except those authorised by law to all contract labourers on the date fixed for disbursement of wages to them.

C. Right to receive over-time (OT) wage at double the rate of ordinary wages, for work in excess of the scheduled hours of work i.e. nine hours a day and forty-eight hours a week.

D. Right to earn wages for all seven days in a week for six days of work and right to enjoy a paid day of rest (weekly off).

E. Right to earn wages for all thirty/thirty-one days in a month for twenty-six days of work and right to enjoy four paid days of rest (monthly off).

VII Right to freedom of expression, freedom of association, freedom to pursue avocation of one's choice and freedom of movement from one part of the territory of India to another.

The fifth dimension

Human rights or entitlements are relevant for all categories of people who are placed in a normal working and living environment such as:

I. Normal boys and girls, adolescents and youth.
II. Normal men and women (including elderly).
III. Members of SC, ST and OBC communities.
IV. Members of linguistic, cultural and religious communities.
V. Physically, orthopaedically, visually, audio-metrically and mentally challenged persons.
VI. Victims of autism, cerebral palsy and spasticity.
VII. Transgenders.
VIII. Victims of learning disability (dyslexia).

The sixth dimension

Human rights or entitlements are as relevant for individuals who work and live in a free environment as those who are made to live in a controlled environment such as

I. Children in Open Shelter Homes under S43 of JJ (Care and Protection of Children) Act, 2015.
II. Special Homes for rehabilitation of children in conflict with law, who are found to have committed an offence and who are placed there by an order of Juvenile Justice Board under S48(i) of JJ (Care and Protection of Children) Act, 2015.
III. Place of safety for persons above the age of eighteen years or children between the age of sixteen and eighteen in-conflict-with law and those accused of and convicted for committing a heinous offence (S49(1) read with S.15 of JJ (Care and Protection of Children) Act, 2015.
IV. Children's Homes for the placement of children in need of care

and protection for their care, treatment, education, training, development and rehabilitation (S.50(1)) of JJ (Care and Protection of Children) Act, 2015

V. Under-trial prisoners who are accused of having committed an offence, who are undergoing trial and who have been lodged in a jail (sub-jail, district jail, special jail, central jail, open jail, etc.)

VI. Persons who have been convicted and sentenced at the end of their trial to undergo imprisonment for a specified period and who have been lodged in a jail (sub-jail, district jail, special jail, central jail, open jail, etc.)

VII. Persons who have varying degrees of mental illness and who have been admitted to mental health hospitals for treatment, recovery and rehabilitation.

VIII. While human rights such as right to decent living accommodation, food, potable water, personal hygiene and environmental sanitation, leisure and recreation, literacy, health and medical care are common between persons in a normal environment and persons in a controlled environment, those kept in a controlled environment are in need of the following additional rights, considering the special nature of the controlled environment where they are kept and special nature of treatment which such stay warrants for them such as:

1. Regular visits by the officers of custodial/correctional institutions to ensure that (a) all special arrangements are in place (b) special care and attention peculiar to the controlled environment are being administered (c) there is a fine balance between requirements of discipline and security on the one hand, and human resource development (literacy and skill training), health and well-being including frugal comfort on

> the other (d) there is a foolproof arrangement for ventilation and redressal of grievances of the inmates (e) Psychological counselling at periodic intervals to those who are victims of drug abuse with a view to withdrawing them from the malady (f) all mentally ill persons are effectively treated, enabled to recover, are discharged in time and sent to their hearth and home provided their address is made available to the mental health hospital authorities (g) continuous monitoring of the physical and mental health of persons who are lodged in jails as well as mental health hospitals to ensure that further crimes are prevented, rigorous custodial discipline is maintained and that such persons do not languish in the controlled environment for a long time due to avoidable delay in completion of investigation, framing of charges and commencement of trial but are enabled and facilitated to reform and rebuild themselves through occupational therapy so that as and when effectively treated, recovered and discharged, they can lead a normal, productive, profitable and autonomous existence.

In *D K Basu Vs State of WB*,[1] Supreme Court of India had observed that custodial torture is a naked violation of human dignity that destroys the self-esteem of a victim. It also observed that torture is a calculated assault on human dignity. In the same judgment, the Court had observed, 'Custodial death is perhaps one of the worst crimes in a civilised society governed by the Rule of Law. The Supreme Court and NHRC have jointly and individually established that prohibition of torture is absolute

1 AIR 1997 SC 610

and may not be suspended, no matter how heinous the crime for which someone has been arrested. It is a right from which the government is not permitted to derogate, even in emergency.

In *Nandini Satpathy Vs P L Dani*,[2] the Supreme Court observed:

> To strike a balance between the needs of law enforcement on the one hand and the protection of the citizen from oppression and injustice at the hands of the law enforcement machinery on the other is a perennial problem of State craft.

The apex court further observed:

> An under-trial or convicted prisoner cannot be subjected to a physical or mental restraint which is not warranted by punishment awarded by the Court and which is in excess of the requirement of the prison discipline or which constitutes human degradation.[3]

In *Prem Shankar Vs Delhi Administration*,[4] the Supreme Court made an important observation on handcuffing of prisoners:

> It is hoop to punish harshly and humiliatingly and to vulgarise the viewers also. Iron straps are insult and pain…writ large, animalising the victim and keeper. Such treatment offends human dignity. For a self-respecting man death is preferable to dishonour. Handcuffing is condemned as inhuman, unreasonable, over-harsh and arbitrary.

In *ADM Jabalpur Vs Sivakant Shukla* case, Justice Hriday Ranjan Khanna had observed:

---

2 AIR 1978 SC 1025

3 Sunil Batra Vs Delhi Administration AIR 1978 SC 1675, Sitaram Vs State of UP AIR 1979 SC 745 Sunil Batra Vs Delhi Administration AIR 1980 SC 1579 Javed Vs State of Maharashtra AIR 1985 SC 231 Sher Singh Vs State of Punjab AIR 1983 SC 465

4 AIR 1980 SC 1534

> Sanctity of life and liberty was not something new when the Constitution was drafted. It represented a facet of higher values which mankind began to cherish in its evolution from a state of tooth-and-claw to a civilised existence. Likewise, the principle that no one shall be deprived of his life and liberty arbitrarily without the authority of the law was not the gift of the Constitution. It was a necessary corollary of the concept relating to the sanctity of life and liberty which existed and was in force before coming into force of the Constitution.

In *Nilabati Behera Vs State of Odisha*, the apex court observed that prisoners and detainees are not denuded of their fundamental rights under Article 21.

In *Sunil Batra Vs Delhi Administration*, Justice DA Desai speaking for the majority had observed:

> There was no provision, like the eighth amendment of American Constitution, in Indian Constitution which forbids cruel and unusual punishment. But conviction should not degrade the convict to a non-person, vulnerable to major punishments imposed by the jail authorities without observance of due procedural safeguards. The Court had a duty towards a prisoner as he was in prison under its order and direction.
>
> We cannot be oblivious of the fact that the treatment of a human being which offends human dignity, imposes avoidable torture and reduces the man to the level of a beast.

In the same judgment, the apex court held that personal liberty of a person who is incarcerated is to a great extent curtailed by punitive detention. The liberty to move, mix, mingle, talk, share company with co-prisoners, if substantially curtailed, would be a violation of Article 21 unless it has the backing of law'.

There are three ways to look at the concept of human dignity which, according to Supreme Court and NHRC, is the quintessence of human rights. These are:

First: According to the National Law and Natural Rights theory, dignity exists merely by virtue of a person's humanity, not his/her social status, caste, class, clan, sect, gender, faith and belief.

Second: The concept relies on the well-being of a human being and demands that government provide the basic conditions of that well-being.[5]

Third: This concerns respect and recognition. It is rooted in the recognition of personal identity and respect accorded by the society and the broader community. Repeated reference to 'dignity' and 'life beyond animal existence' in successive judgments of the apex court is in principle an acknowledgement that life, liberty and dignity go together.

Prof. Upendra Buxi, an eminent jurist, describes dignity in terms of 'persona' of an individual and autonomy. Viewed from this angle, dignity is co-terminus with empowerment with the following implications:

- Respect for one's ability to make one's own free choice;
- Respect for the intrinsic worth of the choice so made;
- Respect for one's need to have a free and informed choice;

In *Maneka Gandhi Vs Union of India (*1978 AIR 597), the apex court made a creative interpretation of Article 21 and conferred a fundamental right on every person not to be deprived of life or liberty except in accordance with the procedure prescribed by the law and that such a procedure has to be 'just, fair and reasonable'.

---

5 This has been emphasised in Francis Corallie Muller Vs Union Territory of Delhi AIR 1981. SC 746

In subsequent judgments:[6]

The broad principles laid down are:

- Any treatment meted out to an accused while he is in custody which causes humiliation and mental trauma corrodes the concept of human dignity;
- Life means something more than mere survival or existence or instrumental value for human beings, but to lead a life with some extrinsic worth, honour and dignity;
- Principle of human dignity is integral to the right to life as it is inherent and intrinsic to human beings;
- Human dignity rests on the recognition of the physical and spiritual integrity of a human being, his or her humanity and value as a person irrespective of the utility he or she can provide to others;
- At the root of dignity is the autonomy of private will and the person's freedom of choice and action;
- There are two facets of dignity, i.e., intrinsic value and instrumental value;
- Viewed in terms of intrinsic value, human dignity is an entitlement or a Constitutionally protected right;
- Viewed in terms of instrumental value, dignity and freedom are entertained, each being a facilitative tool to achieve the other;

---

6 - Prem Shankar Shukla Vs Delhi Admn (AIR 1980 SC 535)
- Mehamood Nayya Azam Vs State of Chandigarh(AIR 2012 SC 2573)
- National Legal Services Authority Vs. Union of India and Others (2014, 5 SCC. 438)
- Shabnam Animal Welfare Board Vs Union of India and Others (2015, 6SC 702)
- Naz Foundation Case
- KS Puttaswamy (Retd) and another Vs Union of India and Others (WP (Civil) 494 of 2012)

- Dignity is so fundamental that it permeates the core of the rights guaranteed as fundamental rights in Part-III of the Constitution.

It is this close correlation between freedom and dignity as very appropriately observed by the apex court which is the key insight to this work as would be abundantly clear from the subsequent chapters.

Section II

ISSUES (FAQs)

A Dialectical Exercise

Question 1

What is the correct understanding of a law and a legal framework?

Answer: Law represents a framework, an enabling mechanism, an instrument embodying certain fundamental principles of governance. Article 13 of the Constitution states that law includes any ordinance, order, by-law, rule, regulation, notification, custom, or usage having the force of law in the territory of India.

Every legal framework is the product of a particular point of time and is expected invariably to reflect the political and economic ethos obtaining at that point of time.

Every law anticipates certain trends and embodies certain principles relevant to those trends within its framework. No law in that sense can be said to be foolproof, since it is not possible to anticipate all the trends relevant for all times and get the same incorporated in the framework of law.

The rationale of enacting a particular law in a particular domain and fashion at a particular point of time can be questioned subsequently but objectively viewed, such questioning cannot take away the perspective and wisdom with which the law was enacted at the relevant time.

Question 2

What is the distribution of powers in the Seventh Schedule of the Constitution which empowers the Central and State Governments/Union Territories to make a law in a particular area i.e. labour?

Answer: Labour figures in the Union and the Concurrent list (List I and List III) of the distribution of powers in the Seventh Schedule of the Constitution [Article 246(I)]

- It does not figure in the State List (List II)
- The items which figure in the Union List (List I) are three in number such as:
  Item 55: Regulation of labour and safety in mines and oil fields
  Item 61: Industrial disputes concerning union employees
  Item 81: Inter-State migration
- The items figuring in the Concurrent List are:
  Item 22: Trade unions, industrial and labour disputes.
  Item 23: Social security and social insurance, employment and unemployment.
  Item 24: Welfare of labour including conditions of work, provident fund, employers' liability, workmen's compensation, invalidity and old age provisions and maternity benefits.
  Item 25: Vocational and technical training of labour.

This has the following implications:

- For the items which figure in the Union List, only the Union Government is empowered to enact a law.
- For the items which figure in the Concurrent List, both the Union Government and the State Governments have been empowered to enact laws
- This is one of the reasons which accounts for the single largest number of laws having been enacted in India in the field of labour.

Question 3

Where does bonded labour figure in this list?

Answer: Bonded labour does not figure anywhere in the list. However, bonded labour as a form of forced labour figures in Article 23, which comes under Part III of the Constitution under the caption 'Right against exploitation'. The expression 'exploitation' implies the use of one person by another by force for a selfish motive. This imparts a human rights dimension and goes beyond the restrictive dimensions of labour. Human dignity and respect for it is the quintessence of human rights while exploitation is exactly the opposite of it. It is also deemed to be an offence punishable in accordance with law.

Question 4

If this is so, how was a law on abolition of BLS enacted by Parliament?

Answer: Article 35(a)(ii) of the Constitution clearly stipulates that Parliament shall have—and the Legislature of a State shall not have—power to make laws for prescribing punishment for those acts which are declared to be offences under this part.

It further says that Parliament shall, as soon as may be after the commencement of the Constitution, make laws for prescribing punishment for acts referred to in sub-section (ii).

This makes it abundantly clear that enactment of a law for abolition of BLS has a special dispensation in the scheme of distribution of powers in the Constitution referred to in the Seventh Schedule and above.

Question 5

What are the various stages in the making of a law?

Answer: The process of enactment of a law in India in the field of labour has to conform to the principle of tripartism (in pursuance of India's ratification of ILO Convention 144). In terms of actual operation, this involves consultation with the tripartite constituents, i.e., Central Government, Employers and Workers Organisations. At the end of the process of tripartite consultation and on the basis of a consensus which may emerge at the end of such consultation, a draft note for the Cabinet is prepared by the administrative Ministry/Department i.e. MoL&E and is circulated among all concerned Ministries/Departments. The note, along with the draft legislative framework and the comments of the concerned Ministries/Departments, are placed before the Cabinet through the Cabinet Secretariat for consideration. After obtaining approval of the Cabinet, the draft legislative framework is converted in shape of a Bill in consultation with the Department of Legal Affairs and Department of Parliamentary Affairs for introduction, consideration and passage thereof by both Houses of the Parliament. The discussion which follows in the wake of such introduction brings out the differences in perception and ideology of the respective parties which might have already come out to some extent at the time of the earlier executive as well as tripartite consultation. Sometimes, the Bill may be referred to a Parliamentary Standing Committee or a Select Committee or a Joint Parliamentary Committee (JPC), as the case may be, for further and more in-depth discussion and scrutiny. Very often at the close of the discussion in Parliament and discussion/scrutiny by the Standing Committee/Select Committee/JPC, as the case may be, and the recommendations of the latter, the legal instrument which eventually emerges essentially remains a product of compromise. That, however, is the logic, if not the irony of the functioning of the Parliamentary system of democracy and is inevitable.

Question 6

What is the genesis of Bonded Labour System (Abolition) Act?

Answer: Article 23 of the Constitution of India deals with prohibition of traffic in human beings, *begar* and other forms of forced labour. It reads as under:

- 'Traffic in human beings and *begar* and other similar forms of forced labour are prohibited and any contravention of the provision shall be an offence punishable in accordance with law'.
- Traffic in human beings is trading with human beings like commodities for exploitative purposes such as commercial sexual exploitation, forced/bonded labour, forced transfer of organs, forced begging, adoption, marriage and domestic help, etc.
- It is a flagrant violation of the Philadelphia Declaration of June, 1944 which clearly and unambiguously affirms that 'Labour is not a commodity'.
- It is an obscene affront to human dignity and decency and is one of the worst violations of human rights.
- The UN Convention against Transnational Organised Crime was adopted in November 2000.

- Two Protocols were adopted by UN at Palermo in Italy in quick succession supplementing the above Convention in December 2000.
- These are:
  - Protocol to prevent, suppress and punish trafficking in persons, especially women and children;
  - Protocol against smuggling of migrants by land, sea and air.

There is a detailed definition of trafficking in the first Protocol which is as under:

- Trafficking is an action with intention;
- Trafficking is a means of recruitment;
- Trafficking is for a specific purpose like exploitation.

Exploitation is the end object/product of trafficking. It includes the following:

- Any act of physical exploitation; or
- Any form of sexual exploitation, slavery, or practices similar to slavery, servitude; or
- Forced removal of organs.

Slavery is co-terminus with forced/bonded labour in as much as:

- In slavery, one person possesses or controls another person in such a way as to significantly deprive that person of his/her individual liberty with the intention of exploiting that person which is akin to forced/bonded labour.

Prior to its amendment, S370 of Indian Penal Code, 1860 dealt with buying or disposing of any person as a slave. After amendment, S370 as it figures in Criminal Law (Amendment) Act, 2013 reads as trafficking of persons.

The Criminal Law (Amendment) Act has broadly adopted the definition of trafficking-in-persons as given in the first Protocol to the UN Convention adopted in December 2000.

Regretfully, the Criminal Law (Amendment) Act begins with definition of trafficking-in-persons and ends with the most stringent punishment against traffickers without providing measures for:

- Rescue/release of victims;
- Repatriation of victims and their restoration to parents, if they are children and to families if they are adults;
- Rehabilitation—physical, economic and psychological;
- Re-integration to family, community and society.

To go back to Article 23, the acts which are declared to be an offence under that Article are;

- Trafficking in human beings;
- *Begar* and
- Other similar forms of forced labour

Article 35(a)(ii) reads as under:

> Parliament shall, as soon as may be, after the commencement of the Constitution, make laws for prescribing punishment for the acts referred to in sub-clause (ii) i.e., for prescribing punishment for those acts which are declared to be offences under this part.

The Constitution of India 'was enacted and adopted' on 26 November 1949 (Preamble to the Constitution).The implication of 'as soon as' is immediately or in quick succession.

The first initiative at the central level was taken on 16 December 1949 when R K Siddha, Member, Constituent

Assembly of India, moved that a Bill to provide punishment for forced or compulsory labour be referred to a select committee.

The Bill was circulated for public opinion. It was introduced and discussed in the Central Legislature. It was, however, eventually withdrawn and could not see the light of day.

B R Ambedkar was independent India's first Union Labour and Law Minister (1946–49). When the senior officials of the Ministry of Labour approached him with the idea of initiating steps for enactment of a law, as required under Article 23 read with Article 35 (a)(ii), he was firmly of the view—justifiably so — that law cannot abolish a social evil like bonded labour. He was of the view that an enquiry committee will tour round the country, marshal evidence and submit its report. This process will generate a lot of awareness in the minds of both the perpetrators of the crime as well as the victims. Thereafter, it will be meaningful to take such legislative or administrative action as may be necessary in the light of the findings of the enquiry committee.

Ambedkar's idea could not be translated to action during his term as Union Labour Minister. He was succeeded by Jagjivan Ram. The latter thought that it would be imprudent to start a nationwide enquiry in view of the unsettled conditions in which Indian States as well as Provinces were left in the wake of independence and partition.

The idea of having a committee for a nationwide enquiry was, therefore, dropped. Instead, a Special Officer was appointed with a clear mandate. He examined all the materials on record and submitted a detailed report. The report was examined and again a view was taken that what was needed was a sense of critical social consciousness in the minds of the people against recourse to and prevalence of forced labour and not enactment of law.

No initiative was, however, taken to launch a country-wide campaign to generate such critical social consciousness against prevalence of forced labour. Seven years after the commencement of the Constitution, Suppression of Immoral Traffic in Women and Girls Act (SITA) was enacted in 1956, later renamed as Immoral Traffic (Prevention) Act which underwent two amendments in 1978 and 1986. This Act cannot, however, be said to come strictly within the ambit of Article 23 on account of the following reasons:

- This was enacted by way of discharge of the legal obligation arising out of ratification of the UN Convention for the Suppression of Traffic in Persons and of the Exploitation of Prostitution of others (1950);
- It does not define trafficking in persons;
- It does not prohibit trafficking as such but prevents immoral traffic i.e., commercialisation of the vice of sexual exploitation of women and girls;
- It comes down rather harshly on a poor and innocent victim soliciting sex but not so much on the pimps and customers.
- It does not provide any measure for rescue/release, repatriation, rehabilitation and re-integration of the victim.

ILO Convention 29 of 1930 had come into force years earlier; it was ratified by Government of India on 30 November 1954, casting a legal obligation to enact a law, formulate a policy and introduce a programme of action in the wake of the said ratification. No such initiative was taken for twenty-two years. The matter was allowed to rest.

Then came the proclamation of Emergency on 26 June 1975 under Article 352 of the Constitution. Barely a week after the proclamation, Item 4 of the Twenty Point Economic Programme dealt in clear, categorical and unambiguous terms with elimination of BLS. The exact wording in which the announcement to the nation was made, was 'Bonded labour system stands abolished and shall be declared illegal wherever it exists'

In her All India Radio (AIR) broadcast to the nation on 1 July 1975, the Prime Minister said:

> The practice of bonded labour system is barbarous and will be abolished. All contracts and other arrangements under which services rendered by such bonded labourers are secured will be declared illegal.

Thus, hesitation and indecisiveness of yesteryears was replaced by an affirmative and decisive political action after a long interregnum of twenty-seven years; the same was characterised by a lot of grit and courage, political will, commitment and determination at the highest level of government.

'Better late than never', so runs the English adage. Developments followed in quick succession.

A Labour Ministers conference was convened on 19 July 1975 to discuss all incidental steps which were required to be taken to fulfil the promises made by the PM to the nation through her announcement of the Twenty Point Programme; the conference was addressed by the PM.

The officials in the Ministry of Labour worked with a feverish pitch to draft an ordinance to give effect to PM's announcement of the Twenty Point Programme relating to abolition of BLS.

- Bonded Labour System (Abolition) Ordinance was promulgated by the President of India on 25 October 1975.[1]

---

1 Under Article 123(2)(a) of the Constitution, an Ordinance shall be laid before both Houses of Parliament and shall cease to operate at the expiration of six weeks from the re-assembly of Parliament

The BLS (A) Bill was introduced by the Union Labour Minister late K V Raghunath Reddy on 12 January 1976 in Rajya Sabha and 27 January 1976 in Lok Sabha. The Bill was passed by both the Houses of Parliament, received the assent of the President on 9 February 1976 and was deemed to have come into force on 25 October 1975, the day the BLS (A) Ordinance had been promulgated.

The statements made by the Union Labour Minister on the floor of both Houses of Parliament provide a rich insight to understand the nature and character of exploitation inherent in BLS:

> The system of bonded labour is the most anomalous remnant of feudalism still vitiating our society. Freedom can never endure the enclaves of bondage, a civilisation with an army of exiles never lasts.

The Minister further continued to explain the genesis of the system:

> The mechanics of the system are well known. A poor peasant or an agricultural worker takes a small loan. His dues accumulate very fast under exorbitantly high rates of interest. Soon he finds it impossible to extinguish his debts; he disposes of his property but still continues in debt. He then begins to work for the creditor but at absurdly low wages and hopes to repay the debt by the fruits of his labour but the cruel logic of usury eludes him. His children and grand-children also begin to work for nominal wages to liquidate the debt. Generation after generation become virtual slaves to the creditor. The entire future of the family gets mortgaged to a small loan taken in the remote past. The debt becomes his destiny.

The Minister continued:

> This is how the system based on usury and feudal

> exploitation perpetuated an unequal exchange system for ages. The bonded labourer has no access to any commodity or capital market. He ceases to be a free economic agent. He is reduced to an appendage of feudal property. The debt dehumanises him. He lives like a sub-human being, a thing.

Question 7

In tracing the genesis of BLS (A) Act, you have dealt with trafficking in human beings. What about *begar* and other similar forms of forced labour as have also been referred to in Article 23?

Answer: The dictionary meaning of 'beggar' is a penniless person who gets reduced to acute impoverishment. *Begar* is a form of acute forced labour where the victim gets impoverished due to non-payment of wages or remuneration. In an address delivered at the Constitution Club of India dated 22 April 2017 captioned 'Celebrating Hundred Years of Champaran, 1917', noted historian Prof. Irfan Habib has brought out what *begar* meant to lakhs of indigo cultivators of Champaran:

> As indigo prices and planters' profits fell, the latter began correspondingly to increase the rent burden of the peasants invoking their rights as zamindars.

Alongside these extractions, the planters made full use of the traditional zamindari practice of *begar*, forced, unpaid or ill-paid labour, requisitioning at will the peasant's cattle, plough and carts compelling them to provide labour for their plantations.

The above description brings out graphically how an indigo cultivator who never received remunerative wages for his labour was driven to desperation and an extreme form of impoverishment in the hands of a severe exploitative system.

We may now proceed to deal with other similar forms of forced labour. This is defined in ILO Convention 29 which reads

> Forced labour is work or service which is extracted from any person under the menace of any penalty for which the said person has not offered himself voluntarily.

ILO Convention 105 of 1957 has no proviso, no exceptions and has immediacy and totality of abolition as its primary hallmark. It calls for immediate and complete abolition of any form of forced or compulsory labour in the following specified categories such as:

- Forced labour as a measure of political coercion or education or as a punishment for holding or expressing political views or views ideologically opposed to established political, social or economic system;
- Forced labour as a means of mobilising and using labour for the purpose of economic development;
- Forced labour as a means of labour discipline;
- Forced labour as a punishment for having participated in strikes;
- Forced labour as a means of racial, social, national or religious discrimination.

The above ILO Convention has several redeeming features such as:

- It provides a broad-based definition of forced labour which covers all and does not exclude any form of forced labour;
- It recognises that all forms of forced labour constitute a violation of the rights of man as in the UN Charter and Universal Declaration of Human Rights, 1948;
- Labour cannot be employed as a means of political coercion against those holding or expressing certain political views;

- No one, far less labour, who is on the right side of the law can be punished merely because he/she belongs to a particular group.
- Right to strike is a fundamental right of the working class and no one can question, far less take away that right. None, therefore, can be punished by way of being subjected to forced labour merely on account of participation in a strike;
- India ratified the above Convention in May 2000.
- There is a Constitutional provision i.e. Article 39(e) occurring in Chapter IV of the Constitution dealing with Directive Principles of State Policy which looks at forcing or compulsorily subjecting someone to work from a slightly different perspective:

> The State shall, in particular, direct its policy towards securing that the health and strength of workers, men and women and the tender age of children are not abused and citizens are not forced by economic necessity to enter avocations unsuited to their age or strength.

The implication of this seminal Constitutional provision is quite clear in as much as:

- Every work is a source of great excitement and joy if and as long as it is performed in a physical environment which is clean, safe, hygienic, free from dust, heat, noise, smoke, fume, various toxic and poisonous substances, pollution and accidents;
- If it is performed under conditions which are normal, natural and conducive to health, safety, morals and well-being of the individuals performing the job, without there being any coercion or regimentation, deceit and fraud, unwarranted interference, abuse, cruelty and torture.

Supreme Court of India in *PUDR Vs Union of India and*

Others[2] has in a judgment delivered on 18 September 1982 (popularly known as Asiad workers case) brought out a few other implications of forced labour in the following words:

> Any factor which deprives a person of the choice of alternatives and compels him to adopt a particular course of action independent of his/her option or volition may be regarded as force. If labour or service is compelled as a result of such force it would be forced labour.

Moreover:

> The word force must be construed to include not only physical or legal force but also force arising from the compulsions of economic circumstances which leave no choice of alternatives to a person and compel him to provide labour or service even though the remuneration received for it is less than minimum wage.

Again:

> When a person provides labour or service to another for a remuneration which is less than minimum wage, the labour or service provided by him falls within the scope and ambit of forced labour under Article 23.

These observations are relevant as far as adult workers are concerned. As far as children are concerned, they can also be victims of forced labour in certain circumstances such as:

- Children/adolescents who discharge household chores at the cost of education which they should receive at a particular age as a matter of highest priority;
- Children/adolescents who are forced to leave their homes to take up some work outside on account of repressive home environment

2 WP No. 8431 of 1981

as also on account of unwarranted parental interference with their studies and day-to-day life and whose parents dub them 'lazy, lethargic, good-for nothing' as their performance in school examinations does not come up to the expectations of parents;

- Child/adolescent beggars (who are recruited by a gang to do forced begging);
- Children/adolescents who are recruited and forced to perform as artistes in circus; employment of children in circuses has been prohibited by Child Labour (Prohibition and Regulation) Act as it stands amended in 2016;
- Children who are recruited and forced to be used as camel jockeys;
- Children who are victims of forced adoption, forced domestic help and forced marriage;
- Children who are recruited and forced to part with their body organs;
- Children who are forcibly recruited for war and insurgent activities;
- Children who are recruited and used as drug peddlers, messengers, carriers of food, water, letters, etc.;
- Children who are recruited to perform in reality dance shows in an inappropriate manner (which stands prohibited by issue of an executive order by the Ministry of Information and Broadcasting in July 2019).

Question 8

In addition to ILO, what are the other international instruments which have dealt with forced labour or similar forms of forced labour?

Answer: Two important realisations dawned on the collective consciousness of the international community at the end of the horrors of the Second World War (1939-45). These were:

I. Governments of a few nation-states have arrogated to themselves the power, authority and capacity to inflict tyranny, repression, violence and brutality of an un-imaginable kind on innocent citizens belonging to a few other nation-states in the name of religion, nationality and ethnicity. This needs to be nipped in the bud.

II. Laws must be enacted and institutional mechanisms must be put in place with a view to putting an end to such tyranny, injustice and oppression on the one hand and to promote, protect and preserve inalienable human rights on the other.

Birth of the United Nations on 24 October 1945, that of all specialised agencies of UN, proclamation and adoption of the Universal Declaration of Human Rights on 10 December 1948 by the General Assembly of the UN followed by adoption of an International Covenant on Civil and Political Rights and International Covenant on social, economic and cultural rights in 1966 could be attributed in no small measure to this realisation.

Article 1 of the Universal Declaration of Human Rights proclaims that 'All human beings are born free and equal in dignity and rights'. Article 4 of the Declaration further stipulates, 'No one shall be held in slavery or servitude; slavery and slave trade shall be prohibited in all forms'.

International Covenant on Civil and Political Rights has similarly prohibited slavery, slave trade and servitude in all its forms. It clearly states 'No one shall be required to perform forced or compulsory labour'.

The UN Supplementary Convention on Abolition of Slavery, the Slave Trade, Institutions and Practices Similar to Slavery (1956) defines debt bondage as under, which in spirit is identical to the definition given in Section 2(g) of BLS (A) Act:

> The status or condition arising from a pledge by a debtor of his personal services or of those of a person under his control as security for a debt, if the value of those services as reasonably assessed is not applied towards the liquidation of the debt or the length and nature of those services are not respectively limited and defined.

It defines serfdom as:

> The condition or status of a tenant who by law, custom or agreement is bound to live and labour on land belonging to another person and to render some determinate service to such other person, whether for reward or not and is not free to change his status.

A few other international instruments of an earlier period have used a different language for slavery or slave-like-practices or forced labour and variants thereof in the following manner:

League of Nations Anti-Slavery Convention (1926)

The Treaty of Versailles was signed at the end of the First World War (1914-18) and gave birth to League of Nations. The League of Nations Anti-Slavery Convention in Article 1(1) defines slavery as the status or condition of a person over whom any or all of the powers attaching to the right of ownership are exercised'. The Convention also prohibits all aspects of the slave trade, including all acts involved in the capture, acquisition or disposal of a person with intent to reduce him or her to slavery [Article 1(2)].

Philadelphia Declaration (June 1944)

> Labour is not a commodity...All human beings

> irrespective of race, creed or sex have the right to pursue both their material well-being and spiritual development in conditions of freedom and dignity, economic security and opportunity.

The Declaration adopted at the end of the War of American Independence (4 July 1776)

> All men are created equal, that they are endowed by their creator with certain inalienable rights, that among these are life, liberty, and pursuit of happiness...Governments are instituted among men to secure these rights.

Question 9

Arising out of these, would you like to identify a commonality of vision, purpose and goals of human rights and human development?

Answer: The commonality of vision, purpose and goals of human rights and human development may be listed as under:

i. Freedom from discrimination by gender, race, ethnicity, social and national origin, faith, belief and political ideology.
ii. Freedom from want characterised by stable and durable avenues of employment, timely payment of living wage principally in cash, a decent livelihood and quality of life measured by happiness.
iii. Freedom from fear of threats to personal safety, security, intimidation, torture, arbitrary arrest, detention and violent acts.
iv. Freedom from injustice and flagrant violation of 'Rule of Law' characterised by equality before law and equal protection of laws.
v. Freedom to develop and realise infinite possibilities and potentialities which every human being has in him/her in an abundant measure.
vi. Freedom of thought, expression, association, movement and participation in decision making.

vii. Freedom from exploitation and access to decent work--physical, economic, psychological and emotional.

Freedom and development, according to Prof. Amartya Sen, are goals which are cherished by every human being.[3] Freedom and development contribute to achievement of other goals which are valued by every human being such as security, social and national integration. Prof. Sen brings out clearly the consequences of lack of freedom such as:

- Lack of substantive freedom relates directly to economic poverty which robs people of the freedom to satisfy hunger, to achieve the desired levels of nutrition or to obtain remedies for treatable diseases or the opportunity to be adequately clothed or sheltered or to have access to potable water or sanitation;
- Lack of freedom links closely to the lack of public facilities and social care such as absence of organised arrangements for healthcare, educational facilities and effective institutions for maintenance of law and order, peace and tranquillity;
- Lack of freedom directly results from a denial of political and civil liberties by authoritarian regimes and from imposed restrictions on the freedom to participate in the social, political and economic life of the community.

Question 10

What is the terminology used in BLS (A) Act relevant to the central objectives of the law?

Answer: In the history of labour jurisprudence in post-independent India, BLS (A) Act is one of the most progressive and pro-victim legislations ever enacted.

3 In his book *Development and Freedom*, 1999

It has twenty-six operative provisions which are simple, easy to understand with a clear definition of bonded debt, bonded labour, bonded labourer and BLS. These terminologies are crucial to understand the central objective of the law.

- Bonded debt means an advance obtained or presumed to have been obtained by a bonded labourer under or in pursuance of BLS.
- Bonded labour means any labour or service rendered under BLS.
- Bonded labourer means a labourer who incurs or is presumed to have incurred a bonded debt and who renders bonded service.
- BLS is the totality of unequal exchange arising out of unequal relationship between a creditor and a debtor.
- The creditor is economically and financially strong, resourceful, influential and has complete command over resources–both movable and immovable.
- The debtor is landless, assetless, resourceless and defenceless.
- He/she is in need of money for fulfilment of personal consumption related, ceremony related and development related needs.
    - Personal consumption needs would mean food, health, medical care, house rent, electricity, clothing, shelter;

  Ceremony related needs would mean:

  - Festivities associated with birth, naming ceremony, birth anniversary ceremony, engagement ceremony, marriage, year-round festivals, death of a member in the family and expenses related to funeral rites.
  - A lot of social prestige is associated with these ceremonies and any member of the community regardless of rank or status or availability of resources will not hesitate to live up to the call of social prestige even if it means incurring loan/debt/advance from the landlord/moneylender of the area.

Development related needs would mean:

- Expenses related to agriculture (seeds, fertiliser, pesticides, agro-chemicals, agro-appliances), animal husbandry, veterinary, dairy;
- Expenses related to education of children, health, nutrition and medical care.

Since the debtor has very little to fall back upon, he/she approaches the creditor for a loan/debt/advance. The creditor is too keen and eager to advance such loan/debt/advance but not without his pound of flesh, like the character Shylock in Shakespeare's *Merchant of Venice*. An agreement will have to be entered into between the creditor and the debtor spelling out the amount loaned/advanced, the rate of interest, the period of re-payment and consequences of non-payment. The agreement may be written or oral, partly written or partly oral.

The terms of the contract are seldom shared with the debtor; besides, even if the agreement is reduced to black and white, it always remains with the creditor. Since the debtor does not have any collateral to offer against the said loan/advance, he/she has to mortgage his/her services or services of any or all family members to the creditor.

Four consequences flow from such mortgage as enumerated in S2(g) of the Act:

- Denial of wages or nominal wages.

or

- Denial of the freedom of employment or other means of livelihood for a specified or unspecified period.

or

- Denial of the fundamental right to move freely throughout the territory of India as guaranteed under Article 19(d) of the Constitution.

or

- Denial of the right to appropriate or sell at market value any of the debtor's property or product of debtor's labour or the labour of a member of debtor's family or any person dependent on him.

Explanation

I. Nominal wage means a wage less than fixed and notified minimum wage by the appropriate government and where no such minimum wage has been fixed and notified, wage which is normally paid for same or similar labour to labourers working in the same locality.

II. The above four consequences of debt bondage as given in S2(g) of the Act are alternatives and not conjunctives.

In other words, an element of loan/debt/advance together with one of the four consequences as in S2(g) is enough to establish the incidence of BLS.

While disposing of WP 2135 of February 1982 filed by Swami Agnivesh, President, Bandhua Mukti Morcha, Supreme Court has given a broad, liberal and expansive interpretation of the law. According to the apex court, it is not necessary to prove beyond doubt the element of loan/debt/advance; it should be presumed to be in existence. In the words of late Justice P N Bhagwati who wrote the main judgment in the BMM case:

> Whenever it is shown that a labourer is made to provide forced labour, the Court would raise a presumption that he is required to do so in consideration of an advance or any other economic consideration and he is, therefore, a bonded labourer.

Again:

> This presumption may be rebutted by the employer and also by the State Government, if it so chooses but unless and until satisfactory evidence is produced for rebutting this presumption, the Court must proceed on the basis that the person is a bonded labourer entitled to the benefit of the provisions of the Act.

In this case, which relates to stone quarry and crusher workers of Faridabad of Haryana State in the 1980s, the State Government had contended that the workmen in stone quarries and crushers might be providing forced labour but they were not working under BLS. Supreme Court had outright rejected this contention of the Government of Haryana on the following grounds:

> It would be extremely difficult, if not impossible, for the labourers to establish that they are bonded as they would have no evidence at all to prove that any advance or economic consideration was provided to them by the employer concerned. The latter would also disown having given any advance or economic consideration to labourers.

This is how the apex court removed the artificial distinction between forced labour and bonded labour.

Question 11

Could you give a few illustrations to highlight how the unequal exchange system works havoc for the victims of BLS?

Answer: The unequal exchange system is fully reflected in the fourth consequence appended to Section2(g) of BLS (A) Act, which will be abundantly clear from the following three illustrations:

Illustration 1

- 'X' is a grower of paddy.
- Since 'X' is landless he grows paddy on the land of others as a share-cropper.
- 'X' does not have resources to buy seed, fertiliser, agro-chemicals and other agro-appliances.
- 'X', therefore, is left with no alternative but to take a loan from a rice mill owner to grow paddy.
- There is a minimum support price (MSP) fixed by the Government for sale of paddy; such MSP may be in the range of ₹2,000-2,500 per quintal.
- The rice mill owner who gives the advance will do so only on the condition that the grower of paddy sells paddy grown by him at half the minimum support price fixed by Government.
- Willy-nilly, 'X' will have to agree to such a condition since he has no other alternative.

Illustration 2

- 'Y' is a fisherman belonging to the SC community.
- 'Y' goes for fishing in river Ganges in Bhagalpur, Bihar.
- The river Ganges flows between Bhagalpur and Kolkata over a stretch of 2,500 km and is a rich reservoir of fish.
- For riparian fishing, 'Y' needs a boat, a net, fish feed and other things for which he has no resources.
- 'Y' therefore, is left with no alternative except to take an advance from a moneylender.
- The moneylender agrees to advance the loan to Y on the condition that he agrees to sell the catch at half the prevailing market price to the former.
- Since fish is a perishable commodity and 'Y' has no deep freezer

for healthy storage of fish, 'Y' willy-nilly subscribes to the said condition which is imposed on him by taking advantage of his resourcelessness and economic helplessness.

Illustration 3

- 'Z' belongs to ST community and lives with his family in an area adjoining a forest in Malkangiri district in South Western Odisha.
- For his livelihood, 'Z' goes to the interior forest with members of his family, including children.
- They leave in the early hours of the morning.
- They traverse long distances in a difficult terrain which is full of insects and snakes with the possibility of fatal injuries due to insect/snake bite.
- They do not have the skills for any other alternative avocation or any other option for an alternative livelihood.
- The minor agricultural and forest produce which they grow and collect after spending several hours with all the potential risks and hazards are:

  Minor agricultural produce: *Rajma* (both red and white), white beans, red gram, Niger seed, turmeric, ginger, Annatto seed, tamarind.

  Minor forest produce: Pungam seed, *gum karaya*, *Nux vomica*, Sal seed, *tendu* leaf, resin, lac, honey, dry *amla* pulp, hill brooms, *mohul* flower and seed.

They neither have the space to store the produce nor the capacity, skill and resources to convert them into value-added end products soon after its collection. They, therefore, willy-nilly, are forced to part with these in favour of middle-men at terribly unremunerative prices; these middle-men approach them on the eve of the collection season, pay some nominal advances and mop up the entire produce. In the wake of KS Bawa Committee's recommendations in early 1970s, institutional mechanisms such as Large Argicultural Multi-Purpose Co-operative Societies (LAMP), Tribal Development Co-operative Corporation(TDCC) and Girijan Corporation have no doubt been in place for more than four decades but they have not been able to promote, protect and safeguard their interests.

What does unequal exchange system mean in such a situation? Such economic transactions and the terms under which they are conducted are totally to the advantage of the creditor and to the total disadvantage of the debtor for the following reasons:

- The debtor is in immediate need of resources (cash) for his biological survival; he cannot wait;
- The debtor does not have the skill or the countervailing power to bargain/ negotiate for a remunerative price; he does not have the means to process them for value addition and offer for sale at a better price;
- On account of his pervasive ignorance and illiteracy, he is unable to understand and internalise the tricks of the game and intricacies of market forces and often gets overpowered by the latter.

Question 12

What are the other forms of bondage (other than debt bondage)? Please give illustrations.

Answer: The other forms of human bondage (in addition to debt bondage) are:

- Customary bondage;
- Inter-generational bondage;
- Bondage arising out of inter-State distress migration;
- Bondage arising out of trafficking.

These are elaborated as under:

Customary bondage

- Victims of customary or social bondage render certain services to other members of the community with or without any remuneration or without remuneration which is equivalent to notified minimum wage or nominal wage;

Examples of such customary bondage are:

- *Bajgees* of Uttarakhand (drum beaters) pledge their services to the community to beat drums at the time of a community festival;
- *Yogins* of Andhra Pradesh and Devdashis of Karnataka and Maharashtra (which stand banned under the law) are forced by ignorant, illiterate and custom-bound superstitious parents to pledge their services as dancers to a supernatural or mystic power since childhood;
- *Rudalis* of Rajasthan have pledged their services to the community to mourn rather artificially at the time of death of any member of the landlord's family in the village;
- Barbers and washermen of Odisha perform similar functions (cut nails, clean clothes, anoint the feet of ladies, be the bearer of palanquins, discharge various obligations at the time of festivities associated with births, deaths, engagement, sacred-thread ceremony, marriage, etc.);
- Yet another form of customary bondage called *Vitti chakri* which is prevalent in 15 districts of North Karnataka (from Bidar to Davangere) since time immemorial is as repulsive as any other form of customary bondage narrated above. Under this system, a member of an agricultural household is required to render free service for a minimum of three hours a day to the household of the landlord. The duration goes up to a full day in times of marriage, death and village ceremonies/festivals. There

is no specificity in the nature of work which can extend from the household to the farm, cattle shed and any other as may be directed. Noted NGO Jeevika/Vimukti Trust which has been active in the field of elimination of BLS in Karnataka for over two decades has identified approximately 3,387 victims of this abominable customary bondage and has taken up the issue with the State Human Rights Commission (SHRC). All of them need to be identified and released as victims of BLS and appropriately rehabilitated. This will be possible only with a positive direction from SHRC, Karnataka where the matter is currently *sub judice*;

- These obligations have been sanctified by social customs and traditions since time immemorial for which there is no written code;
- The remuneration paid for such services invariably in kind is grossly inadequate and computed in terms of its cash value will be much lower than notified minimum wage; where no such wages have been fixed and notified, it is much less than wages for same or similar nature of work performed in the neighbourhood.

Inter-generational bondage

Inter-generational bondage basically means that the obligation to repay the debt taken by forefathers devolves on the debtor or successors of the debtor (grandfather, father, son, grandson, great grandson, etc.) by succession. Inter-generational bondage is also responsible for child bondage (son of a carpenter becomes a carpenter, so also in the case of a cobbler, blacksmith, painter, etc.) sought to be achieved through inter-generational transfer of skills. The following factors contribute to or accentuate inter-generational bondage:

- Agreements entered into are mostly oral;
- Even if there is documentary evidence, the documents remain

with the creditor or his minions (*piyada, munshi, gumasta*);
- The contents of the document are never shared with the debtor;
- Pervasive ignorance, illiteracy and lack of countervailing power put the debtor in the dock; he does not have the skill to understand how usury and the quixotic logic of arithmetic behind usury operate.

Bondage arising out of inter-State distress migration

- Migration *per se* may not lead to a situation of bondage but distress migration from one State to another through deceit and fraud which pushes the recruited migrant worker to in-voluntary labour in an exploitative situation where he does not have the freedom to leave either the worksite or the employer may end up with one of the worst forms of human bondage. The characteristic features of such a situation are:
  - Existence of an originating point and a destination point;
  - Process of recruitment of persons who are landless and assetless, are in need of employment, are heavily indebted to the village landlord/ money lender, have very little or no economic assets to fall back upon and who agree to go to the destination point for work on receipt of advances from the recruiting agent;
  - The loan/debt obtained from the village landlord/ moneylender gets liquidated with the advance taken by the migrant worker from recruiting agents;
  - Absence of any written contract explicitly spelling out the terms of the contract (nature and duration of work, duration of employment, wages, spread-over,[4] weekly off, or over-time wages, etc.);

---

4 A term used in labour law to indicate a period of rest after prescribed hours of work

- Work sites at the destination point are sometimes unilaterally and arbitrarily changed much against the wishes of the workman;
- Licence and registration certificate from competent authorities are not obtained at the time of recruitment;
- Muster roll, wage register, register of deductions and fines, register of overtime and register of advances as also register of contractors are not maintained.[5]
- While accountability of recruiting agents and principal employers/ contractors is diluted, the migrant workers with long hours of work, denial of all statutory benefits, denial of freedom to leave the worksite, denial of option to change the employer due to element of debt are reduced to the level of worst victims of BLS;
- Children of migrant parents remain the worst victims of educational deprivation while women who accompany their husbands are reduced to non-persons (their names are not entered in the muster roll) as also victims of sexual harassment at the workplace.

Bondage arising out of trafficking

This has something to do with the ethos and spirit of the age where all the finer instincts of human beings characterised by kindness and compassion have been replaced by voracious greed and rapacity. All norms of civilised human behaviour and respect for human dignity and decency are thrown to the winds in the mad rush for material affluence.

The instinct of one human being to torture other human

---

5 See Rule 48, 49, 52 of ISMW (ROE&COS) Rules, 1980

beings and take recourse to deceit, fraud, coercion, violence and regimentation is the dominant one which is on the increase. Placed in such a milieu, the problem of identifying, rescuing, releasing and repatriating victims of trafficking from multiple forms of exploitation is becoming far more complex and challenging compared to migration related human bondage. The challenge is further compounded by the following factors:

- Unlike migration which involves only two points i.e. originating point and destination, trafficking involves a third, i.e. transit;
- Operations at all the three points are shrouded with a veil of secrecy and confidentiality;
- The principal traffickers are sly, resourceful and manipulative; they are past masters in the art of coercion, regimentation, chicanery, deceit and fraud;
- They remain in the background and exercise remote control, leaving the primary task of recruitment, transportation and placement to be discharged by the agents;
- The latter also remain mostly invisible, inaccessible and unaccountable;
- They operate as part of a powerful network--national as well as global;
- Seventy-five per cent of the trafficking cases (boys and men) were tricked by the promise of lucrative jobs while girls are deceived by the false promise of marriage;
- The traffickers keep on changing their modus operandi taking into account the typical vulnerability of victims;
- As of now, unlike inter-State migrant workmen, there is no composite omnibus law to deal with all aspects of trafficking, i.e.,prevention, rescue/release/repatriation/ rehabilitation and re-integration of victims to the mainstream family, community and society.

Question 13

Are attached agricultural labourers and share-croppers victims of BLS?

Answer: In the explanation attached to Section 2(b) of BLS (A) Act, examples of attached agricultural labour have been given as: *Halia, Barmasia, Hali, Holya, Hari, Harwai, Kamiya, Paleru, Padiyal, Sagri, Sewak/Sewakia, Seri, Vetti.*

The terms *barmasiya/halia* are used in Odisha, *hali* in Madhya Pradesh, *hari/seri* in Punjab, *holya/ harwai* in Chhattisgarh, *kamiya* in Bihar, *sagri* in Rajasthan and *padiyal* in Tamil Nadu.

In concrete operational terms, attached agricultural labour system may be explained in the following manner:

- An agreement, mostly oral, is entered into between the *bhumiswami*(landholder) and the agricultural labourer;
- By the terms of the agreement, the agricultural labourer pledges his/her services together with services of all or any of the family members to the landlord;
- They are required to work round the clock without any spread over in the household, farm house, barn, cattle shed, pond, water tank, trees grown around the household and the farm, and do all types of odd menial jobs which may not have been specified in the contract;
- Even though they grow the food grains, harvest them, raise the plants, rear the cattle by feeding and watering and attend to a number of miscellaneous chores in the household to which they are attached by the contract, they do not own anything and are not entitled to enjoy any of the usufructs from the land which they raise;
- The contractual wage for the agricultural labourer and for the members of the family is fixed for the whole year which

is invariably much lower than the minimum wage notified by the appropriate government for agriculture as a scheduled employment;

- During the currency of the contract, the agricultural labourer and his family members are not free to leave the landlord and go to another landlord or go in for an alternative avenue of employment and livelihood.

A share-cropper is also an agricultural worker. As an agricultural worker, he tills the soil, sows the seeds, applies fertiliser and pesticide, carries out de-weeding and transplanting operations and harvests the food grains. As a share-cropper, he gets a share of the produce which varies from State to State (usually 25–50 per cent; it could also go beyond). Share-croppers are known by different names in different States like *bataidar* in Bihar, *bhagchasi* in Odisha and *bargadar* in West Bengal.

Under less favourable circumstances, they provide agricultural implements and inputs, different kinds of unpaid labour/service to the landowner as and when needed or demanded but what they receive in terms of remuneration, mostly in kind, is a pittance.

Regardless of whether one is an agricultural worker or a share-cropper, one has to depend heavily on the consumption loan given by the employer-cum-landowner. Prof. Amit Bhaduri in his seminal work 'Analysis of Semi-feudalism in East Indian Agricultural Frontier, Calcutta'[6] has graphically analysed the situation of perpetual indebtedness for both, i.e., agricultural worker and share-cropper. To quote from that brilliant piece of historical research:

6 (Now Kolkata) published on 19 September 1973

> Suppose the produce of land operated by a *bargadar* is 100 mounds of paddy and his minimum consumption requirement is twenty-eight mounds. If he gets forty per cent of the produce, then his legal share is forty mounds. But there is an outstanding past debt of twelve mounds. He has, therefore, to pay back twelve mounds as principal after harvest plus say another twelve mounds as interest charged at 100 per cent. Thus after paying back (twelve plus twelve) twenty-four mounds out of his legal share of forty mounds, he is left with only (forty minus twenty-four) sixteen mounds. Since his annual consumption need is twenty-eight mounds, he must borrow again (twenty-eight minus sixteen) twelve mounds thereby perpetuating a constant cycle of indebtedness. However, many share-croppers are not even so fortunate and get more and more into debt which they can never pay back--one bad harvest, some extra borrowing due to family emergencies like illness or social obligations and the *bargadar* is in the grip of hopelessly accumulating debt which he can never pay back.

A deeper analysis of the factors contributing to their plight and predicament is called for. Prof. Utsa Patnaik, who is widely recognised as an authority on the issues of agrarian crisis, food security and poverty, perceives the problem differently at different phases of history. To illustrate:

> The principal contradiction during the colonial period was between 'the Indian people as a whole and imperialism and its local comprador allies.

The contradiction after independence lies between the mass of working peasantry and labourers on the one hand and the minority of landlord, traders and moneylenders who monopolised control over land and money capital'.

The current scenario may be described as one of highly skewed distribution of land, continuing direct/indirect dependence of nearly two-thirds of the population on agriculture and poor development of the means of agricultural production. This has ensured continuance of semi-feudal relations of production in agriculture. The choice today is between ending tenancies altogether and conferring rights of land ownership to the tiller as in the highly equitable Kerala model or retaining tenancy and affording the best possible protection to tenurial rights such as non-ejection from land, apportionment of an absolutely fair share of the produce in case of share-croppers, no cheating in weighment and quality of food grains. Wherever such a fair share has to be paid, payment of remunerative and living wage to all agricultural workers principally in cash must be enforced at any cost so that they do not get indebted and eventually bonded.

Question 14

What are the central and subsidiary objectives of BLS (A) Act?

Answer: The central objectives of BLS (A) Act are:

- Abolition of BLS (Section 4);
- Promoting the welfare of the freed bonded labourers by securing and protecting the economic interests of such persons (Section 11);
- Preventing relapse to bondage under the erstwhile or any other master/bonded labour keeper of those who have been rescued/ released and rehabilitated (Section 11);
- Implementing measures for rehabilitation of all released bonded labourers--physical, economic and psychological (Section 14(b));
- Prosecution and conviction of principal offenders of the crime and that of other accomplices (Sections 16-20);
- Preventing occurrence and recurrence of social and economic

exploitation of weaker sections of society (members of SC, ST and OBC) who often get into a situation of bondage due to circumstances beyond their control (Preamble).

The subsidiary objectives which in effect amount to provision of substantial reliefs and concessions to the victims of BLS are:

- Liability to repay bonded debt stands extinguished (Section 6);
- Creditor not to accept payment against extinguished debt (Section 9);
- Every attachment made before commencement of the Act and not fully satisfied before such commencement, for the recovery of any bonded debt shall stand vacated under Section 6(4);
- Possession of any property belonging to a bonded labourer/member of his family/other dependent, if forcibly taken over by the creditor for the recovery of bonded debt before commencement of the Act, shall stand restored after such commencement under Section 6(5);
- Any suit or proceeding for the enforcement of any obligation under BLS including a suit or proceeding for the recovery of any advance made to a bonded labourer pending on the date of commencement of the Act shall stand dismissed under Section 6(9);
- Property of a bonded labourer under any mortgage, charge, lien or other encumbrance in connection with any bonded debt immediately before the commencement of the Act shall be restored to the possession of the former on such commencement under Section 7(1);
- A freed bonded labourer is not to be evicted from any homestead or other residential premises which he was occupying immediately before the commencement of the Act under Section 8(1);
- If after the commencement of the Act such person is evicted by the creditor from any homestead land or other residential premises, the Executive Magistrate in charge of the sub-division within which such homestead or residential premises is situated, shall

restore possession of such homestead or residential premises to the bonded labourer under Section 8(2);

- Every bonded labourer who has been detained in civil prison, whether before or after judgment shall be released from such detention forthwith under Section 6(10).

Question 15

To what extent have these objectives been fulfilled?

Answer: A law is merely a framework, an enabling mechanism which sets the pace and tone of a set of activities in pursuance of the provisions contained in the framework and with the help of institutional mechanisms set up thereunder.

In pursuance of the provisions of the BLS (A) Act, notifications were issued by most of the State Governments vesting District Magistrates with powers under Sections 10, 11 and 12 of the Act.

Notifications were also issued vesting the Executive Magistrates with powers of a Judicial Magistrate, first or second class in pursuance of provisions of Section 21(1) of the Act.

Most of the State Governments, both on their own as also on the directions issued by the Supreme Court, took steps to constitute vigilance committees at the district and sub-divisional level under Section 13.

The Act was amended in April 1985 to make it abundantly clear that contract labour and inter-State migrant labour may also come within the purview of the law if they fulfil the conditions of BLS as defined in Section 2(g).

A centrally sponsored scheme providing for apportionment of funds between Central and State governments on 50:50 basis for rehabilitation of freed bonded labourers was launched in May 1978. The per capita rehabilitation assistance which was fixed at ₹4,000 and which was to be released in four installments was subsequently enhanced to ₹6,250 from 1 January 1986, to ₹10,000 from 1 April 1995 and to ₹20,000 from 1 May 2000. The revised notification also provided that the entire sanctioned amount was to be released in one single installment. This has now been converted from 17 May 2016 to a Central Scheme (100 per cent Centrally funded) with liberal scales of rehabilitation assistance such as:

- Per adult male beneficiary: ₹1 lakh.
- Special category beneficiaries such as children including orphans or those rescued from organised forced begging rings or other forms of forced child labour and women: ₹2 lakh.
- Extreme cases of deprivation/marginalisation such as transgender or women/children rescued from brothels, massage parlours, trafficked and disabled persons: ₹3 lakh.

The scheme provides for grant-in-aid support in addition to rehabilitation assistance of the following nature:

1. Assistance for survey of a district to identify victims of BLS: ₹4.5 lakh per district.
2. Assistance for awareness generation per State: ₹10 lakh.
3. Assistance for conducting evaluation studies: ₹1 lakh per evaluation study.
4. Creation of a permanent corpus called Bonded Labour Rehabilitation Fund for ₹10 lakh to be placed at the disposal of the District Magistrate.
5. Immediate subsistence assistance of at least ₹5,000 to be paid to the rescued person out of the District Bonded Labour Rehabilitation Fund.

The entire per capita rehabilitation assistance along with the subsistence allowance as per revised scales is to be released in one single installment.

Between 1981 and 2012, the Supreme Court of India has pronounced as many as twenty-six judgments with a number of seminal directions. Through these judgments and directions issued, the apex court has given a very broad, liberal and expansive interpretation of the law. The apex court has also dispelled a number of doubts, disputes, misgivings and reservations and has put the enforcement of the provisions of the law vis-a-vis the role of State Government, DM, vigilance committees, NGOs and all other stake-holders in a proper and holistic perspective.

Supreme Court vide its judgment on a PIL treated as a WP[7] in *People's Union for Civil Liberties Vs State of Tamil Nadu* and others under Article 32 of the Constitution and more specifically vide order dated 13 May 1994 and 11 November 1997 entrusted to NHRC the responsibility of monitoring and overseeing the extent of implementation of the provisions of BLS (A) Act by different State/UTs.

In a subsequent order of the apex court dated 5 May 2004 delivered by Chief Justice of India S Rajendra Babu and Justice GP Mathur, six additional directions were issued. While five directions were meant for State Governments in matters of identification, rescue/release and rehabilitation of the victims of BLS, in the first direction they were asked to cooperate with NHRC and send periodic status reports in the form prescribed by the Commission once every six months.

Between 7 October 2004 and 7 December 2008, the

7 WP(Civil) No 3922/85 read with WP (Crl) No 153/82, WP © No 166/95, 380/96, SLP (C) 9795/96

Chairperson, Member-in-charge of the subject of bonded labour and Special Rapporteurs (Chaman Lal, K R Venugopal and the author) visited all major States, conducted in-depth reviews and have submitted over one hundred review reports to the Commission. These were sent to the State Governments by the latter for compliance. Their Action Taken Reports (ATRs) were received, reviewed by the Commission and the State Government were advised again and again to comply with the recommendations made by the Commission.

Additionally, the Commission has been conducting well-organised training programmes at the national, state, divisional and district levels for better familiarisation and sensitisation of DMs, ADMs, SDMs, SPs, SHOs, members of VCs, all other district level officers and Magistrates concerned with implementation of BLS (A) Act and all other poverty alleviation/employment generation/credit disbursement programmes which have a bearing on the livelihood, income and quality of life of bonded labour beneficiaries. Fifty such workshops have been conducted by the Commission so far.

As desired by the apex court,[8] the Commission has apprised the former through a detailed report on the current status of enforcement of BLS (A) Act in different States towards the latter half of 2009.

Despite operational constraints, some NGOs who are genuinely good, reliable, committed to social action and have a good track record of social work, who live in remote, interior and inaccessible pockets and who are otherwise non-political or

8 Vide proceedings dated 6 February 2009 in WP (C) No.3922/85

apolitical entities have set very good examples (though limited in number) of identification, rescue/release, repatriation and rehabilitation of bonded labourers,

Here the silver linings end and the grey areas begin. These are:

- VCs are yet to be constituted in all the 719 districts and over 3,000 sub-divisions of the country.
- They are not being reconstituted whenever due, i.e., after expiry of two years of the life of the first Committee.
- Contrary to the provision made in Rule 4 of BLS (A) Rules, they do not continue to meet till they are reconstituted.
- Due to procedural hassles, a long interregnum prevails between the expiry of the old committee and its reconstitution which adversely affects implementation of various provisions of the law with which VCs are intimately involved.
- Such persons who eventually find their way to either district or sub-divisional level committees do not have the educational qualification, professional experience and expertise, far less the understanding and commitment, empathy and sensitivity as would enable them to do justice to their mandate as members of a VC.
- The meetings of the VCs remain mostly ceremonial and not businesslike.
- The committees do not have with them a list of industries, establishments, occupations and processes which will have the potential of engaging victims of BLS.
- No serious efforts have been made in the direction of collection of this vital information in the district/sub-division relevant to BLS (A) Act from the concerned officers of respective departments.
- The VCs might have been able to do a semblance of justice to their mandate if they would have adhered to the following modalities of action such as:

- Going to the field for collection of intelligence about prevalence of BLS in a few selected and sensitive pockets;
- Carrying a simple questionnaire to be addressed to the households or establishments or both;
- Collecting, compiling and analysing relevant information so collected in course of field visits to arrive at a final conclusion about prevalence of BLS and status of marginalised sections of the society in a particular area, i.e., free and unfree;

- By not undertaking field visits, the VCs fail to discharge their primary mandate i.e. conducting a survey as required u/s 14(e) of the Act to identify the victims of BLS;
- Such surveys, wherever conducted, have been directionless and have not produced the desired results; mostly nil reports have been submitted at the end of the survey.
- Instead of involving good NGOs to complement and supplement the efforts of the VCs as clearly emphasised by the Supreme Court in *Neerja Chaudhary Vs State of MP and Others*[9] judgement of 8 May 1984, the task of conducting a field level survey is entrusted to lower echelons of bureaucracy i.e. officers of Revenue or Labour Departments.
- Such functionaries, devoid of knowledge of the provisions of law and the sensitivity to conduct a survey, as also on account of their deep-rooted collusion with the landed gentry (who invariably are the bonded labour keepers) and bias/prejudice against the poor make a mockery of the law and the procedure established by law.
- This is what resulted in much less number of bonded labourers coming to the surface after survey than what exists on the ground.
- Despite the DMs having been vested with wide powers u/s 10,11

9 In WP (Crl) No 1263 of 1982 (AIR 1984 SC 1099)

and 12 of BLS (A) Act, the district administration in most of the districts seems to be in a denial mode about existence of BLS.

- It, in particular, seems to be suffering from the following mindset:
  - BLS is a thing of the past;
  - With enactment of a central law, it is deemed to have been abolished lock, stock and barrel;
  - All that was required to be done has been done and there is nothing more which is left to be attended to;
  - Conducting fresh surveys would open up vestiges of a feudal past;
  - That will bring discredit to the administration; it will also be a slur on the image of the State Government.

Such a negative stand seems to be the dominant trend despite late Justice Bhagwati counselling the State Governments and district administrations that acknowledging existence of BLS neither brings any slur on the State Government nor any discredit to district administration; instead, it comes quite handy in providing timely relief to a very large number of helpless victims of a feudal practice. Provision of such relief should bring a lot of happiness, satisfaction and joy to administration.

Precisely on account of such mindsets, fresh surveys are not being conducted and the number of added victims of BLS between 2000 and 2018 appears to be very small and virtually remains the same.

Even prior to this in late 1990s and early 2000, as the following illustration would show, the entire outcome of the process of identification of victims of BLS seems to have been negative.

In late 1990s, a district level survey was conducted in Tamil Nadu with the help of NGOs and 38,000 victims of BLS were found. When the cases were placed before the Executive Magistrate appointed under S21(1) and vested with powers of a Judicial Magistrate, as many as 25,000 cases were dropped, leaving 13,000 persons without any speaking order and application of mind.

A similar survey was conducted in 2000-01 in Malkangiri in South Western Odisha and 701 bonded labourers were identified. When the cases were presented before the sub-divisional officer competent to take a decision, he dismissed all cases except nineteen on the following premises:

- Between the alleged bonded labour keeper and alleged victim, there is a relationship of father-in-law and son-in-law and it could not be a bonded relationship.

Such a perception is undisputedly flawed for the following reasons:

- BLS in the BLS(A) Act does not rest on the premise of biological/ social relationship;
- The bonded labour keeper and the victim may have such a biological/social relationship but that does not take away the ingredients of BLS as in 2(g) of BLS (A) Act;
- If such ingredients exist, BLS will be conclusively established.

The more important questions emerging out of the decision to dismiss such a large number of cases presented on the strength of a thorough survey are:

- Where would these helpless and hapless persons go?
- Whom would they look up to in terms of their release and rehabilitation?
- It is particularly unfortunate as they would have got the impression in course of the survey that they are working under bonded labour conditions and they deserve rescue/release/rehabilitation;

- They would now be demoralised that they are not going to be released as victims of BLS and have to be reconciled to their lot.

The above examples (they are only illustrative and not exhaustive) go to show that the central objectives of the law could not be fulfilled to a large extent for reasons which were largely human failures related to mindsets and were fully remediable;

It may be apt to quote in this context from the Preamble to Unesco Constitution:'If wars begin in the minds of men, it is in the minds of men that foundations of peace will have to be laid'.

Question 16

What is the difference between normal migration and distress migration?

Answer: Migration is the act or process of moving from one country, region or place of abode to another. Such movement can be in search of better employment, better wages, better means of livelihood and better standard of living as also for sale of one's skill or endowment. Distress migration is actuated by conditions of disadvantage such as:

- Drought or dry spells for a prolonged period;
- Loss of, or damage to crops;
- Lack of stable and durable avenues of employment which should be full, freely chosen, productive and remunerative;
- Quest for sheer biological survival.

The distress or disadvantage arises out of and also gets accentuated on account of the following:

- Long distance between originating and destination point;
- Recruitment of a person on payment of advance without any written document;

- Women and children (including infants and toddlers) being often required to accompany the male migrant worker as they cannot be left behind;
- Alien character of the destination point in terms of climate, weather, language, local customs and traditions, court procedures, etc.;
- Women accompanying male migrant husbands remain vulnerable to sexual harassment at the worksite;
- Children accompanying their parents are invariably pushed involuntarily to work and remain victims of educational deprivation;
- Long hours of work without any spreadover, denial of weekly-off, non-payment of OT wage for work in excess of the scheduled hours of work and denial of all other statutory facilities and amenities such as housing accommodation, first-aid, specialised medical treatment, protective clothing, crèche for children, passbook, safety appliances, etc.

Question 17

What are the commonalities and differences between migration and trafficking?

Answer: The commonalities between migration and trafficking are:

- Movement from one geographical point to another;
- Factors which contribute to both, such as low-end poverty, socio-economic deprivation, traditional and cultural practices;
- Shifting the location of the worksite from one point to another;
- Those who recruit people for migration and those who traffic them may be oracles of too many promises and allurements but are invariably not the authors of their fulfilment;
- Both migration and trafficking may involve cross-border operations;

- Both may entail forced/bonded labour.

The differences are:

- There may be movement in both migration and trafficking but there is no freedom of movement in trafficking;
- There is invariably an element of payment of advance in migration but there is no such payment in trafficking;
- There is a semblance of option, discretion and volition in migration in general as opposed to coercion, regimentation and use of force in trafficking;
- The duration of work/employment is specified in migration whereas the same is not so specified in trafficking;
- Commercial sexual exploitation, forced transfer of organs, forced begging/adoption/marriage, drug peddling, etc., constitute the exclusive domain of trafficking.

  Migration with both inducement and application of force, total deprivation of basic human rights at the destination point, denial of freedom to leave the work-site, change of employer and forfeiture of the freedom to pursue alternative avenues of livelihood makes migration co-terminus with trafficking for forced/bonded labour.

Question 18

Why is distress inter-State migration (which is often associated with human bondage) objectionable?

Answer: Freedom of movement from one part of the territory of India to another and freedom to pursue an avocation of one's choice is a fundamental right guaranteed by Articles 19(d) and 19(g) of the Constitution. Migration is the movement of human beings in pursuit of certain cherished objects such as better employment, better wages and better standard of living and, therefore, apparently there is nothing wrong or objectionable *per se* in migration.

Besides, migration provides an outlet and opportunity for flowering of one's imagination, ingenuity, endowment and skills for better earning and better quality of life. Migration becomes objectionable only when it takes place in a distress situation when the person moving out to a worksite at the destination point is helplessly driven against his wishes due to poverty. Migration becomes objectionable when it leads to exploitation characterised by:

- Deprivation of the irreducible barest minimum needs (food, housing, potable water, hygiene, sanitation, nutrition, medical care, leisure and recreation);
- Confined to one point, movements outside the workplace being under constant surveillance and being generally restricted/denied.

It becomes objectionable on account of:

- The element of loan/debt/advance is extended by the recruiting agents to the migrant worker invariably without any written contract;
- This binds the worker to one employer and one workplace;
- The worker forfeits the freedom to leave the assigned worksite and work at an alternative worksite with a different employer for a better livelihood even when his treatment by the existing employer is abusive, oppressive and inhuman;
- The migrant worker will always be told that he cannot leave the worksite until and unless the debt incurred by him has been fully liquidated;
- The debt cannot be fully liquidated due to the quixotic logic of usury which eludes all reason and rationality.

It becomes objectionable on account of:

- Abusive and oppressive treatment by the employer, contractors, sub-contractors and their minions which is often demeaning and degrading.

- Long hours of work without any spread-over, without any weekly off and without OT wages for work in excess of scheduled hours i.e. nine hours a day and 48 hours a week;
- Low wages (often lower than notified minimum wage);
- Unauthorised deduction from wages for payment of commission to middle-men;
- Absence of creche and anganwadi for early childhood education of children accompanying migrant parents (as they cannot be left behind) and care of health and nutrition of children (3-6 years);
- Absence of facility for education of children in their own mother tongue accompanying migrant parents (6-14 years);
- Absence of food security;
- Purchase of food grains (rice, wheat, *jowr, bajra, ragi*) from open market at exorbitant prices, avoidable expenses incurred in undergoing medical check-up and treatment of self and family members, pushing the migrant workers to the brink of further indebtedness.

It becomes objectionable on account of:

- A difficult and hazardous work environment;
- Non-provision of safety appliances to the workers;
- Occurrence of man-made accidents causing injury and resulting in death and incapacitation;
- Non-reporting of accidents as required under S10B of Employees' Compensation Act, 1923 (as amended in 2009);
- Non-payment of ex-gratia and employees' compensation as may be due to the legal heirs of the deceased.

It also becomes objectionable due to non-payment of

statutory dues as required under Sections 13-16 of Inter-State Migrant Workmen (Regulation of Employment and Conditions of Service) Act, 1979 such as:

- Journey allowance;
- Wages during journey period;
- Displacement allowance;
- Protective clothing;
- Prescribed medical facilities;
- Suitable residential accommodation.

Question 19

What is trafficking in human beings?

Answer: The dictionary meaning of trafficking is trade or dealing in some specific commodity or service often of an illegal nature.

- Labour trafficking means trading in human beings with an ulterior motive (for profit through exploitation) which stands prohibited in the Philadelphia Declaration of June 1944 as also in the UN Convention against Transnational Organised Crime adopted on 15 November 2000.
- The definition of 'traffic in persons' as given in the Criminal Law (Amendment)[10] is broadly the same as in the first Protocol to the UN Convention against Transnational Organised Crime (referred to above) which was adopted at Palermo (Italy) in December 2000.
- Such traffic-in-persons is for four types of exploitation such as:
    - Physical exploitation;
    - Any form of sexual exploitation;
    - Slavery or practices similar to slavery or servitude;
    - Forced removal of organs.

---

10 Act of 2 April 2013 by way of amendment of S370 of IPC 1860

There are three principal components of labour trafficking such as:

- it is an action with intention;
- it is a means of recruitment;
- it is for a specific purpose.

The action component has the following sub-components:

- recruitment;
- transportation;
- transfer;
- harbouring and receipt of persons.

The 'means of recruitment' component has the following sub-components:

- threat;
- use of force;
- other forms of coercion;
- abduction;
- deception;
- fraud;
- abuse of power;
- position of vulnerability;
- giving or receiving payments or benefits.

All these are directed to achieve the consent of a person having control over another person. As a matter of fact, consent of the person being recruited is of no consequence as use of force or coercion does not call for any consent. The 'specific purpose' component is directed towards exploitation of the person recruited under the four heads as specified earlier.

Question 20

What are the redeeming features of the Criminal Law (Amendment) Act, 2013?

Answer: The redeeming features are as under:

- After the Constitution of India was adopted on 26 November 1949 and in pursuance of the provisions of Article 23 read with Article 35(a)(ii) of the Constitution, this is the first enactment to deal with trafficking in human beings;
- In terms of its scope and content, it has adopted the UN Supplementary Convention, 1956 in letter and spirit;
- The latter defines 'institutions and practices similar to slavery' to include;
- Debt bondage;
- Serfdom;
- Deprivation of the rights of women and children;
- The definition of trafficking is almost identical with the definition given in Article 3 of the Protocol attached to the UN Convention against Transnational Organised Crime adopted at Palermo to "prevent, suppress and punish trafficking"; it is a clear and comprehensive definition;
- It makes trafficking in persons a cognisable and non-bailable offence with a stringent punishment which may go up to life imprisonment.

Question 21

The phenomenon of trafficking is invariably associated with forced/bonded labour and the latter also ends up with trafficking. Do you have any example to illustrate this point?

Answer: A true story would serve as a useful illustration of the above point. A young girl of fifteen belonging to the community of drummers (they are called *bajgee*s in Uttarakhand who are required to beat drums during festivals as a matter of discharge of community obligation) belonging to the SC community and also landless is married off to another *bajgee* in a neighbouring village of Uttarakhand.

The girl's father demands and receives ₹2,000 as bride price from the girl's husband. The husband takes the girl home to his village and puts her to work on a strip of land belonging to the local Rajput moneylender to whom he is indebted. At a usurious rate of interest, ₹2,000 taken as a loan from the Rajput moneylender assumes astronomical proportions in due course. Both husband and wife who work on the land of the moneylender are reduced to the level of bonded labourers in as much as:

- o They cannot leave the moneylender until the loan amount has been fully liquidated;
- o It can never be fully liquidated as (a) there is no written contract (b)the victims do not either know or precisely remember how much loan they took (c) how much has been paid (d) how much is outstanding towards principal and interest;
- o The Rajput moneylender unable to recover the amount (both principal and interest) suggests to the husband that the young bride should be sent down to the plains for a year or so for prostitution;
- o An agent is arranged to take the woman to Delhi where she is sold to a brothel keeper for ₹3,000. The loan is paid off and the balance amount is shared between the agent and the moneylender;

With this the transaction is complete. It also sees the conversion of debt bondage to prostitution through the trafficking route;

- After a year or so, as was the understanding with the Rajput moneylender, the young bride is brought back as a bonded labourer to work for the master along with her husband. This completes the cycle of debt-bondage-trafficking for sexual exploitation-debt-bondage.

Question 22

What are the problems, constraints and challenges which have been experienced or are likely to be experienced in handling the issue of trafficking in human beings?

Answer: Trafficking is a multi-faceted or multi-dimensional social evil as also a major challenge.

In dealing with this evil, one has to confront, grapple and eventually overcome extremely powerful manipulative forces which have national and international net-works, abundance of both money and muscle power, often invisible, inaccessible and completely non-accountable. Such an encounter entails tremendous hazards to the life and limb of those who come forward to brave such risks.

This is what explains as to why many NGOs who are otherwise genuinely committed to social action through anti-trafficking operations are not in the field as the prospect of success in this domain of social action is not as bright as it is elsewhere.

It may, however, be noted that NGOs are only one of the players in the game; there are many others such as police, passport/visa officials, immigration officials, railways/bus authorities, airport authorities whose cooperation and collaboration is a must to do justice to anti-trafficking operations. Such cooperation, collaboration and functional co-ordination does not easily obtain in the field and that is what explains why human traffickers invariably have a field day.

The following are some of the outstanding challenges in the field of anti-trafficking operations.

I. Lax law enforcement

To quote a UN document:

> Very little action is taken by the police or the judiciary against traffickers. With regard to the evidentiary procedures involved in trafficking cases, the women and girls who are victims of trafficking are the primary witnesses against the perpetrators. In cases involving organised crime, they are extremely vulnerable and in fear for their lives.

II Collusion between law enforcement agencies and traffickers

When the fence starts eating the crops and when the protector becomes the devourer, the doors of justice will be automatically closed on all sides and there will be no hope of any deliverance for the poor, innocent and helpless victims of trafficking. If the law enforcement officers such as police, border security force, passport/visa officials, immigration and airport officials are hand-in-glove with the procurers, recruiting agents, traffickers, pimps and brothel owners on account of which the latter get off the hook and escape with impunity after committing the crimes, the law breakers will undoubtedly have a field day.

III Multiple points of operation

Traffickers operate at three points: source, transit and destination. These points are spread over long distances with a difficult terrain which makes traffickers invisible, inaccessible and unaccountable; they also make anti-trafficking operations formidable or extremely difficult.

IV Impenetrable networks

Widespread network of traffickers facilitates trading in human beings. The latter are responsible for housing the victims in homes at a transit point with a railway connection thus ensuring their train journey to the collection points and handing them over to another network of agents at the lower point.

V Multiple layers/tiers through which traffickers operate

The layers/tiers through which traffickers operate are:

- Master trafficker or the kingpin;
- Primary trafficker or the procurer;
- Secondary traffickers;
- Spotters or the chain of grass roots-level intelligence gatherers.

The master traffickers, prime movers, arch manipulators, principal profiteers and master criminals remain throughout untraceable and untraced. The underworld connections through which trafficking networks operate also remain equally untraceable and untraced

VI Special problems of border areas

The border areas (West Bengal, Bihar, Meghalaya, Nagaland, Manipur and Mizoram) which are most ideal for trading in human beings remain porous and it is next to impossible to seal them as we seal an envelope. This is on account of the following:

- Long stretch of thousands of kilometres;
- Inadequate policing;
- Collusion of law enforcement officials with the traffickers.

  To sum up, soft laws, lax enforcement, collusion of law enforcement officials, difficult geography and topography individually and cumulatively contribute to committing of trafficking crimes and the perpetrators of such crimes escaping unscathed.

Question 23

Why is trafficking in human beings, especially in women and children highly objectionable and totally unacceptable?

Answer: This can be looked at primarily from three angles namely:

- The very idea or concept of trafficking;
- Horrendous methods adopted;
- Mala fide purpose or intention;
- Overall consequences or impact which is too terrible for words;

I. **The very idea or concept**

- Trafficking in human beings may be an old, global and lucrative business phenomenon but as an idea or concept it is most bizarre and obnoxious;
- Associated with commercial sexual exploitation, forced/ bonded labour, slavery or practices similar to slavery, forced transfer of organs, it is the most brazen and egregious violation of human rights;
- It is an obscene affront to the dignity and rights of women and girls which are non-negotiable.

II. **Horrendous methods adopted:**

- The methods adopted in recruitment for trafficking are highly immoral and unethical such as:
    - Drugging;
    - Kidnapping;
    - Abduction;

  - Material inducement;
  - Deception (alluring people with fake job offer);
- Using marriage bureaus (5.9 per cent of the respondents in a survey conducted by NHRC in early 2000 were deceived by false promises of marriage) for forced marriages;
- Using placement agencies (their activities are mostly unregulated except in a few States like NCT of Delhi, Chhattisgarh and Jharkhand);
- Using tutorial agencies.

III. **Mala fide intention behind trafficking**

- The basic ulterior motive behind trafficking or trading in human beings is associated with profiteering through exploitation.
- Such exploitation which takes place by traffickers establishing complete control over their victims assumes multiple forms such as:
  - Forced/bonded labour;
  - Exploitation of prostitution of others;
  - Circus;
  - Camel jockeying;
  - Begging;
  - Domestic help;
  - Adoption;
  - Organ donation;
  - Marriage;
  - Child sex abuse;
  - Child pornography including pornographic performances.

IV. **Overall consequences or impact**

For children, trafficking puts childhood at its dead end. Practices like camel jockeying are cruel, inhuman and barbarous. Circus artistes bear the brunt of insufferable indignity, physical and sexual abuse, long hours of work, unhygienic and poor accommodation, loss of sleep and complete lack of freedom to leave the establishment despite such repression and violation of human rights. The plight and predicament of begging children who are physically disabled baffle description. As a profession it is illegal and immoral; it is also most degrading and dehumanising. Children who are recruited as domestic help are subjected to horrendous working conditions; they are also victims of educational deprivation. Children who are recruited for adoption are forced to forfeit the natural love and affection of biological parents. They have to reconcile themselves to the whims and caprices of adoptive parents. Organ donation may result in death of the donor due to lack of post-operative care. Foreigners who engage middle-men to recruit young girls for marriage, abandon the victims after some time and the girl is entirely at the mercy of the broker who sells her to brothel owners.

The brutal exploitation and suffering of trafficked children produces a terrible mental and emotional trauma for the survivors which manifests in:

- Malevolence;
- Helplessness;
- Withdrawal;
- Dissociation;
- Loss of confidence in self;
- Loss of confidence in others;
- Frustration and disillusionment with the whole world.

The victims who are traumatised (the trauma is worse in case of children) develop psychiatric disorders which include:

- Post-traumatic stress disorder;

- Depressive disorder;
- Psychotic disorder;
- Eating disorder.

Trafficked victims are stigmatised as outcastes; they face all-round isolation from the family, community and society. They are vulnerable to HIV/AIDS infection, drug addiction, teenage pregnancy and high risk abortion.

The victims are also compelled to lead illegal and immoral lives. Illegality taints every dimension of their lives. Criminalisation severely stigmatises them and intensifies victimisation.

Question 24

What are the implications of the two judgements of the Supreme Court Court of India while disposing of WPs 51, 75 and 186 filed by Bachpan Bachao Andolan?[11]

Answer: The pith and substance of the writ petitions were as under:

- Children from the poverty-stricken areas of Nepal and backward districts of India are trafficked to the circus and entertainment industry:
- Once inside the circus arena, they are trapped for the rest of their lives, leading a 'vagrant, tiresome and catastrophic existence';
- Despite a dialogue with and understanding from Indian Circus Federation (ICF), children continued to be trafficked to circus industry;
- Child artistes in the industry continued to be in bondage and unlawful confinement resulting in perpetual sexual harassment of girl artistes;

11 Dated 18 May 2001, delivered by Justices Dalbir Bhandari and AK Patnayak

- There are no labour or welfare laws which protect the rights of these children. There is no direct legislation which is vested with powers to deal with the problems of children who are trafficked into the circus industry. The police, labour or any other State agency is not prepared to deal with the issue of trafficking of girls from Nepal. The net result is that children are physically, emotionally and sexually abused in circus establishments;
- Additionally, poor accommodation, poor quality of food, overwork and loss of sleep, poor sanitation, no healthcare, occupational risks, poor remuneration and denial of all-round development need special attention.

Observations of the apex court

- Two million children aged 5-15 are forced into commercial sexual exploitation around the world; 5 lakh children are forced into the sex trade annually;
- Girls in the age-group 10-14 years are most vulnerable;
- India is home to 19 per cent of the world's children, with 440 million children being below 18 years;
- 40 per cent of India's children are vulnerable; 15 per cent of CSE workers in India are believed to be below 15 years and 25 per cent15-18 years;
- Women and children do not come to the brothels on their own but are brought through systematic, organised and illegal trafficking networks;
- Traffickers tend to work in groups and children who are being trafficked often changed hands to ensure that neither perpetrators of the crime nor the victims get caught during transit;
- Groups of traffickers include gang members, police, pimps and even politicians, all working in a nexus;

- The trafficking networks are well organised and have linkages both within the country and neighbouring countries.

Directions issued by the apex court

- Every Magistrate before whom a child is brought must be conscious of the provisions of the Juvenile Justice (Care and Protection of Children) Act, 2000;
- He must find out whether the child is below 18 years; if so, the child cannot be accused of an offence u/s 7 or 8 of ITPA;
- The child then will have to be protected under JJ Act;
- The Magistrate has a responsibility to ascertain and confirm that the person produced is a child by accurate medical examination;
- The definition of a child in Section 2(k) of JJ Act means a juvenile or a child as a person who has not completed 18 years of age;
- The child then should be handed over to the CWC to be taken care of by the latter;
- The performance of the CWC must be overseen by the High Court with a committee of not less than three judges and two psychiatrists;
- A minor trafficked child must be classified as a 'child in need of care and protection';
- There should not be any joint proceedings of a juvenile and a person who is not a juvenile;
- Courts must be directed that the same lawyer must not represent the trafficker as well as the trafficked minor;
- Evidence of a child should be taken *in camera*. Courts must protect the dignity of the children. The children's best interest should be of the highest priority;
- In order to implement the fundamental right of children under Article 21-A, it is imperative that the Central Government must

issue a suitable notification prohibiting the employment of children in circus within two months;

- Simultaneous raids should be conducted in all circuses to liberate the children and check the violation of their fundamental rights;
- The rescued children should be kept in care and protection homes till they attain the age of 18 years;
- The Union of India (respondent) is directed to talk to the parents of the children and in case they are willing to take their children back to their homes, they may be directed to do so after proper verification;
- The Union of India (respondent) is directed to frame a proper scheme of rehabilitation of rescued children.

Implications of the judgement[12]

- Several path-breaking directions were given in the said judgment such as:
  - Every case of missing child should be treated as the case of a trafficked child;
  - Every complaint in this regard should be registered as an FIR under S154 CrPC and follow-up investigation should be taken up immediately;
  - Every police station should have a police officer specially instructed, trained and designated as a Juvenile Welfare Officer under S107 of JJ (Care and Protection of Children) Act, 2015);
  - A para-legal volunteer should be made available by NALSA for every police station to keep a watch over the manner in which complaints relating to missing children are being dealt;

12 Delivered by Justice (late) Altamas Kabir, former CJI, Justice Vikramajit Sen and Justice SA Bobde dated 10 May 2013 by way of disposal of WP Nos 75 and 186

- A network should be created between NCPCR, SCPCR,Child Protection units at the District and Block level, all juvenile police units, all JJBs, all CWCs and all police stations.

Bhuvan Rivu, advocate for the petitioner in this case, ably piloted the case and carried it to a logical conclusion which was totally victim-centric.

Question 25

What has been the contribution of NHRC to action research in the domain of prevention and suppression of trafficking in human beings ?

Answer: NHRC was founded on 12 October 1993. A focal point on trafficking and women's right was created in 2001 with Justice Sujata Manohar in charge. Lack of reliable data on the nature and extent of trafficking—both within and outside India—was felt as the main hurdle in formulating a workable strategy to combat trafficking. To bridge this, a path-breaking action research project was commissioned in NHRC which was funded by USAID, supported by UNIFEM and executed by the Institute of Social Sciences (ISS). Sankar Sen, IPS, former DG, Investigation, NHRC and Head, Human Rights Division, ISS was the co-ordinator of this study and PM Nair, IPS, then IG, Police, Bihar was selected on deputation and appointed as Nodal Officer of the Project.

After four years, a report titled 'Trafficking in Women and Children in India' was published.[13] There are few research documents which can match the depth, comprehension, grass roots-level realism and piercing insight with which this document was written.

---

13 By Orient Longman in 2005. The report has 26 chapters spread over 748 pages

In Chapters 25 and 26, there are as many as 75 suggestions and recommendations which may be summarised as under:

- Trafficking should be viewed from a human rights perspective and not from the narrow, restricted angle of prostitution;
- The new approach should be holistic, participatory, convergent, rights-based and not paternalistic;
- A National Policy and Programme of Action should be formulated in implementation of which good, reliable, committed, non-political or apolitical NGOs should be the key players;
- A new self-contained and comprehensive law should be enacted by way of replacement of the existing archaic legislative framework;
- All national, governmental and non-governmental initiatives should be in the best interests of the victims;
- Guidelines should be formulated on minimum standards of care, attention, protection, rehabilitation and re-integration of the victims with the mainstream family, community and society;
- Similar guidelines should be formulated for all service providers, law enforcement officials, judicial officers, prosecutors, medical professionals, psycho-social professionals, counsellors and officials manning after-care homes;
- Minimum standards should be laid down in the area of:
  - prevention;
  - rescue/release;
  - rehabilitation;
  - re-integration;
  - counselling;
  - providing alternative and decent livelihood options;
  - economic and social empowerment of the victims.

MOUs need to be signed between the nodal agency i.e.

Ministry of Women and Child Development and other Ministries such as:

- MHRD;
- Law;
- Labour;
- Finance;
- Social Justice and Empowerment;
- MEA;
- Health and Family Welfare:
- ICT.

Trafficking being a national and global concern with multiple stake-holders and players, it is urgent and imperative that there is total functional co-ordination between Ministries/Departments and NGOs as also among NGOs within the State, across the States and across borders;

Some of the other preventive and corrective measures suggested are:

- The existing Child Helpline against trafficking needs to be strengthened;
- Panchayats at all levels should act as watchdogs and maintain constant vigilance and surveillance against trafficking and traffickers. They should also be made responsible to create and maintain a fairly accurate and updated database on inter-State migration, trafficking of girls and women and movement of placement agencies;
- Vulnerability mapping of both source areas and demand areas also need to be undertaken;
- A web portal should be developed by NHRC. This should be set up under one of the existing government agencies like the National

Crime Research Bureau (NCRB) and should have separate pages on:

- missing persons;
- suspected traffickers;
- intelligence and alert notices;
- fact-sheets of researchers;
- surveys conducted;
- conferences and workshops being held by various agencies and proceedings thereof;
- data on resource persons;
- anti-trafficking networks;
- NGOs.

Question 26

What has been the role and contribution of Integrated Anti-Human Trafficking Project of MHA with UNODC in April 2006?

Answer: On 12 December 2012, India ratified the UN Convention on Transnational Organised Crime and its two Protocols including the one on trafficking.

Ratification of an international treaty by a Member State of UN casts an obligation for (a) enactment of a law (b) formulation of a national policy and (c) adoption of a national programme of action.

Though laws like SITA and later ITPA were already on the statute book since 1956 (amended in 1978 and 1986), they were weak and deficient in many respects. The gaps, omissions and ambiguities in these laws were partially bridged by Criminal Law (Amendment) Act which came into force from 2 May 2013. It amended Section 370 of IPC, provided for the first time a clear definition of trafficking in persons on the model of the UN

Protocol on Trafficking as also stringent and deterrent penalties against traffickers but remained weak in terms of rescue/release, repatriation, rehabilitation and re-integration of victims/survivors.

These weaknesses were sought to be corrected by the Union Ministry of Women and Child Development by conceptualising, drafting and introduction of a comprehensive and self-contained Trafficking of Persons (Prevention, Protection & Rehabilitation) Bill first in 2016 and thereafter in 2018 integrating for the first time trafficking with forced/bonded labour, child labour, forced marriage, commercial sexual exploitation, drug peddling, begging and recruitment of children for war. Regretfully, the Bill could not be passed and lapsed.

As far as policy and programme of action are concerned, there are broadly two issues which emanate from NHRC's Action Research Study Report on Trafficking captioned 'Trafficking in Women and Children in India' (2004) which necessitate formulation of such a policy and programme of action, apart from discharge of the international treaty obligation. These are:

- a very low level of awareness about the crime of trafficking among the police personnel at all levels;
- a very low order of priority being accorded to the crime due to pre-occupation of police with crimes such as murder, rape, arson, breakdown of law and order.

These factors provided the driving force behind formulation of a project on 'Strengthening the law enforcement response in India against trafficking in persons through training and capacity building'.

This was a joint three-year project of the MHA, GoI and UNODC w.e.f. April 2006. The project aimed at raising, through a series of training programmes, the level of awareness of law enforcement officials and building their capacity for better investigation and a more effective manner of launching prosecutions and carrying them to a logical conclusion.

The following four constituted project activities:

- Training of police and prosecutors on anti-human trafficking (Art. 10 (2) of the UN Protocol on trafficking);
- Putting SOPs and protocols in place;
- Setting up of Anti-Human Trafficking Units (AHTUs);
- Advocacy and networking among the stakeholders (supporting Shelter Homes, etc.).

Five States, to start with, namely Andhra Pradesh, Bihar, Goa, Maharashtra and West Bengal, which represent source, destination and transit areas for human trafficking, were selected to come under the project.

This has been a very well thought-out, timely and appropriate institutional mechanism to deal with anti-trafficking operations such as rescue/release, repatriation and restoration of victims/survivors to the custody of families/parents. P M Nair, IPS, then IG Bihar, who was the principal investigator-cum-researcher in NHRC's anti-trafficking project and his wife Bhamathe Balasubramiam, former Additional Secretary, MHA had played a key role in conceptualisation, creation and operationalisation of the institutional mechanism. In 2016, she received international recognition from the US Government for her outstanding contribution to anti-trafficking operations. So far there are 262 AHTUs at the Central and 91 AHTUs at the State level.

The plethora of functions being currently discharged by the AHTUs are:

- Rescue/release of victims/survivors;
- Post-rescue care and attention of the rescued persons with a view to empowering them;
- Preventing the incidence of re-trafficking;
- Sensitising, capacity building and training of police and prosecution personnel, especially at the grassroot level to improve law enforcement response to the organised crime of human trafficking;
- Developing a comprehensive database on the criminal activity of trafficking of human beings by effective use of information and communication technology;
- Sharing of information across stakeholders, States and other organisations for effective implementation of anti-trafficking measures relating to its criminal aspect and promoting best practices in these areas;
- Enhancing cooperation between law enforcement agencies, concerned government departments and NGOs who have the expertise and capacity to assist trafficking victims.

So far over 500 training programmes have been conducted and over 15,000 persons (police and prosecutors) have been trained. The project has assisted in developing resource books about protocols and standard operating procedures. Manuals for Training of Trainers (TOT) programmes have been developed by BPR&D and three national-level TOT workshops have been conducted. A cascading approach (a trainee of today becomes the trainer of tomorrow) has been adopted in conducting the training programmes (both TOT as well as grass roots-level training programmes).

For manning of AHTUs according to a prescribed pattern, the State Governments have made available police personnel and officials from other departments.

The following table provides a glimpse of the positive outcome of training of personnel and AHTUs being in position for more than a decade.

- Anti-Human Trafficking cases registered: 934
- Rescue operations held: 372
- Total number of victims rescued: 1,637
- Minors among those rescued: 269
- Total number of traffickers and exploiters arrested: 1,947
- Number of customers among those arrested: 821
- Traffickers convicted: 30
- Places of exploitation closed: 34
- Number of rescued persons for whom the process of rehabilitation has been initiated: 876

The problems, constraints and challenges faced by AHTUs are:

- To date, there is no self-contained, integrated and comprehensive law covering all aspects of anti-trafficking operations i.e. rescue/release, repatriation, restoration, rehabilitation and re-integration of victims/survivors with family, community and society as a whole;
- There is no comprehensive national policy and programme of action on physical, emotional, psychological and economic rehabilitation of rescued/released victims;
- AHTU's role ends with rescue/release, repatriation and restoration of victims; no funds have been placed at their disposal for rehabilitation and re-integration of victims which involve psychological counselling and engagement of psychiatrists, clinical psychologists and psychiatric social workers for sufficiently long periods across States, districts and dispersed locations which require substantial funds.

An important silver lining which is visible on the horizon is on account of a very positive announcement made by Minister, WCD Smriti Irani on 2 November 2019 that (a) anti-human trafficking units and women's help desks (WHD) will be set up in all districts (719) with the help of Nirbhaya Fund (b) a sum of ₹100 crore will be made available for this purpose by GoI.

Question 27

Why is bonded labour system considered to be highly objectionable and totally unacceptable?

Answer: Every individual in the society has a right to grow, rise, prosper, expand and diversify by effectively harnessing his/ her own imagination, ingenuity, creativity and capacity for innovation in a climate of freedom, dignity, spontaneity and security.

Exercise of such a basic right cannot, however, be at the cost of others, by demeaning, degrading and dehumanising others and in particular, the poor, deprived, disadvantaged and marginalised sections of the society by taking recourse to deception, fraud, coercion and regimentation.

That would amount to exploitative labour or forced labour which may be attributed to man's infinite greed and rapacity to rob others of their basic dignity and rights at an enormous cost to humanity.

Every worker is primarily a human being and is entitled to the irreducible barest minimum to grow, thrive and sustain himself/ herself and members of his/her family through a safe, clean, and congenial work environment which is free from dust, heat, smoke, noise, pollution, accidents and occupational diseases and to work and live with dignity, decency, equality, security and freedom from discrimination.

He/she has infinite possibilities and potentialities. Given a climate of freedom, constructive counselling, encouragement and incentives, these can be optimally harnessed and would enable every worker to contribute his/her very best to the well-being of the enterprise and growth of the economy.

If one set of human beings (including workers) are robbed of their freedom, dignity and decency by the whims and caprices of another set, by an arrogant and irresponsible exercise of power and authority, they will cease to be human beings.

In case of children who are pushed involuntarily to harsh, arduous drudgery and hazardous work at the cost of their education, health, psyche and well-being, petals of childhood will wither away in wilderness before blossoming to the flowers of youth and manhood.

Such children will be reduced to physical and emotional wrecks.

Forced/bonded labour is perverse and abominable for the following reasons:

- All men are created equal and are endowed with certain inalienable rights;
- None has the moral and ethical right to rob another of the right to life, liberty and pursuit of happiness;
- Any hindrance to human beings to pursue their material well-being and spiritual development in conditions of freedom, dignity and security is unwarranted interference with one's natural potential for growth and must be stoutly resisted.

This is how forced/bonded labour is:

- Repugnant to civilised human conscience and existence;
- It is the most flagrant violation of inalienable human rights;
- It is an obscene affront to human dignity and decency;

- It is anti-podal to the concept of decent work propounded by former Director General ILO Juan Somavia;
- It is an outrageous and unpardonable crime against humanity.

Question 28

What are the factors contributing to continuance of BLS?

Answer: Historically speaking, it is evident from a number of writings that slavery in ancient India was an integral and essential feature of the inequitable social structure. The all-powerful State did not make any perceptible effort to bring about any drastic change in the hierarchical social structure based on the caste system which promoted irrational subjugation of persons of lower caste to upper ones and inevitable slavery. Medieval India did not mark any perceptible departure from the inequitable economic and social relationship which obtained in ancient India. As a matter of fact, it acquired a new dimension due to rapid increase in rural indebtedness. The seventeenth century was marked by frequent famines. Each outbreak of famine drove thousands of landless and assetless people without purchasing power and without any food security to a stage of desperation, starvation, indebtedness and bondage.

The beginning of the colonial era in the eighteenth century brought in the repulsive 'hereditary servitude' in many parts of South India. The zamindari system introduced by the colonial rulers in the later half of the eighteenth and early part of the nineteenth century remained in place for nearly 200 years and pauperised millions of artisans, craftsmen, spinners, weavers, potters, carpenters, cobblers and blacksmiths; rack-renting, absentee landlordism, poverty, indebtedness and bondage were the inevitable offshoots of zamindari system. The colonial rule did not create forced labour; it merely reinforced it. Elimination of forced/bonded labour was never high on the political or economic agenda of colonial rulers. The primary motive which ruled out such elimination was to maintain intact the status quo in an inegalitarian social order through political loyalty and revenue paying capacity of the non-cultivating upper caste absentee landlords or slave owners or bonded labour keepers.

Against this historical backdrop, it may be appropriate to precisely identify the factors responsible for growth of BLS. These are:

- A highly stratified social structure with layers and sub-layers (which acts like a labyrinthine maze in the impregnable societal fortress) based on artificial considerations of class, caste, clan, sect and so on;
- Caste-based discrimination, exploitation of and violence against those who are at the lower strata of the society for no fault of theirs;
- Lack of avenues of stable and durable employment giving rise to distress migration;
- Excessive seasonality of employment;
- Difficult nature of landscape (like Palamu in Jharkhand which has acidic soil without any capacity to retain water) which reduces investment in land and any appreciable return from such investment in land;
- Concentration of land-holdings in the hands of a few to the deprivation of many;
- Lack of easy access to resources or inputs of development like irrigation (both flow and lift) and land development;
- Non-enforcement of the provisions of MW Act and payment of wages in kind in a highly monetised economy does not make it possible to defray certain expenses (purchase of essential

commodities from a fair price shop, children's textbooks, uniforms, payment of tuition fee, medical check-up and treatment);

- Payment of wages in kind is fraught with the possibility of cheating by way of under-weightment and poor quality of food grains;
- Land of tribals usurped by non-tribal elements (lease, sale, transfer etc) is not easily restored in time to the former;
- Urgent, imperative and inescapable mortgage of ancestral land to the creditor for obtaining loans and advances for ceremonial and consumption expenditure which leads to alienation of land and conversion of small and marginal farmers as also rural artisans into share-croppers and landless agricultural labourers;
- Non-registration of share-croppers;
- Absence of any effective machinery for just and fair adjudication of land disputes resulting in pauperisation of the landless;
- Policy, law and prevailing practices are ineffective to prevent distress migration which provides the surest gateway to debt bondage;
- Not making credit available to the rural poor on reasonable terms and conditions on account of the ill-perceived notion of traditional bankers that (a) the poor are poor managers of assets (b) the poor cannot easily repay their loans as recorded by Prof. Mohammed Yunus, 2006 Nobel Laureate for Peace in his outstanding Grameen Bank experiment;
- Age-old diehard social customs, traditions and deep-rooted personal and social prejudices against organisations of the rural poor through which they can acquire visibility and voice and articulate their needs and concerns;

• National Food Security Act came into force on 5 July 2013. This is no doubt a landmark legislation as it fulfils one of the essential ingredients for enjoyment of the right to life

(Article 21). The State in India is implementing massive food, livelihood and social security programmes –some of the largest in the world (like ICDS). However, as reported by NC Saxena and Harsh Mander, Commissioner and Special Commissioner of the apex court respectively in their eighth report to the Supreme Court:

> All these programmes are plagued by corruption, leakage, errors in selection, delays, poor allocation and little accountability. They also tend to discriminate against and exclude those who need them most, by social barriers of gender, age, caste, ethnicity, faith, disability and State hostility to urban poor migrants, street and slum residents and unorganised workers.'

As has been observed time and again, members of the ST community numbering over 100 million prefer to consume certain food grains like *jower, bajra, ragi*, which are not available through PDS and, therefore, have to be purchased from open market at unaffordable rates. This taxes the limited income of the members of ST who have to incur loans to buy them from the market for their biological survival. They get into indebtedness which often leads to bondage.

According to a report of Dr Kerlin A Holloway, Regional Advisor, WHO, about 70 per cent Indians spend out of their private income on medicines and healthcare services in comparison to 30-40 per cent in other Asian countries like Sri Lanka. The erstwhile Planning Commission in India had admitted that about 31 million Indians were pushed to poverty because of ill health every year; 30 per cent of the population in India do not go in for any treatment due to financial constraints; and 20 per cent of the ailments in urban areas remained untreated due to financial constraints. It had further observed that about 47 and 31 per cent of the hospital admissions in rural and urban India respectively were financed by loan and sale of assets. Such loans lead to indebtedness and the latter to bondage.

Question 29

How do we identify victims of BLS? What is the rationale of such identification? What methodology should be adopted for an accurate identification?

Answer: Identification of the victims of BLS is not the same as identification of voters with indelible ink as at the time of casting one's ballot through the EVM. It is not the same as counting the heads in a decennial census operation.

Such identification in its true sense and ultimate analysis is

- Discovery of an unfree person;
- Restoration of the identity of a person who has been reduced from a full being to a half-being or non-being;
- Retrieving a victim from ignominy and obscurity, one who has bartered away his/her freedom for some petty loan/advance but who is not aware of the consequences of such indebtedness and unfreedom.

Why do we proceed to identify them? We do so as a part of the total process which should lead to its logical conclusion with rescue/release, repatriation (in case of inter-State migrant workmen) and rehabilitation of the victims—physical, psychological and economic.

We do this so that the victims may be able to lead an independent and autonomous existence where debt will no longer be the architect of their destiny.

We also do so as the victims can ill-afford to grapple with and overcome the adversarial elements which surround their lives due to ignorance, illiteracy and socio-economic backwardness.

We do this so that it would lead the victims to a situation where given two alternatives to development and economic empowerment, the persons who stand liberated from bondage should be able to have an informed, rational and judicious choice of that alternative which will be in their best interest.

The million-dollar question: How do we identify these unfortunate denizens of humanity whom former Union Labour Minister KV Raghurath Reddy (1974-77) calls the 'exiles of civilisation' and lift them from the morass of poverty and unfreedom to the mainstream of a civilised human society so that they can realise the dignity, beauty and worth of their human existence?

There are two aspects in the entire process of identification. One is the methodology and second is the institutional mechanism.

- Vigilance Committees at the district and sub-divisional level constitute the institutional mechanism under S13 of BLS (A) Act.
- Under S14(e) of the Act, the VCs have been mandated to conduct surveys for identifying victims of BLS.
- The Act and Rules are, however, silent on the procedure to be followed for such surveys.
- Late SR Sankaran, former Principal Secretary, Department of Social Welfare, Government of Andhra Pradesh, had conceived of one such methodology with a lot of imagination, insight and sensitivity. In the hierarchy of the steel frame of Indian bureaucracy it is difficult to come across yet another civil servant who could be more passionately committed to the total well-being of the oppressed and the depressed and who could inspire and motivate

scores of current and succeeding generations of bureaucrats with the ideals of total professional thoroughness for dedicated service to the poor and deprived sections of humanity tinged with probity, rectitude and self-abnegation, spartan simplicity, austerity and commitment.

It is a tragedy that his seminal work for alleviation of the misery and suffering of the poor and marginalised notwithstanding, he had to pay a heavy price for the most unorthodox, unconventional and exemplary manner of handling land reforms and bonded labour issues in Andhra Pradesh in mid and late 1970s.

- As a Socio-legal Investigating Commissioner of the Supreme Court in October-November 1983 and January-March 1984 (when the author was serving Government of India as its DG LW/JS in the MoL&E) he had the opportunity of translating the original circular of late Sankaran from Telugu to English, circulating it to all DMs of 460 districts then (now 719) and later adopting it with suitable modifications to suit local conditions obtaining in the stone quarries of Vijayawada and Faridabad which he was mandated to visit, interact with the workers in the quarries and crushers and report to the apex court about the conditions in which they were working and their current status—free or unfree.
- On 15 October 2012, the Supreme Court, while disposing of *PUCL Vs State of Tamil Nadu*[14] and others has categorically observed that guidelines on the methodology for identification of bonded labourers formulated by late Sankaran in his capacity as Chairman of the Expert Group constituted by NHRC, be followed and implemented by all States/UTs with suitable modification to suit local conditions.

---

14 WP (Civil) No 3922/85

- The procedure to be adopted by any DM for identification of the victims of BLS may be as under:
  I. In one of the meetings of the district-level VC, the DM may constitute as many task forces as necessary to investigate the incidence of BLS in all parts of the district with special emphasis on dry, drought-prone and migration-prone areas which are sensitive to this social malady.
  II. Each task force should have a minimum of two persons—one seasoned, experienced and sensitive official and another person who will represent a good NGO from the area which is non-political or apolitical, which has a track record of social work and which is sensitive to the bonded labour issue.
  III. The task force may be assisted by the local police in all its operations.
  IV. Two separate questionnaires—one meant for interrogating the employer of the establishment and another for having an interface with the workers in a simple, friendly and informal manner should be designed.
  V. A brief one-day orientation programme should be organised by the DM for the members of the task force. Subject matter specialists who have professional competence, communication skills, empathy and sensitivity to the bonded labour issue may be invited to such a training workshop to act as resource persons. The questionnaire should be introduced in the workshop and the members given orientation how to administer questions, how to record responses, how to analyse the responses and arrive at the right conclusion on the status of the persons with reference to the relevant provisions of BLS (A) Act and Rules, judgments/directions of Supreme Court and guidelines issued by the NHRC and MoL&E.

VI. The task force (S) should proceed to the pockets which have BLS, selected on the basis of local intelligence.

VII. While the first member of the task force should address the questions in a simple and non-invasive manner, the second member should record them verbatim in black and white.

VIII. The questionnaire for interrogation of the employer of the establishment concerned should include the following questions:

- Name
- When the establishment came into being
- What is the total employment strength? (with break-up of regular, contract and casual employees) as also that of women, men, children (if any) and adolescents?
- If there are workers from outside States, what is their number, break-up between women, men and children, when and how were they recruited and for what period, the terms and conditions of recruitment
- Was a licence obtained by the recruiting agents under S8 of ISMW (ROE&COS) Act if inter-State migrant workmen have been employed?
- Was a registration certificate obtained by the principal employer of the establishment under S4 of ISMW (ROE&COS) Act?
- Were any advances paid at the time of recruitment? If so, what is the quantum?
- Is there any documentary evidence of the advance? If so, in whose custody is the document kept?
- Has a copy of the same been shared with the migrant workers who have been recruited?
- Have the following registers been maintained for all

regular/contract/casual employees:

- Muster roll;
- Wage register;
- Advance register;
- Overtime wage register (Rule 26(1) of Central Minimum Wage Rules, 1950).[15]

- Additionally, have the following registers been maintained for the inter-State migrant workmen?
  - Register of Contractors;
  - Register of Persons employed;
  - Register of deductions.
  - (Rule 53 of ISMW (ROE&COS) Rules, 1980).
- Are wage slips being issued in Form XI to every person employed at least a day prior to disbursement of wages? (Rule 26 (2) of Central Minimum Wage Rules)
- What is the quantum of wage payable to regular, contract and casual employees as also semi-skilled, skilled and highly skilled employees vis-à-vis the notified minimum wage?
- How and when wages payable are adjusted with the advances paid at the time of recruitment and subsequently after arrival of the workers at the work-site?
- Independent of the adjustment of wages which are payable with advances already paid, do the employees have the freedom to leave the work-site and the employer

15 I have referred to the relevant provisions of the Central Minimum Wage Rules 1950 being fully aware that the MW Act has been repealed and has been replaced by a Code of Wages. However, Rules under the Code are being framed and will take some time. I have included the above four registers as they are basic to any establishment employing inter-State migrant workmen

for any reason whatsoever?

- Like the middle-men/agents who recruited the workers from another State, are there middle-men at the work-site too? If so, what are their duties and responsibilities?
- Is there a system of payment of commission to these middle-men, if any?
- Is the same deducted from the wages of the workers?

The questionnaire for interrogation of workers/ employees

- Name
- Father's name
- Where do you come from?
- To which community do you belong?
- Where are you employed?
- Can you recollect the name of the employer of the establishment in which you are employed?
- How did you land here all the way from your native place (relevant for inter-State migrant workmen only)?
- Did you come of your own or were you recruited by anyone?
- If you were recruited by someone, what are the terms and conditions of the recruitment?
- What were you doing prior to coming here?
- Did the person/agency who brought you here make any promise at the time of recruitment? If so, what are the promises made?
- Have these promises been fulfilled? If so, to what extent?
- For how many days have you been working at this site?
- What is the total duration of employment?
- What is the duration of working hours daily?
- Is there any spread over (period of rest)?
- What is the quantum of wages being paid?

- Are you aware of 'notified minimum wage'?
- Are the wages received by you higher or lower than the notified minimum wage?
- Do you get any OT wage for work in excess of the scheduled working hours i.e. nine hours a day and 48 hours a week?
- Do you get 'weekly off' i.e. full wages for seven days for having worked continuously for six days and a substituted day of rest for being called upon to work on the weekly rest day?
- When do you intend to return to your native place?
- Do you feel free to leave the workplace and the present employer and go in for an alternative employer and alternative means of livelihood?

Even if there is an element of loan/debt/advance in every case of debt bondage in general and in every case of inter-State migrant workmen who get reduced to a victim of debt bondage in particular, care has been taken not to include the question of loan/debt/advance in the questionnaire for the following reasons:

- In Bandhua Mukti Morcha Case,[16] Supreme Court raised a presumption about every loan/ debt/advance;
- According to the apex court, every such loan/debt/ advance is to be presumed to be in existence;
- Such a presumption may be rebutted by the employer or even by the State Government, if it so chooses but until and unless the rebuttal is to the total satisfaction of the Court, the Court must proceed on the presumption that the victim is a bonded labourer entitled to all the benefits of the law.

The above judgment makes it abundantly clear that there is no need to put questions to the victims relating to loan/debt/

---

16 WP No 2135 pf 1982 AIR 1984 SC 802 date of judgment 16.12.1983

advance, such as:

- Was there an element of loan/debt/advance at the time of your recruitment?
- If so, what was the amount advanced as principal?
- What is the rate of interest attached to the principal?
- What is the total amount required to be paid?
- What is the period of repayment?
- How confident do you feel to be able to repay the debt and by what time?

Question 30

Alternative No. 4 attached to Section 2(g) BLS (A) Act brings out the elements of an unequal exchange system. How do we establish these elements at the ground level?

Answer: Even though the questionnaire referred to in the previous question broadly covers all the elements of debt bondage as given in Section 2(g) of BLS (A) Act, alternative No. 4 attached to this Section has a complexity and sensitivity of its own and, therefore, deserves special attention and treatment. To establish the elements of an unequal exchange system which are clearly reflected in this alternative, the following questions need to be addressed to every potential victim of BLS *qua* unequal exchange system. These are:

- Do you have any property to sell?
- Is it movable or immovable?
- Do you have any product to sell?
- Is it perishable (like fish) or non-perishable (food grains stored for some time)?
- What is the market price for the property?
- What is the market price for the product?
- Do you ever get this price for sale of the product?

- If not, what could be the ostensible reason?
- Do you have the freedom to sell your property or product to anyone else at a market price or are you bound by a contract under which you have to sell it only to the creditor?
- Does the creditor dictate the price of the property or product to you; if so, why?
- If so, how does the price dictated by the creditor compare with the prevailing market price?

Question 31

What is the correlation between pre-rescue, rescue, release and rehabilitation? Who should conduct the pre-rescue and rescue operations? What are the components of an action plan towards undertaking a rescue operation?

Answer: The dictionary meaning of both rescue and release is: to free or deliver from confinement, danger or evil. Both have a physical and legal connotation. The process of rescue and release is carried to a logical and legal close with issue of a release certificate by the Magistrate concerned in favour of the individual victim.

Pre-rescue includes all the steps including collection of intelligence, search (to find something lost or missing or something concealed), preparation of a map of the rescue area, finalising the composition of the rescue team, etc., which are required to facilitate conducting an effective rescue operation. There are a few steps in the pre-rescue operation such as:

- Information from the primary source from anyone, including the victim, relative of the victim, friend or acquaintance of the victim can be the basis for planning/conducting a rescue operation;
- Such information can also be obtained from secondary sources such as:

- Survey conducted by the Task Force constituted by a VC u/s 14(e) of BLS(A) Act with the help of social action groups;
- Survey conducted by BPL survey teams or Sarva Shikshya Abhiyan survey teams;
- Data available with good and reliable NGOs who are active in the field of social action;
- Any other helpline (like Child Helpline).

The following guidelines may be followed for collection of intelligence as a part of the pre-rescue exercise such as:

- Utmost secrecy and confidentiality should be maintained both on the information received as also on the source thereof;
- The accuracy of the information should be thoroughly scrutinised before accepting it as a tool of planning or basis of further action;
- The onus of sharing the information with the responsible authority will rest with the person receiving/collecting the information and not with the informant;
- A time limit should be laid down to complete the process of scrutiny or verification of the information so received by the responsible authority and, in any case, not beyond 72 hours.

The following components of an action plan for conducting a rescue operation should be borne in mind, such as:

- The rescue is meant for providing relief to the victims and not for inflicting any harm/injury/trauma to the latter;
- The rescue team should be kept to a minimum;
- A map of the rescue area on the basis of information received should be prepared which marks out where the victims are likely to be found.

The composition of the rescue team may be as under:

- A representative of the concerned administrative department;

- A representative of the District Legal Services Authority;
- An AHTU official;
- Police (Special Juvenile Police Unit/Special Police under ITPA, 1986, as the case may be);
- A representative of the NGO of the area active in the field of social action;
- A medical officer with first aid kit;
- Lady police/lady volunteers for rescuing girl/women victims.

Knowledge of local languages in addition to integrity and incorruptibility of the members of the rescue team is a sine qua non for the success of the rescue operation.

Pre-rescue, rescue/release and rehabilitation constitute a continuum.[17] While pre-rescue operation is meant to ensure accuracy of information on the basis of which a rescue operation is to be conducted, the rescue operation itself should be so designed as to include:

- Details of the location;
- Entry and exit points;
- Ways and means of removing the victim securely;
- Preventing disappearance of the accused;
- Preventing destruction of evidence in support of the crime.

While the central objective of rescue is to free a person and deliver him/her from confinement/captivity/violence/danger/evil, as the case may be, rehabilitation is to restore a person to a condition of good health or restoring the ability of a person to work, earn and maintain a decent livelihood.

---

17 Continuum basically implies that one should follow the other in quick succession, treating time as the essence

The relationship between rescue/release and rehabilitation is as good as the relationship between freedom and security.

Question 32

What is the procedure to be followed in securing rescue/release of the victim?

Answer: This is a highly ticklish and unenviable situation for those who are going to rescue/release the victim. The captor is extremely sly, cunning, resourceful, has wide contacts and can go to any extent to fulfil his vile intentions and interests. Those who are going to secure deliverance of the victim from captivity of the keeper have to take care to ensure that the latter is not harmed in any manner whatsoever.

It is against this backdrop and perspective that the following sequential steps have been visualised:

Step One

Offenders of the law/perpetrators of the crime should be prevented from hiding or destroying incriminating evidence.

Step Two

They should be thoroughly discouraged to move the victims away from the facility and prevented from manipulating and obtaining a statement by force from the victims which will be totally to their advantage and suicidal for the entire rescue operation.

Step Three

Ensure that the perimeter has been fully secured to keep out all unconcerned parties while allowing those whose presence is an absolute must for the inquiry.

Step Four

Ensure that the offenders of the law are prevented from

maintaining any contact with the outside world.

Step Five

Physically separate the trafficked victims from the offender of the law to prevent humiliation, harassment, and intimidation to the victim.

Step Six

Ensure that none (neither the perpetrators, nor the middle-men, nor anyone who is not concerned with the inquiry) is present while the victims are being interrogated.

Step Seven

Conduct the preliminary inquiry in a friendly and convivial manner after taking the victim to confidence and assuring and re-assuring him that the inquiry is being conducted entirely in his interest and that his unreserved cooperation is absolutely essential for its success.

Step Eight

- Facilitate the temporary safe shifting of the victim from the facility to a secure location (such as the police station or office of the Executive Magistrate or a shelter home or a public place like a school building) for a short period for the purpose of documentation;
- Eventually and after rescue/release from captivity, the victim(s) needs to be shifted to a transit camp for at least a week to a fortnight (depending on the condition of the victim) for the following purposes:
  - Check-up of health;
  - Check-up of the level of nutrition;
  - Check-up of the level of educational equivalence;
  - Check-up of the level of skills acquired;
  - Psychological counselling;
  - Complete documentation of the victim's socio-cultural

background, educational and skill equivalence acquired, felt needs, preferences, interests and what will be the best way of rehabilitating him/her physically, economically and psychologically.

The above steps are absolutely necessary as a prelude to psychological and emotional rehabilitation of the victim whose health may have been battered and who may have been emotionally and psychologically traumatised.

Question 33

What is the procedure for arrest of the offender of the law and what checks and safeguards need to be provided to ensure that no excesses are committed?

Answer: Arrest of persons has been dealt in Chapter V of CrPC, 1973 (Sections 41-60A read: 'No arrest shall be made except in accordance with the provisions of the Code or any other law for the time being in force providing for arrest.'

In *Arnesh Kumar Vs State of Bihar* (2014),[18] Supreme Court said:

> No arrest can be made in a routine manner on a mere allegation of the commission of an offence made against a person. It would be prudent and wise for a police officer that no arrest is made without a reasonable satisfaction reached after some investigation into the genuineness of the allegation.

- Section 41 which empowers a police officer to make an arrest without a warrant and an order from a Magistrate has laid down clear guidelines for such arrest as also the considerations which should weigh in the mind of the police to effect an arrest.

18 8SCC 273

- These guidelines can be applied keeping in view the exigencies of the situation relating to human trafficking/bonded labour, as the case may be.
- These are:
  - Arrest if there is credible information that a trafficking / bonded labour offence has been committed;
  - If the officer has reason to believe that the trafficking/ bonded labour offence has been committed.

Additionally, the offender can be apprehended when.
- The police officer is present during the rescue/release operation;
- There is resistance from the employer/bonded labour keeper concerned to release the victim from his captivity;
- The employer concerned refuses to return the mortgaged property to the released bonded labourer;
- It would be best for the Magistrate concerned to issue the order of arrest to the police who are present at the rescue site.

What should be the timing of arrest?
- It is best at the time of rescue operation;
- It can be postponed to a later date only if there is no sufficient evidence;
- If the accused is willing to come to the police station or any other inquiry site voluntarily, he/she may be heard, his/her statement recorded along with statements of other witnesses before effecting arrest.

Question 34

Supreme Court in several of its judgments has highlighted

the principles of 'immediacy' and 'simultaneity' in effecting rescue, release and rehabilitation of victims of BLS. What procedure should be followed by the Magistrate under S21(1) of BLS (A) Act read with Section 10 of the Act in effecting timely release of the victim without any hassle?

Answer: Justice Bhagwati had observed with regret that hitherto a formal, rigid and too legalistic approach has been followed in effecting release of the victims such as:

- For every case of release, there is a formal process of trial linked with the procedure for recording of evidence under the Indian Evidence Act, 1872.
- This is an endless process which is detrimental to the interest of the victims of BLS.
- The victims will never be able to stand up to the tyranny of the law and rigidities of the legal process due to their poverty, illiteracy and socio-economic backwardness.
- In *Neerja Chaudhary Vs State of MP and Others,*[19] the apex court had observed with regret that if the victims of BLS are made to stand in the witness box to depose, they will be inhibited to do so in presence of the same employer or bonded labour keeper with whom they may have to go back to work the very next day. They will be confronted with the prospect of instant discharge/dismissal from employment, apart from facing severe reprisal in multiple forms.
- The Magistrate appointed under S21(1) of the BLS (A) Act should, after perusal of the report of the vigilance committee concerned and all other relevant documents and after proper application of mind should come to a speedy conclusion and

19 WP (Crl) 1263 of 1982 (AIR 1984 SC 1099)

issue a speaking order liberating the victim from the captivity of bonded labour keeper if any of the four conditions u/s 2 (g) has been fully satisfied.

- This should be followed by issue of a release certificate individually in favour of each released bonded labourer, preferably in the language which is intelligible to the victim.
- The content of the release certificate should also be explained to the victim if the latter is totally illiterate.
- Prosecution may be filed against the bonded labour keeper/ offender of the law separately and simultaneously but outcome of such prosecution should not be linked to the rescue/release and rehabilitation of victims of BLS.

Question 35

What are the implications of summary trial as in Section 21 (2) of BLS (A) Act?

Answer: Section 21 (2) of BLS (A) Act reads as under:

- 'An offence under this Act may be tried summarily by a Magistrate'.
- The Magistrate referred to in Section 21 (2) is an Executive Magistrate on whom the State Government may confer the powers of a Judicial Magistrate of the First Class or Second Class for the trial of offences under the Act.
- The following considerations might have weighed in the minds of the framers of the law to go in for trial of offences under the BLS (A) Act summarily such as:
    - A victim of BLS represents abject prostration, being generally landless, assetless, resourceless and defenceless. An overwhelming percentage belongs to SC and ST;
    - For generations, they have been victims of social discrimination and economic exploitation;

- For work without any break, creature comfort, privacy, elementary dignity and decency at the workplace, they have been drained of their *elan-vital*;
- Identification of such a person is extremely difficult and tenuous;
- After such a difficult process, when a victim is identified and brought before the Magistrate in question by the VC, the victim is placed in an extraordinarily difficult situation;
- Such a person cannot be put in the witness box to depose evidence against the bonded labour keeper;
- Inconvenient and uncomfortable questions cannot be put to him; that will demoralise him as for several years he has been a victim of the culture of silence and dependence;
- Besides, the victim has been working for and with the bonded labour keeper for years; he cannot be expected to depose evidence against his employer in the latter's presence;
- He can do so only at the cost of a severe reprisal including physical assault and elimination which may follow soon after the evidence has been deposed.

• Such an unenviable situation for the victim was visualised by the Supreme Court in two landmark judgments as under in quick succession:

 1. *Bandhua Mukti Morcha Vs Union of India and Others*
 Date of judgment: 16 December 1983
 2. *Neerja Chaudhary Vs State of MP*
 Date of judgment: 8 May 1984

The relevant portion of the two judgments brings out emphatically as to how such a trial should be conducted with empathy and sensitivity for the victim:

It would be cruel to insist that a bonded labourer in order

> to derive the benefits of this social welfare legislation, should have to go through a formal process of trial with the normal procedure for recording of evidence. That would be a totally futile process because it is obvious that a bonded labourer can never stand up to the rigidity and formalism of the legal process due to his poverty, illiteracy, social and economic backwardness and if such a procedure were required to be followed, the State government might as well obliterate this Act from the Statue Book.

- The framers of the law in recommending summary trial were further concerned that:
  - There is inordinate avoidable delay in most of the trial proceedings;
  - The cost (social and economic) of waiting will be too heavy for the victims if the proceedings are stretched beyond a normal time limit.
  - Need for adoption of a comparatively simpler procedure which will be less time consuming, less expensive, less invasive, a tool of confidence building and morale-boosting (to the effect that everything in life is not lost; life can be started afresh and be normal and self-reliant) which will be beneficial to the victim.
- Successive other judgments of the apex court have also highlighted while disposing off bonded labour related writ petitions that the following principles are to be observed without exception:
  - Principle of immediacy and simultaneity;
  - Principle of not mixing/linking up the trial of the offender of the law with the urgency and high priority needed for securing rescue/release and rehabilitation of victims;

- Prosecution may be filed simultaneously against the offender, trial may go on separately but the conviction or acquittal of the offender will in no way affect the release and rehabilitation of victims.

To sum up, the following is the nitty-gritty of summary trial in the context in which it occurs in Section 21(2) of BLS (A) Act:

I. The VC places the report of survey conducted u/s 14 (e) of BLS (A) Act before the Executive Magistrate, who peruses the survey report and its findings.
II. If he/she has any doubt, he may raise the same in shape of simple questions to the representative of the VC or a Member of the Task Force who conducted the survey and who would be presenting the survey report.
III. There will be no examination and cross-examination of witnesses by taking recourse to provisions of Indian Evidence Act, 1872.
IV. If the Magistrate comes to the conclusion that the victim is a bonded labourer, he/she should issue a speaking order as also a formal release certificate in a prescribed format preferably in a language intelligible to the victim;
V. The Magistrate should clearly indicate that the victim of BLS is being released u/s 2(g) of BLS (A) Act;
VI. Even though there is no explicit mention in BLS (A) Act of release and issue of release certificate individually in favour of the victim (of BLS), these two should constitute an integral part of the powers and functions of DM u/s 10 of BLS (A) Act which are being exercised by the Executive Magistrate u/s 21(1) of the Act. Additionally, issue of release certificate individually in favour of every victim is fully supported by a number of judgments of the Supreme Court.

Question 36

Do you envisage any major problem in the wake of Section 21 of BLS (A) Act having been struck down in its entirety as Constitutionally invalid by three judgments of High Courts of Madhya Pradesh, Bombay and Madras in 1995, 1991 and 2014 respectively?

Answer: Yes. High Court of Madhya Pradesh (Jabalpur branch) in MP 2522 of 1984 in *Hanumatsingh Kuber Singh Vs Another* passed the following order on 28 October 1995:

- Section 21 of BLS (A) Act is violative of Article 21, 14 and 50 of the Constitution;
- Trial against the petitioners for the offences under the Act by the Sub-Divisional Magistrate cannot proceed;
- All the cases (seven) referred to in paragraph two of the order shall stand transferred to the Court of the concerned Judicial Magistrate;
- As the cases are pending since 1983, they shall be disposed of within six months;
- The parties to the cases shall appear before the Judicial Magistrate, First Class, Petalwad on 1 November 1995.

High Court of Bombay in *Govind Shanwar Chatal Vs Dattatraya Waman Bhanushali and Another* passed the following order on 25 September 1991:[20]

- The State Government was not justified in exercising enabling powers of Section 21 and conferring judicial powers upon the Executive Magistrate for conduct of trial of offences under the Act;
- The notifications issued by the State Government in exercise of powers under S21 are, therefore, required to be struck down;

20 WP (Crl) No. 406 of 1988

- The impugned order dated 13 October 1987 passed by the Executive Magistrate, Vasai in criminal case 165 of 1985 is set aside;
- The proceedings are remitted to the Court of Judicial Magistrate, First Class for trial in accordance with the law;
- All proceedings pending before any Executive Magistrate in the State for trial of offences under the Act on the strength of the notification published by Government of Maharashtra in exercise of powers under S21 shall stand transferred to the Court of Judicial Magistrate at a particular station;
- The Executive Magistrate shall not hereafter exercise the powers to conduct trial of offences under the Act.

High Court of Judicature, Madras in *Gajendran Vs Tehasildar, SDM, Collector and DM, Thiruvallur and Chief Secretary to Government of Tamil Nadu* passed the following order on 3 June 2014:[21]

- The enabling provision contained in Section 21 of BLS (A) Act violates Articles 21, 14 and 50 of the Constitution;
- Consequently, trial against the petitioners for the offences under the Act by the Sub-Divisional Magistrate cannot proceed;
- All the cases referred to in paragraph two above shall stand transferred to the Court of the concerned Judicial Magistrate, First Class;
- As the cases are pending since 1963, they shall be disposed of in accordance with law expeditiously within the outer limit of six months;
- As Section 21 of the Act has been struck down, all cases pending under the Act before the Executive Magistrates or Sub-Divisional

21 WP No. 7650 of 2013 and MPs 1 and 2 of 2013

Magistrates shall also stand transferred to the concerned Judicial Magistrates.

With full respect to the judgments pronounced by the three High Courts, the following submissions are made:

- While 21(1) deals with conferment of powers upon Executive Magistrates, the powers of a Judicial Magistrate of First or Second Class for the trial of offences under the Act, 21(2) deals with summary trial of an offence by the concerned Magistrate;
- Summary trial is not a new concept as two years before BLS (A) Act came into force, summary trial procedure was laid down in Sections 260 to 265 of CrPC, 1973;
- Summary trial admittedly has several advantages such as:
    - It is comparatively simpler than the warrants procedure (Sections 238-247 of CrPC, 1973);
    - It leads to expeditious trial and expeditious conclusion of proceedings;
    - It is less expensive and, therefore, is of great advantage for the victims of BLS who come from the lowest social strata and for circumstances beyond their control, have lost their freedom and been subjected to exploitation and denial of their basic rights.

In all the three cases as cited above, Section 21 in its entirety has been struck down. By implication, summary trial occurring in Section 21(2) has also been struck down which is not in the larger interest of the disadvantaged victims.

Even in cases where Executive Magistrates have been divested of their powers, notification issued by the State Government concerned has been struck down and all cases have been directed to be transferred to the Courts of CJM/Judicial Magistrate, the cases could still be tried summarily by Judicial Magistrates.

Going by the letter and spirit of the judgments delivered by High Courts of MP, Bombay and Madras and the directions contained therein, that does not, however, appear to be the case.

The only possible and feasible solution as it emerges is to amend Section 21 in the following manner:

- 'Executive Magistrate' in Section 21(1) may be replaced by Judicial Magistrate, First or Second Class.
- Cases which have already been disposed of by Executive Magistrates need not be reopened;
- Cases which are pending in the Court of Executive Magistrates may be ordered to be transferred to the Chief Judicial Magistrate who in turn will assign them to one of the Judicial Magistrates;
- The provision of summary trial as in the existing Section 21(2) should be retained;
- A maximum time limit of disposal of all transferred as well as new proceedings should be fixed as six months.
- In disposal of all such proceedings, the observations made by Justice Bhagwati in Bandhua Mukti Morcha case regarding the need for adoption of an unorthodox and unconventional attitude, approach and procedure should be kept in view.

Question 37

What are the components of rehabilitation and how are they to be accomplished?

Answer: It has been observed in the entire process of identification, rescue/release and rehabilitation which are closely inter-related that one should follow the other in quick succession as one is incomplete without the other. The framers of the law had clearly perceived and internalised the three in a continuum on account of the following reasons:

- Identification and rescue/release generally meant for a bonded labourer a world of freedom;
- Associated with freedom is a world of uncertainty and insecurity;
- A freed bonded labourer is generally inhibited to face such a world with strength, courage, resilience and self-confidence;
- The choice between the world of bondage and security (which is more illusory than real) and the world of freedom and insecurity as also uncertainty is undoubtedly a difficult one;
- The abolition of slavery in America in 1862 witnessed a number of slaves belonging to the African-American Community going back to their masters when they were confronted with a situation of uncertainty and insecurity after their release;
- Viewed in this backdrop, the released bonded labourer may prefer to go back to his erstwhile master and the bondage associated with it, unless he/she is assured of some tangible physical and economic security to fall back upon;
- In other words, freedom can be meaningful only when the uncertainty in the aftermath of that freedom is removed and the victim is assured of security of life and livelihood;

Rehabilitation is replacement of insecurity by security, ignorance by awareness, illiteracy by functional literacy, diffidence by confidence, deprivation by fulfilment, persecution and harassment by an intense realisation of dignity, decency, equality and freedom of the victim. Every such rehabilitation has three components:

- Physical;
- Psychological;
- Economic;

It has also three different phases:

- Immediate subsistence allowance after release so that starvation is warded off;
- Short-term measures: Skill formation and skill upgradation which will pave the way for self-employment, income and survival on an autonomous basis;
- Long-term measures: Allotment of a roof above the head, allotment of both homestead and agricultural land, provision of full and freely chosen productive employment, enforcement of minimum wage, access to food security, access to health security, access to literacy and education, credit, technology and market which will lead to economic self-reliance.

Physical rehabilitation is essentially directed towards safety of human life and limb and security. This is particularly relevant for those released bonded labourers who are members of SC and ST communities and who have been victims of social discrimination, neglect, cruelty and atrocities by their non-SC and non-ST employers in the past.

They have to be given protection under SC and ST (Prevention of Atrocities) Act, 1989 as amended in 2015. Legal awareness programmes will have to be launched to make the released bonded labourers belonging to SC and ST aware of the provisions of the following laws relevant for them:

- BLS (Abolition) Act, 1976;
- SC and ST (Prevention of Atrocities) Act as amended in 2015;
- Child and Adolescent Labour (Prohibition and Regulation) Act as amended in 2016;
- Inter-State Migrant Workmen (Regulation of Employment and Conditions of Service) Act, 1979;

- Equal Remuneration Act, 1976;
- Sexual Harassment of Women at Workplace (Prevention, Prohibition and Redressal) Act, 2012.

Similarly, programme literacy will have to be imparted to make them aware of government schemes for allotment of house site and agricultural land, low-cost dwelling units under PM's Awas Yojana, employment under MGNREGA, food security under National Food Security Act, 2013, access to education, health and nutrition, immunisation, potable water and sanitation.

Psychological rehabilitation must go side by side with physical and economic rehabilitation. In essence, it means a process of assurance and re-assurance to the victims that (a) they are free citizens of a free country entitled to certain inalienable human rights, certain irreducible barest minimum needs, facilities and amenities of life and (b) even though freedom was lost for a while, everything is not lost and life can always be started afresh.

Such assurance and re-assurance are extremely important as empirical studies have revealed the following:

- Planned efforts to rehabilitate freed bonded labourers did not yield the desired result on account of the peculiar sociological milieu which makes it extremely difficult for the freed bonded labourers to live and grow with dignity and respect as free citizens of a free country;
- This was found true in contingencies where the erstwhile bonded labour keepers were found to be nursing a grievance against them as with their release an opportunity for exploiting cheap labour was lost;
- This resulted in total denial of employment in a few cases and denial of wages in few others;

- Any protest or resistance to such denial, howsoever subdued, met with severe reprisal characterised by greater persecution and repression.

How complex and difficult is the task of promoting psychological rehabilitation has been lucidly and forcefully summed up by (late) Union Labour Minister KV Raghunath Reddy, while introducing BLS (A) Bill on 27 January 1976 in the Lok Sabha:

> A freed bonded labourer will not have inputs for production or any supply of credit. He will neither have any professional skill that would enable him to pursue an independent livelihood. Even where installed in a profitable activity, he will have no income during the period of gestation. The bonded labourer who is used to a world of domination and servitude will not obviously be aware of his rights. At times, he may not even like to undergo the strenuous process of economic rehabilitation and may even prefer reversion to thraldom.

The first pre-requisite of psychological rehabilitation is that freed bonded labourers must be weaned away from the old habitat and be rehabilitated at a new place where they will no longer be vulnerable to the pernicious influence and organised onslaughts of absentee landlords and usurious moneylenders of the village.

Such freedom can be secured by adopting a group or cooperative approach to rehabilitation on the one hand and formation of collective social action groups on the other.

The following are the distinct advantages of a group approach to rehabilitation as opposed to an individual beneficiary approach such as:

- In a group approach, physical, economic and psychological

components of rehabilitation are holistically combined;

- By bringing freed bonded labourers belonging to SC, ST, OBC, linguistic, cultural and ethnic minorities (wherever such a combination naturally occurs) and rehabilitating them at a common point, the group approach promotes social integration;
- Such an approach also ensures economies of scale;
- It facilitates visit of functionaries of development departments to come to the rehabilitation site, have an open, informal and friendly interface with the beneficiaries, enable them to impart programme, legal, financial, electoral and digital literacy and disseminate relevant development messages;
- It facilitates representatives of banks to visit the beneficiaries at the new site and through an informal and friendly interface with them, exhort them to take up bankable schemes with financial assistance from Mudra Bank for better incremental income and decent livelihood;
- It facilitates opening and maintaining Jan Dhan Yojana accounts of all beneficiaries at the bank proximate to the new site;
- It facilitates pooling of resources from a variety of sources and integrating them imaginatively and skillfully for a permanent, meaningful and effective rehabilitation;
- It facilitates formation of a cooperative society of beneficiaries; in such a society, workers in addition to being workers also become supervisors and eventual owners;
- In such a cooperative set-up, there will be no scope for any rank outsider (like a contractor) coming from outside to brazenly exploit them and deprive them of the fruits of their hard labour as also just and fair entitlements;
- Once the beneficiaries have developed through a healthy combination a sense of unity and solidarity, rapport and

bonhomie, they will no longer be vulnerable to the most unethical and unprincipled manipulation and control from landlords, money lenders and contractors.

Economic Rehabilitation

The three phases of economic rehabilitation are:

- Immediate subsistence allowance after release;
  (This was ₹1,000 when the total package of rehabilitation assistance under the old centrally sponsored scheme was ₹20,000; with enhancement of the total package of rehabilitation assistance to ₹1 lakh, the subsistence allowance has been raised to ₹20,000).
- Short-term measures to help the released bonded labourer to start a fresh lease of life by way of:
  - Allotment of house site;
  - Construction of a low-cost dwelling unit under Prime Minister's Awas Yojana;
  - Allotment of a plot of agricultural land measuring 2.5 acres or one hectare in the minimum;
  - Supply of a pair of bullocks, agricultural implements and inputs to be made available initially free of cost;
  - Insurance for the milch animals and other productive assets, the initial insurance premium being borne by Government;
  - Provision of avenues of gainful employment;
  - Access to health, hygiene, nutrition and sanitation;
  - Enforcement of notified minimum wage under the Wage Code which has come into force w.e.f. 9 September 2019;
  - Food security by ensuring through ration cards easy access to fair price shops under PDS;

Long-term measures to complete the process of economic

self-reliance and socio-economic advancement in life such as:

- Land development including provision of irrigation facility;
- Arranging short-term and medium-term credit;
- Provision of total animal husbandry and veterinary cover;
- Training for new skill formation and upgradation of existing skills (under the skill training programme of GoI such as PMKVY as also programmes of skill training under skill development missions of State Governments);
- Providing a remunerative price support for minor agricultural and forest products relevant for members of ST community;
- Ensuring access to and retention in free and compulsory elementary education of the children of freed bonded labourers;
- Ensuring simultaneous measures for health, medical care, immunisation and nutrition of all family members including those of pregnant mothers and children;
- Protection of civil rights of freed bonded labourers (in particular protection from the vice of untouchability) who on account of being born in lower castes have been victims of social discrimination, caste prejudices and economic exploitation.

In implementation of any worthwhile rehabilitation scheme, a few checks and safeguards need to be adopted so that there is no leakage or wastage in implementation of the latter. These are:

- The scheme should be formulated preferably at the source/origin of the victims of the bonded labour system;
- The preferences, felt needs and genuine interests of the beneficiaries should always be kept uppermost at the stage of formulation of the scheme with full participation of the beneficiaries themselves; such a process alone will convert beneficiaries into participants in the total development effort;

- A proper survey should always be undertaken to identify which one among the three possible alternatives (land-based, productive assets-based and art/craft/skill-based) will be the most suitable one for a beneficiary or a group of beneficiaries if they are going to be rehabilitated by adoption of a group approach;
- In undertaking such an exercise, one should do away with the wrong impression that the victims of BLS are incapable of exercising an informed choice between the three alternatives and are incapable of managing land or productive assets;
- The failures which have been noticed over the years in implementation of development schemes, for the poor, the SC, ST and OBCs are not as much due to lack of competence of the beneficiaries as they are due to absence of proper back-up or support services, forward and backward linkages, training and visit (T&V) and there is no reason as to why with the provision of such back-up support services, BLS victims will not be able to make proper utilisation of these assets and achieve economic self-reliance, which is the ultimate goal of all rehabilitation efforts.

Every rehabilitation effort should be multi-faceted, holistic and integrated and not confined to a single scheme. To make rehabilitation effective, meaningful and permanent, resources should be pooled from a variety of sources and integrated imaginatively and skillfully to create the desired impact. The different aspects which a rehabilitation effort ought to cover are:

- Providing employment (both wage employment and self-employment);
- Ensuring enforcement of notified minimum wages;
- Providing productive assets;
- Ensuring hassle free access to all facility and amenities;

- Providing back-up or support services;
- Ensuring forward and backward linkages;
- Ensuring that all delivery mechanisms in the domain of education, health, medical care, immunisation, nutrition, sanitation, housing, water, energy, animal husbandry and veterinary, social assistance and social insurance, deliver in time, free of charge, without any hassles.

With seventy-third and seventy-fourth Constitutional amendments dating back to 1992-93, involvement of local self-governing bodies in formulation and implementation of all rehabilitation schemes is absolutely essential and must be ensured.

Similar involvement of good, reliable and experienced NGOs who are apolitical and non-political, who are committed to voluntary social action and have a genuine urge, inclination and concern for the poor, deprived and disadvantaged sections of the society is crucial to the success of all rehabilitation efforts.

Simultaneous efforts need to be made to change the attitude and mindsets of local administration and, in particular, of the rural oligarchy who look upon organisations of the rural poor as incipient insurgency. It should be impressed on them that a bonded labourer who is subjected to dual disadvantage—physical coercion and economic dependence and exploitation resulting in an atmosphere of acute fear psychosis in his life can come out of it only through building up of such organisations and the representational security associated with such collectivities.

Question 38

What were the salient features of the centrally sponsored scheme of May 1978 for rehabilitation of freed bonded

labourers (as modified from time to time)? To what extent are they different from the central scheme introduced in May 2016?

Answer: The centrally sponsored scheme for rehabilitation of freed bonded labourers was introduced by Ministry of Labour and Employment in May 1978. It had three components such as:

- Land based;
- Non-land or productive assets based;
- Art/craft/skill based.

The per capita assistance for rehabilitation was fixed initially at ₹4,000, shareable by the Central and State Government concerned on 50:50 basis. The amount was to be released in four installments. A screening committee under the chairmanship of DG (LW)/JS of MoL&E was set up to scrutinise and approve all proposals for rehabilitation assistance to be received from the State Government concerned.

The procedure involved was rather cumbersome and led to in-ordinate delay in processing and according approval to the said proposals for rehabilitation assistance.

In the very first meeting of the screening committee held in August 1982 under chairmanship of the author, then DG(LW)/JS, the deficiencies in the scheme came to surface and the following suggestions were approved:

- it would no longer be necessary for the State Governments to send proposals for rehabilitation assistance to MoL&E for approval;
- Instead, they would be placed before a State-level screening committee to be constituted for the purpose;
- The number of installments in which the rehabilitation assistance was to be released will be reduced from four to one only.

This was ostensibly for the following simple and practical reasons:

- Under the non-land or productive asset-based programme, a cow or buffalo or any other milch animal was to be purchased and distributed in one go and not four times;
- A productive asset before its delivery could not be divided into four parts;
- The per capita assistance itself being extremely low, it does not make any sense to release it in four installments.

The State Governments were accordingly directed to release the full share of the grant-in-aid to the DMs of the concerned districts in one go subject to the condition that (a) the grants released for these districts earlier have been fully utilised and (b) necessary utilisation certificate has been furnished to that effect.

The quantum of per capita financial assistance for rehabilitation of freed bonded labourers has been reviewed and revised from time to time in the following manner as under:

- From ₹4,000 to ₹6,250 w.e.f 1 February 1986;
- From ₹6,250 to ₹10,000 w.e.f 1 April 1995;
- From ₹10,000 to ₹20,000 w.e.f. 1 May 2000.

This has been further revised under a Central Scheme w.e.f 17 May 2016 in the following manner:

- The rehabilitation package shall be ₹1 lakh for every adult male beneficiary;
- The latter shall have the option to either deposit it in an annuity scheme or receive the grant in cash;
- For special category beneficiaries such as children including orphans or those rescued from organised and forced begging rings or other forms of forced child labour and women, the amount

of rehabilitation assistance shall be ₹2 lakh out of which at least ₹1.25 lakh shall be deposited in an annuity scheme in the name of each beneficiary and the balance amount shall be transferred to the beneficiary account through ECS;

- For victims of forced or bonded labour involving extreme forms of deprivation such as transgender or women or children rescued from the venue of ostensible sexual exploitation such as brothels, massage parlours, trafficking through placement agencies or in cases of differently-abled persons in situations where the DM deems fit, the rehabilitation assistance shall be ₹3 lakh;
- Of this, at least ₹2 lakh shall be deposited in an annuity scheme in the name of each beneficiary and ₹1 lakh shall be transferred to the beneficiary account through ECS.

The purpose for which the above rehabilitation assistance would be utilised is as under:

- Allotment of house site and agricultural land;
- Land development;
- Provision of low-cost dwelling unit;
- Animal husbandry, i.e., dairy, poultry, and piggery;
- Collection and processing of minor agricultural and forest produce;
- Education of children.

A bonded labour rehabilitation fund shall be created at the district level by each State with a permanent corpus of at least ₹10 lakh at the disposal of the DM which should be renewable. The fund will be utilised for extending immediate help to the released bonded labourers.

Penalties recovered from the perpetrators of the crime of forced/bonded labour on conviction may be deposited in this fund. From out of the proceeds of the fund, immediate assistance of at least ₹5,000 may also be disbursed if the DM is satisfied that the nature of the case so warranted.

Additionally, 100 per cent central assistance is available under the central scheme of 17 May 2016 for the following purposes:

1. **Survey:**

   The amount of assistance for survey of bonded labourers per district shall be ₹4.5 lakh (as against ₹2 lakh which was available under the centrally sponsored scheme of May 1978).

   The above amount can be utilised to finance involvement of NGOs to be enlisted for identification of victims of BLS. The scheme provides for a detailed break-up of the items under which the above amount is required to be spent.

2. **Awareness generation**

   The expenditure on generation of awareness of the provisions of the Act and the scheme, judgments of the apex court and other related issues can be reimbursed on case-to-case basis subject to a maximum limit of ₹10 lakh per each State. The scheme provides for a detailed break-up of the items under which the above amount is required to be spent.

3. **Evaluation of the content, quality and impact of the programme.**

   The existing norms for sanction of grants upto ₹1 lakh for each evaluation study subject to a maximum of five evaluation studies per State in one financial year have been maintained. The scheme provides for a detailed break-up of the items under which the above amount is required to be spent.

Modalities of submission of proposals, sanction and release of funds under the central scheme.

This process involves the following stages:

- The DM shall submit claims to the National Child Labour Project (NCLP) set up at the district level;
- Each such proposal shall have (a) details of cash and non-cash assistance and rehabilitation facilities to be provided by the State Government (b) quantum of penalty awarded to the accused under the summary trial as provided u/s 21(2) of BLS (A) Act;
- In cases where summary trial has not been concluded but the DM/SDM has arrived at a prima facie finding and proof of bondage, the proposal for cash assistance shall not be stopped for want of details of conviction. However, final disbursement of cash assistance shall be made upon proof of bondage and other legal consequences as per judicial process;
- On receipt of the claim, the district NCLP shall scrutinise the documents and submit the proposal to MoL&E. The claim shall thereafter be processed;
- The funds will be released by the MoL&E to the district NCLP and the district NCLP thereafter will release the funds to the implementing agencies;
- The accounts of district NCLP shall be subject to the same audit norms as applicable to the NCLP;
- Wherever district NCLP does not exist, the MoL&E shall notify not later than ninety days from the date of notification of the scheme notifying a new NCLP.

Question 39

What are the redeeming features and grey areas in the central scheme for rehabilitation of freed bonded labourers?

Answer

- The redeeming features in the central scheme are:

- It has substantially raised the quantum of per capita rehabilitation assistance (increase of 500 per cent in both the quantum of total assistance including immediate subsistence allowance);
- It has brought women, children, physically and orthopedically challenged victims, victims of trafficking and begging rings within the purview of the scheme;
- It is a scheme resting on cent per cent Central Government assistance which ensures availability of funds better than the earlier centrally sponsored scheme;
- The DM of the district has been given a lot of discretionary powers in contingencies which call for immediate assistance necessary for care and protection of the rescued persons as also in relation to persons other than the victims of debt bondage;
- The amount earmarked for survey for identification of victims has been raised to ₹4.5 lakh;
- The scheme provides for creation of a district bonded labour rehabilitation fund with a minimum corpus of ₹10 lakh which was not there earlier;
- It also provides that penalties recovered from the perpetrators of the crime upon conviction may be deposited in the said special fund.

Objectively analysed, the grey areas in the scheme may be listed here under:

Para 4.3

The Union Government proceeded to enact a law on traffic in human beings, *begaar* and similar other forms of forced labour not because labour is on the Concurrent List but on account of (a) express provision made in Article 35 (a) (ii) read with Article

23 (1) of the Constitution and (b) ratification of ILO Convention 29 of 1930.

Para 7.4 (iii)

Bank accounts are opened in the names of adults and not in the names of children. The observation 'balance amount shall be transferred to the beneficiary account through ECS' is factually incorrect and operationally unsound.

Para 7.9 (viii)

The Juvenile Justice (Care and Protection of Children) Act, 2015 speaks of the following Homes:

- Special Home: Section 18(g) and S48(1);
- Children's Home: Section 50(1);
- Observation Homes: Section 47(1);
- Open Shelter: Section 43(1).

There is no mention of 'Short Stay Home' anywhere in the Act. The reference to 'Short Stay Home' and the source thereof is not clear.

Inappropriateness of certain provisions:

Para 9.3

The provision of DMs submitting claims to National Child Labour Projects (NCLP) is inappropriate for the following reasons:

- NCLP as on date is only a transitional scheme;
- All districts (719) have not been covered by NCLP, the number of NCLPs being 250+ only;
- All children, including working children withdrawn from work are required to be enrolled in formal schools as defined in Section 2(n) of RTE Act, 2009;
- In other words, the possibility of special schools (which do not come within the definition of school as in Section 2(n) of RTE Act) under NCLP to continue indefinitely is extremely limited;

- NCLP societies have very limited project staff who are already overloaded. Given the uncertainty in which they are placed, the proposal as in the central scheme to burden them with additional responsibilities to receive, spend and maintain accounts (which will be for sizeable amount) will be unworkable;
- Besides, rehabilitation of adults is quite different from that of children and NCLP's primary mandate is rehabilitation of children withdrawn from hazardous occupation/process.

Para 9.2

That prosecution and conviction of bonded labour keepers/ perpetrators of the crime and rehabilitation of freed bonded labourers are two different issues not to be linked up and the latter is not to be made conditional on the outcome of the former would be evident from the following judgments of the Supreme Court:

I. *Bandhua Mukti Morcha Vs Union of India and Others*

II. *Neerja Chaudhary Vs State of MP*

III. *Upendra and Others Vs State of MP*[22]

IV. *Santhal Pragana Antyodaya Ashram Vs State of Bihar and Others*[23]

The pith and substance of these judgments in the context of de-linking prosecution/conviction from rescue/release and rehabilitation are:

- It would be extremely difficult, if not impossible for the labourers to establish that they are bonded as they would have no evidence at all to prove that any advance or economic consideration was provided to them by the employer;

22 WP (Civil) 1071 of 198 SCC 66 1986 SCC (Tax) 781, date of judgment 25 September 1986

23 1987 (Suppl) SC 114 WP 1345 of 1983, Date of Judgment: 19 November 1986

- It would be cruel to insist that a bonded labourer would have to go through a formal process of trial with the normal procedure of recording of evidence;
- Rehabilitation must follow in the quick footsteps of identification; if not, released bonded labourers would be driven by poverty, helplessness and despair into serfdom once again;
- There must be a sense of urgency and seriousness of concern in regard to the speed of rehabilitation among officials;
- We would be driving released bonded labourers to starvation unless they are rehabilitated immediately on a permanent basis;
- Implementation of the rehabilitation programme should not wait on account of pendency of a proceeding in any Court including Supreme Court;
- DMs are mistaken in their perception and line of argument that rescue/release and rehabilitation process should begin only after the bonded labour keepers have been convicted.

Article 141 of the Constitution of India reads: 'The law declared by the Supreme Court shall be binding on all Courts within the territory of India'. It is, therefore, patently illogical and not in conformity with the spirit of Supreme Court judgments as cited above that a proposal for rehabilitation is required to have information relating to the quantum of penalty/imprisonment awarded to the accused in the summary trial as provided under Section 21(2) of the Act read with Section 16 of the Act.

It is patently illogical for the following reasons:

- Rehabilitation of released bonded labourers is required to be attended to with 'immediacy' as the key word;
- Despite best of intentions and efforts, conviction for committing an offence may not be secured with the same lightning speed;

- Prosecution at the end of the trial may or may not end up with conviction;
- Conviction may or may not end up with imprisonment;
- Even though no accurate and up-to-date data is available on the actual pendency of all cases in the Courts of Magistrates all over the country, empirical studies on the basis of review conducted by MOL&E, the pendency of such cases may be quite heavy;
- This may precisely be on account of the casual and routinised approach adopted by the Magistrates in trial of cases under S21(2) of BLS (A) Act which was deplored by the Supreme Court in Bandhua Mukti Morcha case;
- If the outcome of prosecution by way of conviction/acquittal of the accused is linked to rescue/release and rehabilitation of bonded labourers, the latter will rarely see the light of deliverance.

Para 10.1

Providing for economic and social rehabilitation of freed bonded labourers is the responsibility assigned to VCs at the district and sub-divisional level (Section 14(1)(b) of BLS (A) Act.

Monitoring the pace and progress of implementation of the central scheme should appropriately be, therefore, of the responsibility of VCs and not of NCLP society. To make this possible, the VCs should be strengthened by way of orientation and training, better mobility, vigilance and surveillance of the problem through a team of agile, alert and aware staff attached to the VCs.

Para 10.2

VC is a statutory body vested with certain powers and functions under BLS (A) Act; it cannot be made subordinate to the NCLP society which is an administrative body.

Para 10.3

Bondage is related to debt; it is also related to customs/traditions. The proforma prescribed under the central scheme under caption 'nature of bondage' corresponds to 'debt bondage' only; customary bondage has been completely lost sight of.

To sum up, what is sought to be given by one hand through introduction of a grandiose central scheme with 100 per cent central funding for rehabilitation of freed bonded labourers, substantially higher scales of rehabilitation assistance as also enhanced scales of assistance for survey and awareness raising is taken away by the other by couching the scheme with too many conditionalities which are rigid, inflexible, unworkable and unsustainable. The central objective of this otherwise well-intentioned scheme can be fulfilled only if the conditionalities are removed and all other inaccuracies and loopholes are simultaneously addressed and made good.

Question 40

What have been the silver linings in implementation of rehabilitation schemes in different parts of the country?

Answer

I. The Cooperative Poultry Complexes (17) implemented in Rangareddy district of the erstwhile undivided Andhra Pradesh and now of Telangana State in the 1980s launched with the imagination and dedicated leadership of D Muralikrishna, the DM, was a model of integration. In one such complex, there are 461 beneficiaries, majority of whom are members of the SC community. In one complex (Dharmasagar) all beneficiaries are freed bonded labourers. Each beneficiary was provided with a stipend of ₹180 per month for a period of six months under TRYSEM as a part of training in rearing of birds. Dwelling units were provided for stay of beneficiaries near the complex so that they can devote their time, energy and attention to management of the project. Training in rearing of birds, giving feed, injection and treatment of all common ailments enabled the beneficiaries to become barefoot doctors or mini-animal husbandry men. All inputs of the project starting with supply of quality chicks, feed, medicines, vaccines and health coverage were fully tied up with the output service, i.e., collection and marketing of eggs by the AP Meat and Poultry Development Corporation. By pooling resources from a variety of sources and integrating them imaginatively and skillfully, the DM demonstrated the effectiveness of group approach to rehabilitation while building up a massive infrastructure and converting the beneficiaries to barefoot doctors and eventual owners of poultry sheds.

II. Similar convergence was demonstrated by the DM, Rangareddy in making available various inputs such as irrigation, soil conservation, provision of quality seeds, back-up support & services, orientation and guidance to the beneficiaries to make land-based programmes of rehabilitation of freed bonded labourers a success in his district.

III. Under Economic Rehabilitation of the Rural Poor (ERRP) in Odisha in the 1980s, a group of bonded labourers who had agriculture as their principal avocation were sought to be rehabilitated at a common point as a group effort. A compact patch of land (10 acres and above depending on availability) was selected, beneficiaries (landless and assetless rural poor, many of whom were bonded labourers) were brought to the point where the patch was located, land measuring 1.5-2 acres was allotted to them, reclamation of waste land was taken up with a complete back-up or support service such as provision of irrigation facilities by sinking dug wells, installation of lift irrigation points, construction of low cost dwelling units under Indira Awas Yojana for housing the freed bonded labourers and their family members. All inputs of agricultural production such as quality seed, fertiliser and pesticide were made available to the beneficiaries and the cropping pattern was judiciously determined. ERRP was a model of integration in fighting rural poverty on the one hand and in facilitating permanent, meaningful and effective rehabilitation of freed bonded labourers on the other.

IV. On similar lines, land colonisation schemes of Kerala and schemes of rural agricultural estates in Bangalore Rural district of Karnataka were modelled for rehabilitation of freed bonded labourers as a group effort. Such a group approach to rehabilitation facilitated the following:

- Social and emotional integration of families belonging to SC, ST, OBC and minorities;
- Pooling of resources from a variety of sources and their integration in an imaginative and skilful manner;
- Easy and meaningful interface of the beneficiaries with the development functionaries and in particular, training and extension officials and banks;
- Imparting programme, legal and financial literacy to the beneficiaries;
- Ensuring economies of scale;
- Protection from organised onslaughts of bonded labour keepers.

V. The experiment of Tribal Project Authority in Dehradun, Tehri Garhwal and Uttarkashi districts of erstwhile undivided UP and now Uttarakhand with fifty-four project workers drawn mostly from the community of SC and ST proved immensely useful. Functioning under the guidance and control of Hill Areas Development Department, these project workers maintained an intensely humane and friendly relationship with all freed bonded labourers of the area allotted to them and functioned as 'friends, philosophers and guides' of the victims of BLS who have been converted to both beneficiaries and participants in the rehabilitation efforts being implemented for them.

Question 41

What constitute offences under BLS (A) Act? What is the procedure for trial of these offences?

Answer: There are five substantive sections in BLS (A) Act for dealing with offences. These sections are elaborated as under:

Section 16. Whoever compels, after commencement of the Act, any person to render any bonded labour shall be punishable.

Section 17. Whoever advances, after commencement of the Act any bonded debt shall be punishable.

Section 18. Whoever enforces, after commencement of the Act any custom, tradition, contract, agreement or any other instrument for extracting bonded labour under BLS shall be punishable.

Section 19. Whoever, being required by BLS (A) Act to restore any property to the possession of the bonded labourer, omits or fails to do so, within a period of thirty days from the date of commencement of this Act, shall be punishable.

Section 20. Whoever abets any offence punishable under this Act shall, whether or not the abetted offence is committed, be punishable with the same punishment as is provided for the offence which has been abetted.

The punishment for an offence committed under Sections 16, 17 and 18 is imprisonment for a term which may extend to three years and also fine which may extend to ₹2,000.

The punishment for an offence committed under S19 is imprisonment for a term which may extend to one year or with fine which may extend to ₹1,000 or with both. Section 19 further says that out of the fine, if recovered, payment shall be made to the bonded labourer at ₹5 for each day during which possession of the property was not restored to him/her.

Procedure for trial of cases:

On the basis of the enquiry report of an officer subordinate to DM, the Magistrate concerned (could be an Executive Magistrate vested with the powers of a Judicial Magistrate, First or Second Class or a Judicial Magistrate, as the case may be), shall start summary trial of the accused under S21(2) of the Act.

The procedure for summary trial has been dealt with in detail in Sections 260-264 and 265 of Cr PC 1973. To start with, the trying Magistrate takes cognisance of the offence under Section 190 Cr PC in the following manner:

- Upon receiving a complaint of facts which constitutes such offence;
- Upon a police report of such facts;
- Upon information received from any person other than a police officer, or upon his own knowledge, that such an offence has been committed.

After taking cognisance of an offence, if the Magistrate concerned feels that there is sufficient ground for proceeding, he/she shall issue summons for attendance of the accused under Section 204(1) of CrPC.

Such a summons shall be issued only after a list of prosecution witnesses has been filed. Every such summons shall be accompanied by a copy of the complaint. If the accused does not appear, and the Magistrate concerned thinks fit, he/she may issue a warrant u/s 204(1)(b) of CrPC.

The Magistrate concerned shall record the following particulars of the case u/s 263 CrPC as under:

- Serial number of the case;
- The date of commission of the offence;
- The date of the report or complaint;
- The name of the complainant, if any;
- The name, parentage and residence of the accused;
- The offence complained of and the offence (if any) proved and in cases coming under clause (ii), clause (iii) or clause (iv) of sub-section 1 Section 260, the value of the property in respect of which the offence has been committed;
- The plea of the accused and his examination, if any;
- The finding;
- The sentence or other final order;
- The date on which the proceedings terminated;
- The Magistrate concerned shall state particulars to the accused u/s 251 CrPC;
- He/she shall ask the accused if (a) he pleads guilty or (b) he has any defence to make;
- The plea of the accused should be recorded u/s 252 CrPC;
- If the accused pleads guilty, without appearing before the Magistrate, and after transmission to the Magistrate by post or by messenger, a letter containing his plea and also the amount of fine specified in the summons, the Magistrate may, in his discretion, convict the accused in his absence on his plea of guilt and sentence

him to pay the fine specified in the summons;

- If the accused doesn't plead guilty, the Magistrate concerned, on perusal of the materials on record before him, and after taking such evidence, if any, as he may of his own motion cause to be produced issue a speaking order either convicting or acquitting the accused, as the case may be (Section 252, 253, 254, 255 CrPC, 1973);

Question 42

At what stage should the FIR under 154 CrPC be filed against the accused?

Answer: If the physical release of a victim of BLS does not take place and there is resistance to such release from the side of the employer/bonded labour keeper, FIR u/s 154 CrPC should be filed against the latter.

FIR should also be filed if the accused is unlawfully compelling any person to work against his wishes (Section 374 IPC).

Whoever not being a member of SC or ST compels or entices a member of a SC or ST to do other form of forced labour other than any community service for public purposes would warrant filing FIR (Section 3(i)(h) of the The SC and ST (Prevention of Atrocities) Act, 1989 as amended in 2015 (Act 1 of 2016).

Question 43

What was the rationale behind Supreme Court taking a stand that regardless of pendency of a proceeding in the Supreme Court, implementation of the rehabilitation programme should not wait?

Answer: In the case *Santhal Pargana Antyodaya Ashram Vs State of Bihar and Others,*[24] the apex court had appointed a Committee

24 WP 1345 of 1983, 1987 (supplementary) Supreme Court cases 141

under the chairmanship of KB Saxena (IAS, retired), a senior official of the Government of Bihar, to investigate into the alleged existence of bonded labourers in Mohanpur and Deogarh blocks of Deogarh district and Saraiyahat Block of Dumka district. The committee after thorough investigation had submitted a detailed report to the Court. In course of investigation, the committee had been able to identify 2,515 bonded labourers and had stated that large number of persons were still working under bonded conditions. The apex court had issued certain directions with a sense of urgency.

The directions issued were:

- All persons who have been found bonded may be released within two weeks;
- A release certificate to each person released would be issued by the Collector;
- These certificates should be handed over to the persons so released simultaneously;
- Each of the released bonded labourers on making an application to the State Government through the Collector shall be paid a sum of ₹3,000 by way of interim relief;
- The released bonded labourers must be rehabilitated by the State Government on a permanent basis;
- Implementation of the rehabilitation programme should not wait on account of the pendency of the case in the Apex court.

The rationale behind delinking rehabilitation of a freed bonded labourer from any other proceeding pending before any other Court is as under:

- Immediacy and simultaneity are the key words in handling cases of rescue/release and rehabilitation of bonded labourers;

- This is because, while everything else may wait, these proceedings cannot wait;
- They cannot wait for the simple reason that a victim of BLS who is landless, asset-less, resourceless and below poverty line and has none or nothing in this world to fall back upon is likely to starve to death until and unless his rescue/ release/ rehabilitation are handled simultaneously and with lightning speed;
- If freedom which follows rescue/release is not accompanied by physical and economic security, the victim will either lapse back to the erstwhile master/bonded labour keeper or migrate. In either of the two contingencies, it will be difficult to trace the whereabouts of the victim;
- The central objective of rescue/release will be defeated.

Question 44

What were the directions of the Supreme Court in interpretation of the law on abolition of BLS and disposal of WPs filed under Article 32 of the Constitution?

Answer: The Supreme Court has original jurisdiction in any dispute concerning Government of India and any State on one side and one or more States on the other and between two or more States. It also has an appellate jurisdiction in matters of appeal from High Courts in certain cases.

Parliament may by law make provision for conferring on the Supreme Court such supplemental powers not inconsistent with any of the provisions of the Constitution of India.

Under the Anglo-Saxon system of jurisprudence, it is only a person to whom a legal injury is caused has a *locus standi* to move the Court for judicial redress; no one else can do so on his behalf.

This narrow and restricted doctrine effectively blocked the

concerns of the poor, deprived and disadvantaged sections of the society being brought before the Courts because the poor lacked the requisite awareness as also the resources to approach the Courts for judicial redress of the wrongs that were being perpetrated on them.

In a seminal decision, the Supreme Court reformed its procedural and jurisdictional rules relating to *locus standi*, making it easier for social action groups to bring litigation on behalf of the poor. It held that where there is a denial of Constitutional or legal rights of the poor who cannot on account of poverty, social exclusion or any other disadvantage, approach the Courts for vindication of their rights, any member of the public or social action group can, while acting bona fide, approach the Court for judicial redress of the injustice or wrong on behalf of the poor.

This need not be done by filing a regular writ petition through a lawyer but by addressing a letter to a Judge of the Court. The latter will entertain it as a WP under Article 32 of the Constitution.

This innovation was permitted by the Court as it was felt that it would be very difficult, if not impossible, for a member of the public or a social action group in any part of India to travel to the Supreme Court or the concerned High Court and engage a lawyer at considerable expense to file a writ petition.

This is how the doors of the Courts were thrown open to a large new class of litigants and a large number of cases began to pour in over the years by NGOs and social action groups on behalf of the poor.

Through such public interest litigation (PILs), not only the rights of the poor have been vindicated and timely Constitutional and legal remedies have been provided but the entire process facilitated a broad, liberal and expansive interpretation of the law without changing the law.

It is in this context that it may be appropriate to quote from an address by late Justice PN Bhagwati delivered on the occasion of a seminar in 1984:

> Our Constitution proclaims equality before the law but to large millions of our people, equality before the law has remained merely a myth or an illusion. There can be no real equality before law unless it is based on social and economic equality. Unfortunately, paternalism and not equalitarianism is the dominant attitude. A poor man is either your dependant or your enemy but never an independent, conscious and assertive individual and hence legal equality has remained merely a paper declaration.

This is the perspective in which public interest or social action litigation took shape in early 1980s in India and has spread its roots over the past three decades. Justice Bhagwati further explains:

> Since we are a democracy governed by the rule of law, whatever change we wish to bring about can only be through the process of law. The legal process must, therefore, be utilised for the purpose of bringing about change in life conditions of the poor. It can be used for a variety of purposes such as:
>
> - To claim entitlements provided by the terms of the statute law but denied in practice;
> - To explore contradictions between prevailing exploitative or repelling practices and existing principles of law;
> - To denounce, corrupt, oppressive or lawless administration;
> - To secure redress against the abuse or misuse of power by those charged with the responsibility to enforce the law, notably the police and public service officials;
> - To articulate claims of new rights and demands.

In all, twenty-six judgments were delivered between 1981 (when WP No 8431 was filed during Asian Games, New Delhi by PUCL) and 15 October 2012 (when the apex court finally disposed off WP No 3922/85 filed by PUCL) and all of them relate to elimination of BLS.

All these judgments may be viewed in a holistic and integrated perspective. The pith and substance as also the spirit of these judgments may be summarised as under:

- It does not stand to the credit of the State Government to disown the existence of BLS on the mistaken notion that it may be a slur on the image of the Government concerned or may bring discredit to administration;
- Instead, if the State Government acknowledges the existence of BLS and makes planned, coordinated and concerted efforts for its complete eradication, it may earn a lot of credit by providing timely relief to the victims;
- VCs at the district and sub-divisional level should be constituted and re-onstituted whenever due under S13 of BLS (A) Act;
- Individuals of character and integrity with proven track record of commitment to social work should be chosen as members of VCs;
- NGOs and voluntary social action groups should be given due representation in these bodies;
- VCs should go to the field, conduct inquiry into specific complaints, collect intelligence about prevalence of BLS in specific occupations and processes and conduct survey for identification of victims of BLS as has been mandated for all VCs under S14(e) of BLS (A) Act;
- No State Government should take a stand that there are no bonded labourers in the concerned State without constituting VCs, without collection of intelligence from the field and without conducting surveys;

- This would tantamount to such recalcitrant States (who are constantly in a denial mode) burying their heads ostrich-like in piles of sand, refusing to take cognisance of the ground-level realities;
- According to a judgment of the apex court (15 October 2012), incidence of BLS is found in the following occupations such as:
    - Brick kilns
    - Stone quarries and stone crushers;
    - Beedi rolling, labelling and packaging;
    - Carpet weaving;
    - Building and construction;
    - Power looms;
    - Cotton handlooms;
    - Fish processing.
- Surveys should, therefore, be undertaken at periodic intervals in sensitive areas;
- A simple, unconventional and unorthodox approach should be adopted both at the time of conducting a survey for identification of victims of BLS, at the time of having an interface with the victims and while presenting the findings of the survey before the Magistrate concerned (Section 21(1) of BLS (A) Act;
- The trying Magistrate should not put the victims in the witness box, should not put inconvenient and uncomfortable questions and ask him/her to depose evidence in presence of his employer/ erstwhile bonded labour keeper which will inhibit him/her;
- He/ she can never stand up to the tyranny of the law and rigidity of the legal process on account of his/ her poverty, illiteracy, indebtedness and backwardness;
- If he/she is forced to make a statement by way of deposition of evidence in presence of his/her employer, he/she may be confronted with the prospect of instant discharge/dismissal from

employment, apart from facing severe reprisal in the hands of the employer concerned;

- The apex court has put simultaneity and immediacy as the key principles in identification, rescue/release, repatriation and rehabilitation of bonded labourers;
- This means that there should be no time gap between identification and rescue/release on the one hand and release and rehabilitation on the other;
- These processes should be simultaneous;
- Such simultaneity would undoubtedly prevent lapse back of the released bonded labourers to servitude under the erstwhile bonded labour keepers; it would also prevent the incidence of inter-State distress migration;
- Release certificates should be issued by the same Executive Magistrate appointed u/s 21(1) of BLS (A) Act and vested with powers of a Judicial Magistrate, First or Second class *suo motu* and individually in favour of each bonded labourer;
- Such a certificate would form the basis of rehabilitation apart from establishing the identity of the freed bonded labourer in question;
- The Executive Magistrate appointed u/s 21(1) of BLS (A) Act and vested with the powers of a Judicial Magistrate, First or Second Class, should take up summary trial of the proceedings in each case with a sense of urgency and seriousness of concern.[25]

---

25 The above provision of Section 21 of BLS (A) Act has since been struck down as violative of Article 50, 21 and 14 of the Constitution by three High Courts of MP (Jabalpur Branch), Bombay and Madras on 28 April 1995, 21 April 1991 and 3 June 2014 respectively However, it is my considered view that till the Section 21 is amended and Judicial Magistrates alone are empowered to try cases, the existing arrangement may continue as otherwise there will be an impasse resulting in huge pendency of cases

The implications of summary trial (by adopting the procedure laid down in Sections 260-265 of the CrPC) are:

- There should be no examination or cross-examination of witnesses by taking recourse to the provisions of Indian Evidence At, 1872;
- The Magistrate concerned should go through the report of the survey team and should issue a speaking order after arriving at a definite conclusion which ideally should be in favour of the victim;
- Release of a bonded labourer from bondage and prosecution of bonded labour keeper/offender of the law should not be linked; the former should not be made conditional on the latter;
- In other words, regardless of whether the bonded labour keeper is convicted or acquitted at the end of the criminal proceedings initiated under S21(2) of BLS (A) Act, it should not affect the process of release and rehabilitation of the bonded labourers;
- The latter as a matter of fact, should receive the highest priority conceivable and possible;

  Every case of release should be followed in quick succession by efforts for securing effective, meaningful and permanent rehabilitation.

In the case of inter-State migrant workmen, the discretion as to whether they would like to be rehabilitated at the destination point or originating point after they have been rescued/released from bondage should be entirely theirs; the State concerned should respect this choice and facilitate its implementation.

The process of rehabilitation strictly according to the preferences, felt needs and interests of the victim should be facilitated by the district administration with utmost expedition and ease. Good, reliable NGOs who are genuinely committed to social action, who are non-political or a-political should be involved in the process of identification and rehabilitation.

Question 45

Which are the landmark judgements relating to BLS delivered by the Supreme Court?

Answer:

Ram Pal Vs Maishi Lal Rajkumar and Others[26]

The WP alleged that certain persons have been held as bonded labourers in a brick kiln of UP's Saharanpur district. The DM was asked to visit the brick kiln and record statements of those persons. He reported to the Court that they intend to go back to some other place of employment but do not wish to avail of any assistance from the State Government by way of rehabilitation. The Court directed the respondents to allow these persons to leave the brick kiln and to ensure that the brick kiln owner does not restrain them from doing so by threat of force or otherwise

PUCL Vs Union of India and Others[27]

The Supreme Court gave the following directions:

- Central Government should ensure that provisions of labour laws are being strictly enforced;
- It need not have to wait for any formal complaint from the aggrieved workers;
- An effective system of periodic inspection coupled with occasional surprise inspection by higher officers should be put in place;
- Through such a system of inspection, it should be ensured that there are no violations of labour laws and that the workmen are not denied the rights and benefits to which they are entitled;

---

26 WP (Crl) 7 of 1982
2 Supreme Court cases (SCC) 349
Date of judgment: 19 January 1982

27 WP 8143 of 1981 AIR 1982 SC 1473 1982 Lab IC 1646 Date of judgment: 18 September 1982

- Immediate action should be initiated against defaulting employers/ contractors as also officers for any laxity and inaction;
- Construction being primarily a hazardous employment, no child below the age of fourteen should be allowed on a site;
- When a person provides labour or service for a remuneration which is less than the minimum wage, it falls within the ambit f forced labour under Article 23 of the Constitution.

Sanjit (Bunker) Roy Vs State of Rajasthan[28]

The apex court gave the following directions:

- If the Rajasthan Famine Relief Works Employees (Exemption from Labour Laws) Act, 1964 excludes the applicability of Minimum Wages Act, 1948 and provides that minimum wages may not be paid to workmen employed in any famine relief work, it would be clearly violative of Article 23.
- When the State extracts labour or service from the affected persons for carrying out famine relief work which is otherwise useful, there can be no justification for the State not to pay minimum wage by taking advantage of the helpless condition of affected persons.
- The minimum wage is fixed per day and not with reference to a particular quantity of work turned out by the workman during the day.
- The minimum wage is not to be fixed on piece rate basis so that a particular minimum wage would be payable only if a certain amount of work is turned out by the workmen.
- Minimum wage must be paid by the employer to the workmen so long as they work throughout the working hours of the day.

28 WP 6816 AIR 1983 SC 328 Date of judgment: 20 January 1983

Bandhua Mukti Morcha Vs Union of India and Others[29]

The judgment contains the following observations and directions:

Observations

- Government of Haryana's contention that the workmen in the stone quarries and crushers might be providing forced labour but they were not working under BLS has no substance;
- Government of Haryana shouldn't have insisted on a formal, rigid and legalistic approach in the matter of implementation of a Statute which is an important instrument for ensuring human dignity;
- A bonded labourer who can never stand up to the rigidity and tyranny of the legal process due to poverty, ignorance, illiteracy and backwardness should not be required to go through a formal process of trial with the normal procedure for recording of evidence;
- The BLS (A) Act, if properly implemented, should have by now secured and fulfilled the objective of total identification, release and rehabilitation of bonded labourers;
- Government of Haryana shouldn't have maintained a stand that there were not at any time any bonded labourers within its territory without constituting VCs at the district and sub-divisional level.

Directions

- There would be no occasion for a bonded labourer to be placed in a situation where he/she is required to supply forced labour for no wage or for nominal wage unless he/she has received some advance or other economic consideration from the employer;

29 WP 2135 AIR 1984 SC 802 Date of judgment: 16 December 1983

- Whenever it is shown that a labourer is made to provide forced labour, the Court would raise a presumption that he is required to do so in consideration of an advance and he is, therefore, a bonded labourer;
- This presumption may be rebutted by the employer and also by the State Government, if it so chooses, but, until and unless satisfactory evidence is produced for rebutting this presumption, the Court must proceed on the basis that the person is a bonded labourer entitled to the benefits of the provisions of the Act.
- Every workman required to carry out blasting operations with the help of explosives should be trained under Mines Vocational Training Rules, must hold first-aid qualification and must carry a first-aid outfit while undertaking blasting operations;
- All cases of occupational injury (caused by accidents) and disease (caused by exposure to dust, heat, fume, noise & toxic substances) should be reported to CIF&B/DGMS/DGFASLI;
- Legal assistance should be provided to the workmen to enable them to file a claim for compensation;
- CBWE should, in addition to VV Giri National Law Institute, hold camps near the sites of quarries and crushers for the purpose of educating the workers about the rights and benefits conferred on them by labour and social welfare laws;
- Anti-pollution measures should be undertaken by the Central and State Government;
- The Central and State Government should issue direction to mining lessees and stone crusher owners to ensure supply of potable water by obtaining the same from unpolluted sources and transporting the same by tankers to the colonies where the workmen live;

- The Central and State Government should ensure that conservancy facilities in shape of latrines and urinals at both work sites and workers' colonies be provided;
- Inspections by the officers of labour law enforcement machinery of both Central and State Government to the quarries and crushers should be arranged once in a fortnight and should ensure provision of medical and legal assistance to the workmen as may be needed;
- The apex court appointed the author as a socio-legal investigating commissioner to visit the stone quarries and stone crushers and enquire of the labourer as to whether they are providing forced labour. He was directed to ascertain (a) whether advances have been paid to the workmen at the time of recruitment and thereafter (b) whether the workmen are in receipt of wages less than the statutorily notified minimum wage and submit a detailed report within three months from the date of the order.

Labourers Working in Salal Hydro-electric Project Vs State of Jammu and Kashmir[30]

The judgement in this case primarily relates to implementation of provisions of CL(R&A) Act in a major hydro-electric project and secondarily, to implementation of provisions of BLS (A) Act.

The following directions were issued:

- The Central government should take immediate steps to ensure that the sub-contractors or piece wagers do not execute any portion of the project work without obtaining a licence u/s 12(1) of CL(R&A) Act;
- They should carry out their obligations u/s 16-21 of CL(R&A) Act read with rules 41-62 of CL (R&A) central rules;

30 WP (Crl) 1179 of 1982 (1984) 3 Supreme Court cases (SCC) 538 Date of judgment 25 April 1984

- The Central government should immediately ensure that canteens, restrooms and washing facilities are provided by the contractors, piece wagers or sub-contractors to the workmen;
- No child below the age of fourteen should be employed in the project;
- Wages to the workmen employed by piece wagers or sub-contractors should be paid directly without the intervention of any intermediary;
- No deduction from the wages except those authorised by the law, i.e., Payment of Wages Act, 1936 should be made;
- Payment of wages should be made in presence of an authorised representative of the Central Government or the project;
- Thorough inspections should be carried out by the inspectorate staff with regular frequency;
- Provisions of ISMW (ROE&COS) Act should be enforced with immediate effect.

Neerja Chaudhary Vs State of MP[31]

The following observations and directions were made by the apex court in the above case:

General observations:

- The district and sub-divisional level VCs should be re-organised and activated;
- Their meetings should be more frequent than now;
- An intensive survey of the areas which have been traditionally prone to the prevalence of bonded labour system should be undertaken by the VCs;

31 WP (Criminal) No 1263 of 1982 AIR 1984 Supreme Court 1099, date of order 08.05.84

- The officers who are posted at different levels to deal with the problem of bonded labour should be trained and sensitised;
- They should develop a sense of involvement with the misery and suffering of the poor;
- Every officer who is placed in charge of identification, release and rehabilitation of bonded labourers should be imbued with a sense of purpose, dedication and responsibility;
- The activities of these officers should be under constant supervision;
- Officers who are socially committed, naturally motivated, inspired by idealism and un-polluted by pulls and pressures should be encouraged by way of suitable public recognition;
- The pace and progress of schemes of rehabilitation under implementation must be evaluated (by way of both concurrent and summative evaluation);
- A sense of urgency and seriousness of concern must pervade the implementation of the programmes including rehabilitation so that benefits of expenditure reach the lowest of the low and weakest of the weak.

Specific directions:

- Release and rehabilitation of bonded labourers should be simultaneous; if not, there is every possibility that freed bonded labourers on the way to rehabilitation would lapse back to the bondage of erstwhile masters;
- Social action groups operating at the grass root level should be fully involved with the task of identification, release and rehabilitation of bonded labourers. They are better suited to attend to these tasks than either the representatives of people (MPs, MLAs and MLCs), Panchayats, Collectors and Divisional Commissioners

on account of the following reasons:

- They have flexibility of structure, procedure and operation;
- Collectors and Divisional Commissioners rely on their sub-ordinates who are in collusion with the exploiting class;
- Panchayats are also dominated and influenced by vested interests;
- Social Action Groups live with and work for the people; they have the pulse of the people on their fingers.

Mukesh Advani Vs State of Madhya Pradesh[32]

The Supreme Court appointed the District Judge, Bhopal as the Inquiring Officer to visit the Raisen flagstone mines. The latter found the following:

- Workmen were being paid less than what was agreed at the time of recruitment;
- The piece rate method of computation of wages was deficient; it resulted in very low average earnings of ₹5-10 per day.
- The unauthorised deduction made from the wages against the provisions of the PW Act left the workmen with little to survive;
- The quarry contractor's contention was that each worker had to repay ₹15,000-16,000 towards advances taken; it is precisely for this reason that the workmen were not free to leave the work site.
- There is no BLS in the flagstone mines of Raisen.
    - The report was flawed and full of ambiguities and contradictions. If as agreed to at the time of recruitment wages were not being paid, if unauthorised deductions were taking place and if the workmen were not free to leave the employer and the work site, they came within the purview of

32 WP 1232 of 1982 AIR 1985 Supreme Court 1363 Date of judgment 2 May 1983

Section 2(g) of BLS (A) Act. The action of employer is also punishable under Sections 406 and 409 of IPC for criminal breach of trust. The basis on which the District Judge, Bhopal, came to his negative conclusion is not clear.

- It appears that the Court issued the following orders without any specific direction on the status of the workers, i.e., whether they're bonded or not, and if bonded, a direction about their release and rehabilitation.

- The Union of India should come out with proposals to prescribe minimum wage on piece rate basis for various operations in flagstone mines;
- The Union of India should issue a preliminary notification under S5 of MW Act, setting out its proposal for information of persons likely to be affected thereby specifying a date not less than two months from the date of the notification on which proposals will be taken into consideration;
- A joint machinery comprising the representatives of the Union of India and the State Government (MP) should be set up to ensure timely and proper enforcement of minimum wage in quarries.

Upendra and Others Vs State of MP and Another[33]

The following directions were issued:

- Rehabilitation must follow the quick footsteps of identification and release;
- A socio-legal investigating Commissioner was directed to visit the villages of Bagaijore, Paisada, Durgapalli, Bhanwarpur, Ichhapur and Singhnapur in Raipur district, ascertain whether there are any more

33 WP (Civil/Criminal) 1071 of 1986 (supplementary) Supreme Court Cases 558 Date of judgment: 25 September 1986

bonded labourers in these villages, identify them and bring their names and particulars immediately to the notice of the Collector, Raipur for the purpose of releasing and rehabilitating them;

- Rehabilitation of bonded labourers should be dovetailed with other development and welfare schemes launched by the Central and State government.

Bandhua Mukti Morcha and Mehboob Batcha Vs State of Tamil Nadu[34]

The apex court expressed its appreciation that the government of Tamil Nadu has come forward with a rehabilitation scheme duly approved by the Sub-Collector, Kodaikanal as well as by the Commissioner appointed by the Court. The Court expressed the hope that the scheme which will benefit 157 families working in Kodaikanal hills will be implemented properly and effectively and that several suggestions made by the petitioner will be taken into account while implementing the scheme.

Chhattisgarh Krishak Mazdoor Sangh Vs State of MP and Others[35]

The apex court directed that 678 persons of Saraipalli tehsil of Madhya Pradesh who were identified as victims of BLS by the socio-legal investigating Commissioner appointed by the Court be released and rehabilitated.

The apex court further directed the State Government to identify bonded labourers afresh (over and above 698 persons)

34 WP 574 and 693 of 1986 (supplementary) Supreme Court Cases 541 Date of judgment: 16 October 1986

35 WP 1330 of 1983 1987 (supplementary) Supreme Court Cases 198 Date of judgment: 9 December 1986

within three months from the date the list containing the names of persons alleged to be bonded labourers is filed by the advocate for the petitioner. It also directed that orders with appropriate certificates of release be passed by the competent authority immediately thereafter entitling them for rehabilitation.

Santhal Pargana Antyodaya Ashram Vs State of Bihar and others[36]

This case has been dealt in detail in response to Question 43.

P Sivaswamy Vs State of Andhra Pradesh[37]

The petitioner had alleged prevalence of bonded labour in stone quarries in several districts of Andhra Pradesh. After taking cognisance of the complaint as a WP, the Court had directed the DM, Hyderabad, AWARE (an NGO), District Judge, Krishna and the author, then DG(LW)/JS, MoL&E, one after the other in quick succession, to visit stone quarries at Kailashapuram and submit a report on the status of the quarry workers and extent of compliance with Mines Act, Mines Rules, Mines Vocational Training Rules, Mines Crèche Rules, CL(R&A) Act and Minimum Wages Act.

On receipt of the report, the apex court issued the following directions were issued:

- 2,200 bonded labourers belonging to Tamil Nadu, Karnataka and Odisha should be released forthwith;
- Government of AP was asked to prepare three separate lists of

---

36 WP No 1345 of 1983
1987 (supplementary) Supreme Court Cases 141
Date of judgment: 19 December 1986

37 WP (Crl) 1574 of 1982 with 1573 and 1187 of 1982 and 54 of 1983 AIR 1988 Supreme Court 1863 Date of judgment: 10 August 1988

released bonded labourers for their repatriation to Tamil Nadu, Karnataka and Odisha;

- Government of AP was further asked to swear an affidavit on the total number of bonded labourers identified, released and repatriated district wise (twenty-three districts) since 1 January 1983;
- Government of AP was directed to set up VCs at all district and sub-divisional levels;
- Social activists and a representative of AWARE were to be co-opted as members thereof;
- Concern was expressed over non-cooperation of the State Government of Karnataka;
- The apex court also lamented that even years after the Constitutional directive contained in Article 23 and coming into force of BLS (A) Act, they have failed to generate appropriate attitudes and dispositions;
- The Court further lamented that a lot of its time, energy and resources are wasted in persuading and impressing on the State Governments about the importance of carrying out their statutory responsibility as also in securing compliance with its directions;
- The Court expressed its inability to entertain repeated complaints of this type and devote its time and attention in monitoring the administration of the Act;
- It summed up the situation as most unsatisfactory.

Sankar Mukherjee and Others Vs Union of India and Others[38]

The judgment in this case primarily relates to implementation of provisions of CL (R&A) Act in brick kins of West Bengal and indirectly relates to elimination of forced/bonded labour. The

38 WP 2123 of 1982 AIR 1990 Supreme Court 532, 1989-SC (2) GJX 0613 SC Date of judgment: 10 November 1989

directions issued by the apex court were as under:

- The system of contract labour is nothing but an improved version of BLS;
- It is surprising that more than forty years after independence, the practice of employing labour through contractors by big companies including public sector companies is still being accepted as a normal feature of employment of labour;
- In the contract labour system, there is no security of service to the workmen and their wages are far below that of regular workmen of the company.

Balaram Das and Others Vs State of MP and Others[39]

On 13 July 1989, the apex court had directed Socio-legal Investigating Commissioner PV Rajagopal to ascertain as to how many out of 3,949 freed bonded labourers have been provided with the benefits of rehabilitation scheme. Rajagopal visited Pithora, Basna and Saraipalli blocks in Raipur district. The Court came to the conclusion that proper attention has not been paid to rehabilitation of freed bonded labourers and issued the following directions:

- Adequate funds should be released under the rehabilitation scheme framed under BLS (A) Act;
- The Collector and such other officers who have been assigned the responsibility of supervising implementation of the rehabilitation scheme shall ensure that the full amount reaches the released bonded labourers;
- All such persons who are willing to have an account opened in their respective names shall have accounts opened and the money shall be credited to such accounts;

39 WP (Civil) 927-928 of 1987 AIR 1990 Supreme Court 44 Date of judgment: 26 September 1989

- Those who do not want bank accounts to be opened shall be paid in cash after proper identification in presence of a judicial officer, if available or before a gazetted Executive officer who will certify the receipt of the amount.

Bandhua Mukti Morcha Vs Union of India and Others[40]

By its order dated 21 February 1991, the apex court constituted a committee with certain specific mandate to be discharged within a prescribed time schedule. The report submitted by the committee on 1 July 1991 indicated inhuman living and working conditions in quarries. The Court considered the report of the committee, fixed the total number of identified bonded labourers around 2,000 (as against 3,993 as stated by the petitioner) and issued a number of directions both for the Union Government and Government of Haryana for compliance as under:

- Quarries are located in a particular area away from habitation. People from different parts of the country are made to live inside the quarries with their family members under unhygienic and insanitary conditions. It should be the responsibility of the employer to look after health of the workmen and that of the members of their families and education of the children as also that of adults in such exclusive locality;
- The employer should also be obliged to provide a definite source of clean potable water for drinking to the workers and their family members;
- The workmen are engaged almost on full-time basis. The report of the committee indicates that majority of the workers are not prepared to return to their States. It is, therefore, necessary to

40 WP 2135 of 1982 (1991) Supreme Court cases 177 Date of final disposal: 13 August 1991

earmark a permanent residential base at or near the work site. It should be an integrated plan encompassing provision of housing, supply of water, provision store, schooling and hospital facility, recreational facility, a police station/outpost, as the case may be;

- In view of the inherent limitation on the part of the Court to monitor compliance with these directions, it should be the obligation of the Welfare State to provide for all these facilities and amenities;
- The operation of stone quarries is more or less concentrated in particular areas. Placing a local officer of appropriate status would help in improving the lot of the workmen;
- Inspection by the competent authority entrusted with welfare would also ensure availability of facilities like schooling, hospital, provision of clean potable water, etc.;
- The State of Haryana must give adequate importance to the pollution problem. The ecology should be viewed both as a local problem as well as a problem of NCT of Delhi;
- The authorities in the State of Haryana must take care to protect the workmen by ensuring compliance with the laws applicable to quarry workers;
- The Union Government could consider raising a special cess against quarry activities to be specifically utilised by way of return to the industry. All statutory and non-statutory facilities and amenities could be provided from out of the corpus of this fund (as is being done in case of miners in coal, iron ore, manganese ore, limestone and dolomite, mica, etc.)

T Chakkalackal Vs State of Bihar and Others[41]

In this case, the apex court has thrown light on some of the

41 WP 10237 of 1992 1993 supplementary (4) Supreme Court cases 211 Date of judgment: 9 October 1992

important provisions of BLS (A) Act and has observed the following:

- The District and Sessions Judge, West Champaran, Bettiah in his report submitted to the Court had observed that those who continued to work with the employer in consideration of an advance and/or in consideration of interest due on such advance for a specified or unspecified period were not bonded labourers;
- The Court found it difficult to accept this interpretation and conclusion;
- Under S6 of BLS (A) Act, the debt stood extinguished and it was obligatory on the part of the employer to return any property of the bonded labourer held by him;
- The survey conducted by the Dy Collector, West Champaran, Bettiah showed that the bonded labourers after their release were forced to refund the bonded debt;
- The Court held that such action on the part of the bonded labour keepers was clearly violative of the provisions of law; the apex court directed the employers to return the property of the bonded labourers--movable or immovable held illegally by them;
- The Court further directed that in every case of release, a release certificate must be issued;
- The freed bonded labourer(s) have the option and volition to work under the erstwhile employer(s) but whenever and wherever they do so, the employers have the obligation to comply with the provisions of the Minimum Wages Act;
- All cases of bonded debt should be investigated and necessary action would have to be taken by the State Government to ensure that the bonded labour keepers return the property forcibly taken by them from bonded labourers;
- This is yet another case of flawed finding on the part of the head

of the Judiciary at the district level after the Bhopal case. It is encouraging to note that the Court in the fitness of things did not accept the finding of the District Judge, West Champaran.

PUCL and Others Vs State of Tamil Nadu and Others[42]

The Supreme Court came to the conclusion in this case that nearly two decades after the enactment of BLS (A) Act, no significant progress has been made by the authorities concerned and that there is not much change in their attitude. The Court, therefore, considered it appropriate to issue certain directions for prompt compliance by all the State Governments through their administrative machinery. The directions issued by the Court were as under:

- To identify bonded labourers as well as to identify the villages where the practice is prevalent;
- To identify the employers/bonded labour keepers and to initiate appropriate criminal proceedings against them;
- To extinguish/discharge any existing debt and/or bonded liability and to ensure them an alternative means of livelihood;
- To appoint an independent body such as local non-political social action group to collect independent information and details of:
  - The prevalence of exploitative practice of bonded labour;
  - Employers or their agents perpetrating the wilful violation of the law by encouraging and abetting the practice of bonded labour;
- To provide employment to such bonded labourers as agricultural workers at the prescribed minimum wage rate and/or provide landless bonded labourers with agricultural land with a view to ensuring an alternative means of livelihood;
- To provide adequate shelter, food and basic education to the

42 1994-SC (2) –GJX-0516-SC Equivalent citation 1994-(005)-SCC-0116-SC Date of judgment: 13 May 1994

children of the bonded labourers, medical facilities to the bonded labourers and their families as part of a rehabilitation package.

Further directions to administration at the national, State and district level included:

- Setting up of VCs in each district;
- Submission of periodic quality reports to the Supreme Court Legal Aid Committee or to any Commissioner appointed by the Court for this purpose;
- Setting up of rural credit facilities such as Grameen Banks, cooperatives, etc., from which short-term interest-free loans can be availed without security;
- Regular inspection by the Labour Commissioner concerned with a view to keeping the contractors who in the past have employed bonded labourers under close watch;
- To initiate criminal proceedings against those employers, contractors or their agents who engage bonded labourers, employ children below the age of fourteen years without adequate monetary compensation and who pay wages below the minimum wage rate as notified under Minimum Wage Act;
- To initiate criminal proceedings against these employers, contractors or their agents who make part payment of wages by way of *kesri dal*—a pulse with toxic elements which is known to cause permanent disability or latherism.

PUCL Vs Union of India and Others[43]

The above WP admitted under Article 32 of the Constitution is based on a report submitted by the NGO Campaign against

43 1996-SC(2) -6JX -0742- SC Equivalent citation(s) 1998-(008)-SCC-0485-SC Date of judgment: 26 March 1996

Child Labour. According to the report, five children were procured by an agent called Rajput on payment of a paltry ₹500-1,500 to poor parents. The children below the age of fifteen years were forced into bonded labour. One of the boys aged eight years was beaten to death. The remaining four boys were not traceable after this tragic occurrence. Subsequently, while three boys could be traced by Maharashtra Police, the fourth is still untraced. The petitioner had claimed that the parents of the boys are entitled to compensation.

The following observations were made and directions were issued by the Court in this case:

Observations:

- A claim in public law for compensation for contravention of human rights and fundamental freedoms, the protection of which is guaranteed by the Constitution is an acknowledged remedy for enforcement and protection of such rights;
- Such a claim based on strict liability made by resorting to a Constitutional remedy which provided for the enforcement of a fundamental right is distinct from and in addition to the remedy in private law for damage for the tort resulting from the contravention of fundamental rights;
- The defence of sovereign immunity being inapplicable and alien to the concept of guarantee of fundamental rights, there is no question of such a defence being available in the Constitutional remedy;
- It is this principle which justifies award of monetary compensation for contravention of fundamental rights guaranteed by the Constitution;
- This is the only practical mode of redress available for the contravention made by the State or its servants in the purported

exercise of their powers and enforcement of the fundamental right as claimed by resort to the remedy in public law under the Constitution by recourse to Article 32 and 226/227 of the Constitution.

Bandhua Mukti Morcha Vs Union of India and Others[44]

The order of the Court in this case was passed on a WP filed by way of PIL under Article 32 of the Constitution. The petitioner sought issue of a writ of mandamus directing the government to take steps to stop employment of children in carpet industry in the State of UP, to appoint a committee to investigate into the terms and conditions of their (children) employment and to issue such directives as are appropriate for total prohibition of employment of children below fourteen years. The Court allowed the WP and issued the following directions:

- The Government of India would convene a meeting of the concerned Ministers of the respective State Governments in charge of labour and their Principal Secretaries to evolve policies and principles for progressive elimination of employment of children below the age of fourteen years;
- They would evolve such steps as are consistent with the scheme laid down in the judgment (1997 AIR SCW 407) and in particular to provide:
    - Compulsory education to all children either by industries themselves or in coordination with the industries by the State Government to the children employed in factories, mines or any other industry, organised or unorganised labour with such

44 WP (Civil) 12125 of 1984 with 11643 of 1985 AIR 1997 Supreme Court 2218 Date of judgment: 21 February 1997

timings as are convenient to impart compulsory education, facilities for secondary vocational and higher education;

- Periodic health check-up;
- Nutritious food.

- Entrust the responsibility for implementation of the principles;
- Report the progress made to the Registry of the Court.

Bandhua Mukti Morcha Vs Union of India and Others[45]

By the order dated 16 December 1983, the Court had issued certain directions (21) and had appointed the author, then Director General (Labour Welfare) to investigate and submit a report to the Court keeping the twenty-one directions in view. The author submitted his report in two volumes in which he had clearly & emphatically reported to the Court that not a single direction had been implemented by the State Government. Subsequently as the recommendations were not complied with by the State Government, the petitioner filed a petition of contempt of court. In the wake of filing of this contempt petition, Dr Mahaveer Jain, a senior faculty member of the National Labour Institute was appointed to inquire into the measures and the extent by which the directions of the Court had been implemented.

The following directions were issued by the Court:

- There is a discrepancy in the assessment of the magnitude of the problem of bonded labour in the stone quarries of Faridabad. While Swamy Agnivesh, the petitioner put the number at 3,993, the Government of Haryana put it 544 as on 30 November 1990;
- With a view to removing the discrepancy, the Court directed that a committee be set up with DG(LW) or any senior officer

45 WP 2135 of 1982 (1991) 4 Supreme Court Cases 174 Date of judgment: 21 February 1999

from the MoL&E, the Chief Judicial Magistrate, Faridabad, Raju Ramachandran, an advocate of the Supreme Court with social service background, an officer of Government of Haryana not below the rank of ADM and Swami Agnivesh representing the petitioner. MR Rohatgi or his nominee advocate, appearing for and on behalf of the brick kiln owners' association, would be permitted to associate himself with the activities of the committee;

- The committee shall within six weeks check the particulars provided in the list by the petitioner, identify the persons claimed to have been victims of BLS and collect all relevant materials in respect of the victims so as to assist the Court to issue further directions in terms of requirement of the scheme to rehabilitate the victims;
- The Haryana officer shall act as the Convener of the Committee and be responsible for providing logistics support to the Committee.

After consideration of the affidavits filed by the Deputy Commissioner, Faridabad and Commissioner, Municipal Corporation, the Court issued the following directions:

- The State Government shall provide necessary funds on the basis of the estimates already approved by the Municipal Corporation;
- On receipt of funds from the State Government, the Corporation may get the job (electrification) done through the agency of Haryana Vidyut Prasaran Nigam (a State-owned Corporation);
- While laying down the pipelines for supply of potable water, metalling of roads as also construction of community toilets, the Corporation shall provide surface drainage in the colony;
- Completion of all the above items of welfare work in the colony is not to be linked with deposit of development charges by stone crusher owners. The job shall be completed by the Corporation independent of it;

- The dwelling units for 141 stone crusher workers shall be constructed by the Corporation with financial assistance from the State Government. The cost shall be recoverable from stone crusher owners;
- In the light of repeated violation of labour laws by the mining lessees including non-payment of minimum wages, the State Government may consider the feasibility of cancelling the leases of the defaulting mining lessees;
- The CJM, Faridabad will file an affidavit within four weeks from the date of all the cases pending in his Court for recovery of the amount as also the stage of the recovery proceedings;
- Suo-motu contempt notice issued to BK Panigrahi, then Dy Commissioner shall stand discharged;
- Suo-motu contempt notice issued to Uma Shankar, then Municipal Commissioner is also discharged. However, he and the present incumbent Krishna Kumar shall continue to attend the proceedings of the Court.

PUCL Vs State of Tamil Nadu and Others[46]

The Court entrusted the National Human Rights Commission (NHRC) with the responsibility of monitoring and overseeing the implementation of its directions as well as provisions of BLS (A) Act in all the States /UTs.

It issued the following directions:

- Fresh surveys to be conducted periodically once in three years in all States/UTs;
- The findings of the survey should be made part of a computerised data base available on the websites of all concerned;

46 WP (Civil) 3922/85 Date of order: 11 November 1997 (7) SCALE (SP) 17

- The responsibility for conducting the surveys is on the district and sub-divisional vigilance committees;
- The latter should submit their report to NHRC once every three years;
- The VCs should be reconstituted once every three years;
- In conducting surveys, brick kilns, stone quarries, stone crushing mines, *beedi* rolling, labelling and packaging, carpet weaving, building and construction, power looms, cotton handlooms and fish processing should warrant prioritised attention of VCs;
- Child labour and educational deprivation of children go together. In the wake of RTE Act, 2009 coming into force, all children in schoolgoing age (five to fourteen) should go to school and no child should be pushed involuntarily to work;
- Children working as domestic help should be withdrawn from the said work;
- Local self-governing bodies should identify, rescue/ release such children and ensure that they get proper education;
- Observance of correct methodology will be crucial to the successful conducting of a survey for identification of victims of BLS;
- The guidelines laid down by SR Sankaran, former Principal Secretary, Government of AP (1975-78) on the methodology of such identification may be followed by all States/UTs with suitable modification to suit local conditions;
- Requirement of funds for rehabilitation of all freed bonded labourers should be assessed by all States/UTs;
- Steps may be taken by GoI to enhance the rehabilitation package from the present limit of ₹20,000 (w.e.f 1 May 2000);
- All DMs should exercise their powers as laid down in Sections 10, 11 and 12 of BLS (A) Act with due diligence, empathy and sensitivity;

- The States of AP, WB, Jharkhand, Bihar and NCT of Delhi are directed to ensure compliance with the orders passed by NHRC as highlighted in its revised report to the Court.

PUCL Vs State of Tamil Nadu and Others[47]

The apex court in this order issued comprehensive directions to all States /Union Territories to check the prevalence of bonded labour system, to identify through periodic surveys victims of bonded labour system and take timely steps for rehabilitation of victims of bonded labour system in a meaningful, effective and permanent manner.

PUCL Vs State of Tamil Nadu and Others[48]

The apex court passed the following order:

> Shri AK Ganguly, learned Amicus Curie has also produced a Declaration on elimination of bonded labour system and child bondage jointly adopted by the Government of Tamil Nadu and Campaign for the Abolition and Rehabilitation of Bonded Labour (CAREBOLA) with the active support of the Ministry of Labour, Government of India at Chennai on 20th and 21st August 1997. All the State Governments are required to file their comments thereto and further action taken in that direction. This be done by all the State Governments within four weeks furnishing copies thereof to learned Solicitor General and Amicus Curie. The learned Solicitor General will have three weeks thereafter to examine the same

47 WP (civil) No 3922/85 Date of order (interim) 6 March 1995 1994 (5) SCC 116

48 WP (Civil) No 3922/85 Date of order (interim) 15 September 1997 (7) SCALE (SP) 16

PUCL Vs State of Tamil Nadu and Others[49]

After receiving the response from the concerned States and UTs, the apex court entrusted the National Human Rights Commission (NHRC) with the responsibility of monitoring and overseeing the implementation of its directions as well as provisions of BLS (A) Act in all the States /UTs.

PUCL Vs State of Tamil Nadu and Others[50]

In this interim order, the apex court issued the following directions namely:

1. All States/ UTs must submit their status report in the form prescribed by NHRC once every six months.
2. All States/ UTs shall constitute VCs at the district and sub-divisional level as required u/s 13 of BLS (A) Act within a period of six months from today, i.e. 5 May 2004
3. All States/UTs shall make proper arrangements for rehabilitating released bonded labourers. Such rehabilitation can be land-based or non-land based or art/craft/skill-based depending on the choice of the freed bonded labourer, his/her inclination and past experience. If the States are not in a position to make arrangements for such rehabilitation, they shall identify two philanthropic organisations or NGOs with proven track record and good reputation who can provide the basic facilities required for rehabilitation of released bonded labourers within a period of six months.
4. The States/UTs shall chalk out a detailed plan for rehabilitating released bonded labourers either by themselves or with the involvement of such organisations or NGOs within a period of six months.

---

49 WP (Civil) 3922/85 Date of order 11 November 1997 (7) SCALE (SP) 17

50 WP (Civil 3922/85 Date of order (interim) 5 May 2004, 12 SCC 381

5. The Union and State Governments shall submit a plan within a period of six months for sharing the money under the modified centrally sponsored scheme in such cases where the States wish to involve such organisations or NGOs.
6. The States/UTs shall make arrangements to sensitise the DM and other statutory authorities/Committees in respect of their duties under the BLS (A) Act.

PUCL Vs State of Tamil Nadu and Others[51]

In this case, while delivering the final order, the apex court referred to the two preliminary orders delivered on 5 and 13 May 2004, guidelines on the methodology of identification of bonded labourers formulated by SR Sankaran, report submitted by the NHRC to the apex court on the basis of reports received from States which present a sorry state of affairs at the ground level, request of NHRC to the apex court to issue specific directions to the States to improve their performance and issued the following directions presented in a summary form such as:

- Fresh surveys to be conducted periodically once in three years in all States/UTs;
- The findings of the survey should be made part of a computerised data base available on the websites of all concerned;
- The responsibility for conducting the surveys is on the district and sub-divisional vigilance committees;
- The latter should submit their report to NHRC once every three years;
- The VCs should be re-constituted once every three years;
- In conducting surveys, brick kilns, stone quarries, stone crushing

51 WP (Civil) 3922/85, Date of judgment 15 October 2012

mines, *beedi* rolling, labelling and packaging, carpet weaving, building and construction, power looms, cotton handlooms and fish processing should warrant prioritised attention of VCs;

- Child Labour and educational deprivation of children go together. In the wake of Right To Education (RTE) Act, 2009 coming into force w.e.f. 1 April 2010, all children in school going age (five to fourteen) should go to school and no child should be pushed involuntarily to work;
- Children working as domestic help should be withdrawn from the said work;
- Local self-governing bodies should identify, rescue/ release such children and ensure that they get proper education;
- Observance of correct methodology will be crucial to the successful conducting of a survey for identification of victims of bonded labour system;
- The guidelines laid down by SR Sankaran on the methodology of such identification may be followed by all States/UTs with suitable modification to suit local conditions;
- Requirement of funds for rehabilitation of all freed bonded labourers should be assessed by all States/UTs;
- Steps may be taken by GOI to enhance the rehabilitation package from the present limit of ₹20,000 (w.e.f 1 May 2000);
- All DMs should exercise their powers as laid down in Section 10, 11 and 12 of BLS (A) Act with due diligence, empathy and sensitivity;
- All State Governments/UTs and DMs should pay particular attention to a proper and effective implementation of the following laws:
    - Minimum Wages Act;
    - Employees' Compensation Act;

- Child Labour (Prohibition and Regulation) Act.

- All local self-governing bodies should report to the DMs if they come across any incidence of bonded labour system and the DM should take appropriate follow up action on such report.
- The States of AP, WB, Jharkhand, Bihar and NCT of Delhi are directed to ensure compliance with the orders passed by NHRC as highlighted in its revised report to the apex court.

Question 46

What bearing does the SC&ST (Prevention of Atrocities) Act have on BLS (A) Act, 1976?

Answer: The SC&ST (Prevention of Atrocities) Act, 1989 was enacted with a view to preventing the commission of offences of atrocities against the members of SC&ST and to establish Special Courts for the trial of such offences as also for providing relief and rehabilitation of the victims of such offences.

The joint survey which was conducted by Gandhi Peace Foundation and VV Giri National Labour Institute in November 1978 had come to a finding that 84 per cent of the bonded labourers surveyed in ten major Indian States belonged to SC&ST.

From this it is evident that any law dealing with problems of SC&ST will have a bearing on their unfree status.

This is confirmed from a bare reading of S3(h) of SC&ST (Prevention of Atrocities) Act, 1989 as amended in 2015:

> Whoever not being a member of a SC or ST makes a member of a SC or ST to do *begar* or other forms of forced or bonded labour other than compulsory service for public purposes imposed by the Government, shall be punishable with imprisonment for a term which shall not be less than six months but which may extend to five years and with fine.

This is a cognisable but non-bailable offence (S438 of CrPC is not applicable).

The offence may be tried by a Special Court/Exclusive Special Court (S.14).

The Act was comprehensively reviewed in 2014 through wide consultation with all stakeholders keeping the following in the backdrop:

- Despite deterrent provisions in the Act, the atrocities against members of SC/ST continue to grow at a disturbing level;
- It was difficult to ensure adequate justice to the victims and the witnesses as they encountered hurdles at every stage of the legal process;
- The implementation of the Act suffered due to (a) procedural hurdles such as non-registration of cases; (b) delay in investigation, arrests and filing of charge sheets; and (c) delay in trial and low conviction rate.

The Act was eventually comprehensively amended in 2015 (Act I of 2016). Among other amendment provisions, setting up of 'Exclusive Special Courts' in addition to Special Courts for trial of offences of atrocities against members of SC/ST was a refreshingly welcome one.

Despite such a progressive amendment, it is regrettable to note that the Supreme Court in its order dated 20 March 2018 had directed the following:

- No arrests under the Act could be made without prior permission;
- Prior permission is to be obtained from the appropriate authority in case of public servants and from the SSP for others;
- A preliminary enquiry should be conducted before registration of FIR.

The above decision of the apex court witnessed countrywide agitations and protests. Review petitions were filed against the above decision. It is refreshing to note that the earlier decision has been recalled by a larger Constitution bench comprising Justices Arun Mishra, MR Shah and BR Gavai on 1 October 2019.

The pith and substance of the directions/observations of the Division Bench are as under:

Fundamental objections to the earlier decision of the apex court:

- Permission of appropriate authority to arrest a public servant is not at all statutorily envisaged;
- It is encroachment on a field which is reserved for the legislature;
- The earlier direction (of the apex court) amounts to a mandate having legislative colour which is a field not earmarked for the Courts;
- The earlier direction (of the apex court) is discriminatory and would cause several legal complications.

Procedural objections to the earlier decision of the Supreme Court:

- There is no provision in the Code of Criminal Procedure (CrPc) or SC & ST (Prevention of Atrocities) Act for a preliminary enquiry;
- Procedurally speaking, according to the earlier decision of the apex court, even if a complaint made out a cognisable offence, a FIR would not be registered until the preliminary enquiry is held; this is uncalled for;
- On account of such a conditionality imposed (by the earlier decision of the apex court) neither the investigation nor the trial can be completed within the specified time;

- Such delay would be adding further to the plight of the downtrodden class.

The latest judgment of the apex court dated 1 October 2019 comes like a breath of fresh air and provides justice and relief to 200+ million members of the SC and 100+million members of the ST. It has tellingly brought out the plight and predicament of members of these communities in the following words:

> As to the prevailing conditions in various areas of the country, we are compelled to observe that SCs/STs are still making a struggle for equality and for exercising civil rights…The members…are still discriminated against in various parts of the country. In spite of reservation, the fruits of development have not reached them, by and large, they remain an unequal and vulnerable section of the society…They have been suffering ignominy and abuse and they have been outcastes socially for centuries. The efforts for their upliftment should have percolated down to eradicate their suffering.

Further, the apex court lamented:

> We have not been able to provide the downtrodden class fundamental civil rights and amenities, frugal comforts of life which make life worth living…
>
> They do labour, bonded or forced, in agricultural fields which is not abrogated in spite of efforts. In certain areas, women are not treated with dignity and honour and are sexually abused in various forms. We see sewer workers dying due to poisonous gases…We have not been able to provide masks and oxygen cylinders. We cannot leave them to die like this and avoid tortious liability concerned with officials/machinery…
>
> They are still discriminated within the society in the matter of enjoying their civil rights.

The apex court made the following observations on its earlier decision/direction:

> We do not doubt that the (earlier) directions encroach upon the field reserved for the legislature and are against the concept of protective discrimination in favour of the down-trodden classes under Article 15(4) of the Constitution and also impermissable within the parameters laid down by this Court for exercise of powers under Article 142 of the Constitution of India.

The apex court ruled that historically disadvantaged groups must be given special protection so that they can be uplifted from their poverty and social condition.

Thus the latest judgment of the apex court dated 1 October 2019 is fully in tune with the laudable intentions of the framers of the SC&ST (Prevention of Attrocity) Act, 1989 as amended in 2015. By striking down its own decision/direction of March 2018 and reinforcing the need to adopt a positive, pro-active and constructive approach to interpretation of the law, it has injected a lot of hope, faith and conviction in the hearts of millions of members of withered and forlorn Dalit and ST communities. This will undoubtedly provide relief to the members of SC/ST, a sizeable percentage of whom work as victims of BLS.

Question 47

What are the lessons to be learnt from numerous judgments of the apex court?

Answer: Between 1981 and 2012 (when the last judgment of the apex court was pronounced on 15 October 2012) as many as twenty-six judgments have been pronounced by the apex court with numerous directions.

In addition to providing a broad, liberal and expansive interpretation of the provisions of BLS (A) Act which has come like a breath of fresh air, the judgments involved interpretation of the following labour laws such as:

- Payment of Wages Act, 1936;
- Minimum Wages Act, 1948;
- Contract Labour (Regulation and Abolition)Act, 1970;
- Inter-State Migrant Workmen (Regulation of Employment and Conditions of Service) Act, 1979;
- Building and other Construction Workers (Regulation of Employment and Conditions of Service) Act, 1996;
- Child Labour (Prohibition and Regulation) Act, 1986 as amended in 2016;
- SC & ST (Prevention of Atrocities) Act, 1989 as amended in 2015.

The judgments of the apex court were pronounced in the wake of filing of WPs on behalf of aggrieved persons. These WPs were filed under Article 32 of the Constitution seeking legal remedies against non-enforcement of specific provisions of law.

Directions contained in the judgments may be divided into the following categories:

- Creation of institutional mechanisms (VCs);
- Not to do certain things (not to deduct from wages unless authorised by law, not to go in for piece-rate work and piece-rate wages, not to engage persons as contract labour as a matter of course, not to push children involuntarily to work, not to ask victims of BLS to depose evidence in the witness box, not to insist on refund of extinguished debt, not to deny the workmen their just and fair entitlements including minimum wages, employees' compensation, journey allowance, displacement allowance and

wages during journey period for inter-State migrant workmen);

- Provision of specific relief to aggrieved workmen with immediate effect;
- Monitoring, supervision and coordination to ensure that
  (a) Right things are done in right time in right manner.
  (b) Directions of the Court and recommendations of NHRC are complied with in letter and spirit without ifs and buts.

PILs and directions of the apex court were necessitated as State Governments/UTs and district administrations were not carrying out duties and responsibilities assigned to them under the law (like constituting and re-constituting VCs whenever and wherever due).

Directions of the apex court were also necessitated as law enforcement authorities often evade and circumvent provisions of the law with a number of alibis and pretexts. They never acknowledge their mistakes, acts of omission and failure even though such acknowledgement with humility could lead to instant correction of mistakes. They comply only when directed by the apex court or the NHRC to do certain things which are mandated for them both under the Constitution and the law. The apex court had to remind them again and again about the mandate assigned to them by the Constitution and the law.

It is indeed ironical that while laxity, inaction, lack of interest and commitment, evasion and circumvention of the law and negligence in discharge of statutory duties and responsibilities were responsible for filing of PIL and entertainment of the same as a WP, the directions of the apex court at the end of the disposal of PIL were remitted to the very same law enforcement machinery whose callousness and insensitivity had necessitated filing of the WP.

This makes honest, transparent and meaningful compliance with the directions of the Court extremely difficult. Such non-compliance invites contempt of court petitions. Disposal of such petitions is time consuming. Even if they are disposed of in time and strictures are issued against the non-complying statutory authorities, it does not create the desired impact. More than anything else, it does not provide any relief to the aggrieved victim who has been waiting for justice and relief for a long period.

Some officers are thick-skinned; they do not get unduly worried about the directions issued by the apex court. It is time that they think, reflect, critically analyse and ask the following questions to themselves:

I. Why is that they dither and vacillate in attending to their Constitutional and legal mandate normally, naturally and spontaneously?

II. Does such evasion and circumvention add to their standing and reputation?

III. If not, why should they not resolve to do what they are mandated to perform without ifs and buts under the Constitution and the law, honestly, sincerely and diligently?

Question 48

What are the implications of the orders of the apex court dated 11 November 1997 entrusting NHRC with the responsibility of monitoring and overseeing the implementation of its directions as well as provisions of BLS (A) Act?

Answer: Monitoring has the following implications:

- Visits to different States/UTs for an on-the-spot inspection/ review of what is being done by the State/UT concerned to implement the statutory provisions as also to comply with the directions of the apex court and submit a detailed report to the Commission;

- The report submitted by the reviewing officer to the Commission is to be considered, approved by the latter if it is in order, and sent to the concerned State Government/UT for submission of an ATR;
- Scrutinising the ATR and assessing the extent to which directions of the apex court and recommendations of NHRC have been complied with;
- Deputing teams of officials from the Commission to investigate into specific complaints received from the victims of BLS or NGOs or anyone on their behalf with a prayer for providing timely relief;
- The Commission on consideration of the report of the investigating officer should issue necessary directions to the State Government for grant of relief to the aggrieved;
- Holding workshops at the national, regional, State, divisional and district level for familiarisation and sensitisation of the officers of concerned departments of the State Governments/UT, DMs, ADMs, SDMs, all other Executive Magistrates and members of VCs;
- Getting studies on elimination of BLS carried out by institutes of social science and research of repute and standing and initiating follow-up action there on;
- Bringing out publications on elimination of BLS, trafficking and child labour (like Manual on Human Rights for use of DMs) as one of the worst violations of human rights;
- Maintaining constant liaison and coordination with the Ministry of Labour for (a) review and revision of centrally sponsored scheme/central scheme as the case may be (b) bringing about amendments to BLS (A) Act and Rules framed thereunder (c) for

better implementation of the law and compliance with directions of the apex court issued thereon from time to time;

- Drawing the personal attention of the CMs of States/UTs at the level of the Chairperson of the Commission concerned to (a) expedite reports of inquiry on complaints which are forwarded by the NHRC to State Governments/DMs concerned (b) expedite disposal of cases pending with the Executive Magistrates who have been vested with powers of Judicial Magistrates, first or second class. (c) constitution and re-constitution of VCs in conformity with the provisions of Section 13 and making them optimally functional under S14 by provision of necessary logistic and budgetary support. (d) conducting fresh surveys for identification of victims of BLS (e) establishing simultaneity between release and rehabilitation (f) paying special attention to the issue of rescue/release, repatriation and rehabilitation of inter-State migrant workmen who have been found working under bonded conditions (g) accelerating the process of rehabilitation of those who have been waiting for rehabilitation for a long time. Such a letter was addressed demi-officially to CMs of all States/Lt Governors of all UTs by Justice (Dr) AS Anand, then Chairperson of the Commission on 12 September 2006.

Question 49

How has the Commission proceeded in complying with the directions of the apex court?

Answer: On the date of pronouncement of the interim order in *PUCL Vs State of TN and Others,*[52] Justice MN Venkatachaliah was the Chairperson of the NHRC. Soon after, he convened a

52 WP 3922/85

meeting of senior civil servants like D Bandyopadhyay, BD Sharma, PS Krishnan, SR Shankaran, KR Venugopal, Anil Bordia, BN Yugandhar, NC Saxena and others. A comprehensive background paper on the subject prepared on the request of the Chairperson of the Commission by the author, then Union Labour Secretary, formed the basis of discussion. A blueprint to translate the mandate of the Commission as entrusted to it by the apex court to concrete action was put in place with the following components:

1. A format in which half-yearly progress reports on the extent of compliance by the State governments with the directions of the apex court and provisions of BLS (A) Act was designed and approved by the Commission.
2. A calendar of training programme for familiarisation and sensitisation of officers/agencies concerned with implementation of statutory provisions was drawn up.
3. A calendar of holding workshops at the national, State, divisional, and district levels for better awareness generation of all stakeholders was drawn up.
4. A calendar of visits to different States and UTs by Chairperson/ Member-in-charge of bonded labour, Special Rapporteurs/ Officers of the Commission for an in-depth review of the pace and progress of implementation of the directions of the apex court and provisions of BLS (A) Act was drawn up.
5. Computerisation of all complaints relating to enforcement of provisions of BLS (A) Act and chalking out a plan for investigation into and disposal of all complaints was to be attended to and accomplished as a measure of high priority; the central computer unit of the Commission is required to act as a watchdog on receipt/registration, processing, investigation and disposal of

all complaints on the basis of the investigation report, a tool of information, storage and sharing as also monitoring the pace and progress of implementation of statutory provisions and the compliance with the directions of the apex court.

S Muralidhar, then an advocate and currently a Delhi High Court Judge, played a memorable role in carrying these initiatives to their logical close.

The author, in his capacity as Union Labour Secretary, was actively involved in the entire process till the monitoring and reporting mechanisms were put in place.

Question 50

What has been the outcome of these initiatives and efforts?

Answer

1. Between 7 October 2004 till date, the Chairperson, Member-in-charge of bonded labour and Special Rapporteurs have undertaken visits to major States like Andhra Pradesh, Bihar, Chhattisgarh, Gujarat, Haryana, Himachal Pradesh, Jharkhand, Karnataka, Kerala, Madhya Pradesh, Maharashtra, Odisha, Punjab, Rajasthan, Tamil Nadu, Uttar Pradesh and Uttarakhand for an in-depth review of the pace and progress of implementation of various provisions of BLS (A) Act and compliance with various directions issued by the apex court and submitted over a hundred fact-finding review reports to the Commission.
2. Elimination of BLS was incorporated as one of the chapters in Human Rights Manual for DMs which is being used for training extensively since 2008, when it was brought out. The author, when he was Senior Advisor, ILO at the relevant time, had contributed a write-up on bonded labour on the request of

LBSNAA Mussourie, which had been drafted by the Commission to compile the manual.

3. Bonded labour and its elimination is also one of the topics for the orientation and training of interns (LLBs, LLMs drawn from different National Law Universities and other Institutions). So far thirty-nine such training programmes for interns have been conducted. The author has been a regular guest speaker on the subject of bonded labour since 2006.
4. Deputy Commissioners of selected States like Punjab (seventeen) and Haryana (fourteen) have been invited and given intensive training on BLS and its elimination at the headquarters of the Commission. The training workshop was conducted by the author on the direction of then Chairperson Justice S Rajendra Babu.
5. Fifty workshops have been held at the national, State, zonal, divisional and district headquarters for familiarisation and sensitisation of all stakeholders with the provisions of the law as also judgments of the apex court. The author has been fully involved in conceptualisation and organisation of a number of these workshops between 2006 and 2011.
6. A DG (of the rank of DG Police at the State level) has been put in overall charge of investigation into complaints as also offences. He is assisted by one DIG, three SSPs, eight DSPs, and twenty Inspectors.
7. NHRC has developed Human Rights Commissions Network.[53] The said portal can be used by the State Human Rights Commissions (25) for online complaints lodging /tracking system and handling of complaints received offline i.e. by hand, post, etc.

   (ii) NHRC net portal is enabling the Commission in timely and efficient handling of complaints for many years. The

53 NHRC net portal https://www.nhrcnet.nic.in)

software has been useful in processing complaints at every stage such as diarisation, registration, entry in the relevant case file for commencement of processing at the appropriate level in the Commission. The software will also assist all other Human Rights Commissions in the country in handling all registered complaints in a timely and efficient manner.

(iii) The Commission has conducted several workshops to get the State Commissions on board on the NHRC Netportal. Of the total 25 State Commissions, 18 are already on board the NHRC Netportal. The Commission is making persistent efforts for on-boarding of the remaining State Commissions so that they can take advantage of the linkage particularly with reference to duplicate checking of complaints received in the National and State Commissions.

This procedure has assumed relevance in view of the following amendment in S13(6) of the Protection of Human Rights Act, 1993 as amended (Act 43 of 2006) which reads as under:

> Where the Commission considers it necessary or expedient so to do, it may, by order, transfer any complaint filed or pending before it to the State Commissions of the State from which the complaint arises, for disposal in accordance with the provisions of the Act provided that no such complaint shall be transferred unless the same is one respecting which the State Commission has jurisdiction to entertain the same.

(iv) The State Nodal officers of human rights (civil and police) can see the details of pending complaints, details of the incidents which occasioned the complaints and orders passed by the National Commission; they can also upload the report to be submitted to the latter.

(v) Between 12 October 1993 (when NHRC was founded) and 15 December 2019, a total number of 18,77,773 cases were registered and 18,56,061 cases were disposed-of, leaving 21,712 cases pending. Of 18,77,773 cases, 1,58,439 cases have been transferred to SHRCs. A total monetary relief amounting to ₹17,85,488,668 in 6716 cases has been awarded by the Commission.

Of the total no. of 18;77,773 complaints since inception, 15,462 relate to bonded labour. Of these, 14387 cases have been disposed leaving 75 cases pending.

The existing system suffers from the following gaps, omissions and deficiencies as far as complaints relating to forced/bonded labour are concerned. These are:

- Under Criminal Law (Amendment) Act, 2013 amending S370 of IPC w.e.f. 2 April 2013, trafficking in human beings can be for forced/bonded labour as one of the objects/intentions. Such complaints cannot be entertained at present as no separate code has been allotted for this purpose;
- While bonded labour constitutes the main head for which a code has been allotted (601), there may be a number of sub-heads or sub-components relating to complaints received under the main head such as:
  - non-payment of wages;
  - non-payment of notified minimum wages;
  - non-payment of nominal wages;
  - unauthorised deduction of amount from the wage, for whatever purpose, like payment of commission to middlemen;
  - denial of free movement of the person bonded from one part of the territory of India to another;

    - denial of search for alternative employer or alternative avenues of employment/livelihood;
    - denial of price of labour or price for the produce of labour.
- Similar break-up should also be available in regard to no. of complaints disposed-of and pending.
- It may be noted that every statistical database constitutes a tool of planning and meaningful corrective action. No such planning for action will be possible if there is no detailed analysis of the various components and sub-components of a database.
- To illustrate, like trafficking in human beings taking place for forced/bonded labour as one of the objects, migration and in particular, distress migration could also, in all probability and possibility, land the migrant in a situation of bondage. The present database does not indicate if there have been such cases where migration has led to bondage. In any case, no separate code has been allotted to either trafficking or migration-related bondage.
- Such indication would have been useful for taking both preventive and corrective action.

It was encouraging to note that the SG is monitoring at his level all pending complaints (including bonded labour complaints) and taking appropriate corrective action reduce the no of pending complains through timely follow up.

On the basis of State-level reviews conducted and feedback as well as ATR received from different States, the overall impressions/observations on the performance of States/UTs in relation to BLS (A) Act may be summed up as under:

Andhra Pradesh (October 2006)

Late SR Sankaran, Principal Secretary, Social Welfare,

Government of AP during 1975-77 made yeoman contribution to identification, rescue/release and rehabilitation of freed bonded labourers. He had set the pace and tone of identification of victims of BLS by conceptualising and issuing a comprehensive circular to all the DMs of twenty-three districts of undivided Andhra Pradesh which was remarkable in terms of its imagination, perception, insight, grass roots-level realism and sensitivity. Regretfully, the programme of rescue/release and rehabilitation suffered a terrible setback after he was sent to Tripura as Chief Secretary in 1978 and many grey areas in operationalisation of the programme cropped up, such as:

- Meetings of VCs became infrequent;
- Fresh surveys were not conducted for identification of victims of BLS;
- Even if conducted (though sparingly), VCs were not being involved in the survey although it is their primary statutory responsibility;
- Meetings of VCs started taking place in closed chambers; they seldom went to the field to conduct survey/inquiries;
- Sufficient orientation was not imparted to all members of VCs at the district and sub-divisional level;
- The rate of success in individual beneficiary-oriented programmes dropped on account of the socio-cultural background of the beneficiaries, absence of adequate guidance and back-up support, inability to stand up to the problems of management of assets and finances and inability to withstand the machinations and sometimes organised onslaught of the erstwhile bonded labour keepers;
- Inter-State migrant workmen (both to and out of AP), continued to be recruited without licence and registration certificate; most of such recruitment was due to distress conditions;

- No institutional mechanism for ventilation and redressal of grievances of these workmen either at the source or destination point has been put in place;
- Sensitisation workshops at the district, block and panchayat levels as decided at the State-level workshop held at Hyderabad on 17-18 October 2006 are yet to be organised; (the workshop anchored by the author had been graced by then Andhra Pradesh Chief Minister, late YS Rajasekhara Reddy);
- Trafficking of girls from Cuddapah, Chenchus of Mehboobnagar and Lambadas who are spread over in various pockets of the State for commercial sexual exploitation continues unabated; no strategy to deal with this social menace is in sight.

An Action Plan for elimination of child labour drafted by the author on the request of the State Government has been put in place since 2011-12 but there is no Action Plan on elimination of BLS.

Tamil Nadu (November 2006):

In the years 1975-76, Anjani Dayanand, Principal Secretary, Social Welfare, had provided excellent leadership and direction to the programme of rescue/release and rehabilitation of freed bonded labourers. In late 1990s, a full-fledged department, i.e., Adi Dravidar Department was put in charge of the programme with a full-time Special officer – PWC Davidar of the IAS. During 2000-03, he established excellent co-ordination and liaison with a number of committed NGOs active in the field of social action. In March 2005, he had brought out an excellent handbook /manual on release and rehabilitation of bonded labourers for guidance of all field functionaires. A State-level Action Plan for elimination of BLS has also subsequently been put in place. The Plan was jointly prepared by IJM Office, Chennai and the author and is reported to be under implementation.

Regretfully, a number of grey areas had also cropped up in implementation of the programme:

- Of the 38,678 persons identified as victims of BLS through survey conducted by the district administration all over the State in 1996-97, as many as 25,503 cases were dropped without any ostensible reason;
- The remaining 13,175 persons are reported to be not yet fully rehabilitated;
- Release Certificates were being issued in English and not in the language spoken by or intelligible to the victim;
- The penalties imposed by the trying Magistrates do not correspond to the provisions of the law and are not proportional to the severity of the crime which is contrary to the direction issued by the apex court;
- Content, quality and impact of rehabilitation of freed bonded labourers have not been evaluated so far, without which it is difficult to have a correct assessment of the current status of bonded labourers who are supposed to have been rehabilitated;
- The erstwhile bonded labour keepers continue to nurse a grievance against the released bonded labourers; they remain hostile to the rehabilitation efforts being made by the district administration; To illustrate, during the visit of Member, NHRC in-charge of bonded labour Justice Y Bhaskar Rao and the author to Kanchipuram in November 2006, it transpired that owners of brick kilns had set fire to a truck which was purchased by availing financial assistance from the Kanchipuram DM and was owned by the co-operative society formed by released bonded labourers (ex-workers of the brick kiln). It transpired that the owner nursed a grudge against the district administration and workers for loss

of cheap labour as a result of rescue and release of the victims;
- Doubts continue to be expressed over implications of the judgments of the apex court like denial of minimum wage would bring a person within the ambit of forced labour and would be an infringement of Article 23 of the Constitution.

Haryana (November 2006)

Government of Haryana has failed to comply with the twenty-one directions of the apex court issued on 16 December 1983 while disposing of WP 2135 of 1982 as would be evident from the following:
- The practice of payment of commission to middle-men (Jamadar) is being encouraged in brick kilns and tile manufacturing units,[54]
- No information is available if VCs are going out to the field to conduct surveys/ inquiries;
- The functioning of VCs has not received due attention of the State-level Committee (which is in place); there is no purposive and meaningful monitoring of the performance of VCs;
- DMs are yet to map out areas of concentration of bonded labourers which are to be found mostly in stone quarries and brick kilns;
- No camps seem to have been organised in these sensitive areas with concentration of potential bonded labourers for promoting the awareness of the latter about labour laws;
- The competent authority did not issue release certificates on its own in favour of identified bonded labourers;
- The competent authority often prevaricates. Issue of release certificate in favour of 103 bonded labourers in Charkhi Dadri in

54 Notification 3/101/84-3 dated 12 June 2003 issued by Labour Department, Government of Haryana

Bhiwani district (an independent district since November 2016) was initially refused by the recalcitrant Magistrate. He eventually complied due to timely intervention of NHRC;

- Workers were recruited from Latehar (now a part of Jharkhand State), Nawada and Lakhisarai districts of un-divided Bihar to work in the brick kilns of Haryana but there is no evidence if the same is taking place on the strength of either a licence u/s 8 or grant of registration certificate under S4 of ISMW (ROE&COS) Act;
- Such recruitment of workmen is patently illegal.

The entire process of adjustment of advances paid by the recruiting agents to the inter-State migrant workmen with minimum wages payable to them is not transparent; it is not shared with the workmen concerned.

The conditions under which loans are advanced initially at the time of recruitment and subsequently after the workmen have landed at the destination point eventually leads to a situation where a migrant worker falls into the trap of debt-bondage;

There is large-scale incidence of attached agricultural labour which has all the ingredients of debt bondage as defined in S2(g) of BLS (A) Act; regretfully, this is neither acknowledged either by the landlord or by the law enforcement agency.

Odisha (December 2007)

Families from KBK region are being illegally drafted to work outside the State under oppressive and exploitative conditions. The problems of women and children accompanying migrant male adult members are harrowing, to say the least, which has not received adequate attention of either the source or destination State.

The last survey for identification of BLS in Odisha was

conducted in 2001-02 in ten out of thirty districts. Not a single bonded labourer was identified in any district other than Malkangiri. Even in Malkangiri, where 701 bonded labourers were identified, all but nineteen cases were dropped on unjustified grounds, making the entire exercise infructuous.

BLS is the outcome of an inegalitarian social structure, inhospitable terrain, large family size (5-10 in tribal areas), low-end poverty and huge gap between earning and expenditure in ceremonies as also day-to-day life leading to indebtedness and bondage. Its eradication calls for radical interventionist strategies which have not been put in place.

A number of loopholes have been found in implementation of MGNREGA Programme: manipulation of muster roll by inserting fictitious names, work being executed through contractors, serious problems in making timely payment of wages and, in particular, payment of minimum wage notified by the appropriate government; these have not been addressed since inception (February 2006).

There is no mechanism for ventilation and redressal of grievances at any level for the aggrieved.

Officers of development departments suffer from peculiar mindsets in acknowledging existence of BLS and taking timely action for its eradication. There is no social communication between officers of the department concerned and the beneficiaries with a view to making them active participants of the development process. This leads to total alienation of the victims.

Even though induced migration and human trafficking are associated with horrors of exploitation and most of those who migrate or are being trafficked would come within the purview of forced/ bonded labour, not a single case has been treated so far as such.

The story of rehabilitation of freed bonded labourers after the 1990s is one of dismal failure, necessitating a second dose of financial assistance. Most of the productive assets distributed to the beneficiaries in 1997-98 have perished. There is no other ostensible means of livelihood for landless beneficiaries other than working on somebody else's land.

There is no accurate and up-to-date database on the current status of persons who have been identified as victims of BLS in another State and repatriated to Odisha for rehabilitation. Minimum rates of wages (both time rate and piece rate) notified by the State Government under MW Act are quite low compared to other States and are not being enforced.

There is no State-level Committee to monitor the quality of rehabilitation in terms of its impact on employment, livelihood, income and quality of life. The whole issue of simultaneous release and rehabilitation and maintaining vigilance over employment, livelihood, income and quality of life of freed bonded labour beneficiaries as emphasised by the apex court from time to time has not received the prioritised attention of the State Government which it deserved.

No Action Plan/Perspective Plan for the elimination of BLS has been put in place even though an Action Plan for elimination of child labour initially drafted by the author (2007-08) is currently under implementation.

Madhya Pradesh (January 2007)

No Action Plan/Perspective Plan for elimination of BLS or child labour has yet been put in place.

The *harwah* system or the system of attached agricultural labour has all the ingredients of BLS but is not acknowledged as such. No fresh surveys have been undertaken for identification of the victims of BLS. Neither have guidelines formulated by SR Sanakaran been adopted with modification to suit local conditions nor has any other guideline been put in place.

Majority of the members of the VCs at Vidisha were found in January 2007 in course of a field visit by the author as Special Rapporteur, NHRC to have been drawn from the trading community who donot qualify to be members of a VC u/s 19 of BLS(A) Act. It is unclear as to how they have found their way to the VC.

No orientation has been imparted to the field functionaries of Revenue, Labour, Health, Education, SC/ST Welfare and other concerned departments of the State Government even though their services are being utilised for identification of victims.

Inter-State migration occurs both from MP to outside States as also into MP from the States of UP, Bihar and Chhattisgarh. The details are:

- From UP: 92
- From Bihar: 70
- From Chhattisgarh: 167

They have been identified, released from bondage and sent back to the States they came from. No information is available as to whether they have been rehabilitated or not. This would require liaison and co-ordination with the States of UP, Bihar and Chhattisgarh.

Similarly, 270 labourers have been identified as bonded labourers, released from bondage and brought back to MP for rehabilitation. No information is available on the current status of rehabilitation of these persons.

There is no State-level committee to monitor such progress in rehabilitation as also evaluation of its impact on income, livelihood and quality of life of the beneficiaries. No screening committee has yet been constituted either at the State or at the district level to screen proposals for rehabilitation of freed bonded labourers.

Registers containing the names and addresses of all freed bonded labourers, avocation/occupation and income of every freed bonded labourer and details of benefits which they have been receiving from the government under different schemes are either not maintained as required under Rule 7 of BLS (A) Rules or a clear picture about the current economic status of freed bonded labourers is not available.

The dilemma faced by the freed bonded labour beneficiaries belonging to the ST community is two-fold. On the one hand, they have large families (average family size is 5-10) with few or no earning members with a number of additional mouths to feed and attendant liabilities of employment on land or otherwise for which they are forced to migrate.

Children accompanying adult parents are involuntarily pushed to work at the destination point and remain the worst victims of both forced labour and educational deprivation. Neither the originating nor the destination State has any strategy for rescue/release, repatriation, rehabilitation and reintegration of these children through education, health check-up, nutrition, psychological counselling and skill training.

There is no mechanism for ventilation and redressal of grievances of these workmen at any level (State, Revenue Division, District, Taluka, Block, GP).

Rajasthan (February 2007)

No Action Plan/Perspective Plan for elimination of BLS has yet been put in place.

Sagri system in Rajasthan is one of the worst manifestations of usury with attendant exploitation of Bhil tribes inhabiting in Chittorgarh, Dungarpur, Banswada, Sirohi and Udaipur districts while Sahariya tribes in large number in similar conditions are to be found in Kota, Bundi and Baran districts. Sagri system was abolished by a State legislation called Sagri System (Abolition) Act, 1961 but it continued to persist.

Vigilance Committees have been bypassed in terms of their responsibility for conducting survey u/s 14(e) of BLS (A) Act. Instead, the responsibility for conducting survey has been entrusted to lower echelons of Revenue, Pachayati Raj and Education Department by a circular dated 4 February 2004 of the State Government.

There is no watch on the working and living conditions of people who were bonded labourers at one point of time, were released and rehabilitated but who have been leading a life of destitution and deprivation even thereafter.

A large number of bonded labourers belonging to Sahariya tribes in Baran district who were rehabilitated in 1975-77 are left today in a precarious condition where their children have grown up, have set up separate homes after marriage, leaving the elderly by the wayside. They deserve a second dose of rehabilitation assistance and the care, concern and consideration from a caring society and State.

The State Government in response to a questionnaire issued by NHRC has reported that 11,327 bonded labourers have been identified and released but did not indicate how many have been rehabilitated, how many are left to be rehabilitated, how many might have lapsed back to erstwhile bondage, whether there is any need for a second dose of financial assistance to prevent them from lapsing back to bondage and so on.

In a district like Bundi, *hali*—a system of attached agricultural labour which is a variant of BLS—is prevalent, but the district administration has not made any effort to identify the victims as such.

There is incidence of both inter-district and inter-State migration in Rajasthan. In either case, it is imperative that surveys are conducted by the district administration to ascertain if the workmen in Rajasthan or outside States are unfree.

The State Government and district administration should simultaneously make a thorough assessment of (a) extent of landlessness (b) stability and durability of avenues of employment (c) adequacy and timeliness of payment of wages principally in cash (d) sustainability of livelihood (e) gap between income and expenditure (f) how to bridge the gap with a view to pre-empting the possibility of occurrence/ recurrence of future debt bondage.

In the unorganised farm sector in general and in dry, drought-prone and desert areas--Barmer, Jaisalmer, Jalore, Sikar, Jhunjhunu, Bikaner and Jodhpur in particular--non-payment and untimely payment of wages to labourers who struggle to make both ends meet is a cause for genuine concern. A special drive to ensure timely payment of notified minimum wages principally in cash requires to be launched.

The Public Distribution System (PDS) should be revamped and managed effectively so as to enable and facilitate farm wage labourers to meet their primary consumption needs from the fair price shops with the wages earned by them.

Food grain banks in tribal areas on the same pattern as in Maharashtra and Odisha may be thought of as a primary means of promoting thrift, reducing dependence on the market and ensuring food security during lean season.

Functional literacy and numeracy should be imparted to freed bonded labourers belonging to ST Community, in particular, through opening adult literacy centres at such places where the Bhils and Sahariyas live. For this, bilingual literacy may be adopted as the principal strategy (imparting instructional lessons in the spoken dialect, to start with, and switch over after 50 per cent of the lessons have been transacted, to the State standard language). Rajasthan has a strong infrastructure in adult literacy programme through Adult Education Associations at the district level in a number of districts dating back to the 1950s and the same could be fruitfully harnessed for this purpose.

Similar initiative should be taken to mobilise and organise all freed bonded labourers and their able-bodied adult family members who are wage earners into SHGs. Vocational skill training programmes should be conducted for members of SHGs and a corpus should be formed so that some of the emergent needs could be met from out of that corpus without turning to moneylenders.

Karnataka (May 2007)

An Action Plan for elimination of forced/bonded labour is in place.The Action Plan was formulated by the State Government in collaboration with Vimukti Trust, a Bangalore-based NGO with a track record of dedicated service to the cause of elimination of BLS for more than two decades. The latter has also collaborated with the State Government in a meaningful manner in specific fields like training of functionaries.

In two years after 25 October 1975 when BLS (A) Act was given effect, the largest number of bonded labourers (60,000+) in the whole country were identified, rescued and released. The same momentum, however, was not maintained in the 1980s and there was no significant addition after the crucial 1975-77 phase.

There was also an avoidable large gap between the number of bonded labourers identified and released and those rehabilitated. In June 2000, BLS in one of its worst forms surfaced when Karnataka Rayat Sangha brought to the notice of NHRC that forty-five stone quarry workers in Hangarhalli in Mandya district were kept in chains under in-human conditions. They were subjected to gruelling manual labour over long hours and had no freedom to leave the workplace. They had to drag themselves in chains to take their food and water as also to ease themselves. Two of the bonded labourers who were recently married (before they started working) were deprived of conjugal pleasure as they were in chains. It is a matter of deep regret and concern that after protracted litigation all the accused and their accomplices were acquitted by Karnataka High Court in January 2017.

This incident had sent shock waves and as a result of re-survey ordered by the State Government throughout the State in 2000-01 and 2001-02, 2,177 bonded labourers were identified.

The State Government has conferred on all DMs the powers of Judicial Magistrate, First Class for trial of all bonded labour offences u/s 21 of BLS (A) Act. Strangely enough and contrary to the spirit of the notification, the SDMs are trying these offences.

Perusal of orders passed by SDM, Davangere in a case pertaining to Hanumath Manjunath is devoid of merit and is contrary to the spirit of multiple judgments of the apex court.[55] The order provides unmerited and uncalled for relief to the bonded labour keepers while instilling a psychosis of fear, anxiety and uncertainty in the minds of a few hapless and helpless child bonded labourers.

55 AIR SC 802 WP 2135 of 1982, AIR 1984 SC 1099 WP 1263 of 1982, AIR 1982 SC 1473 WP 8143 of 1981

It is a brazen transgression of the directions issued by the apex court which under Article 141 of the Constitution of India is binding on all subordinate courts.

Yet another bizarre case of such transgression was noticed in the case of Manjunath (19), son of Balaya, a landless agricultural labourer in Kudur Hobli of Magadi taluk in Bangalore rural district. A field visit by the author as Special Rapporteur of NHRC in May 2007 and interaction with the victim confirmed that it is a clear case of Section 2(g) of BLS (A) Act. Regretfully, neither any release certificate was issued by the Deputy Commissioner, Bangalore rural district after repeated prodding and goading nor any action initiated against the bonded labour keeper.

Even minimum wage notified by the Government of Karnataka was not paid to Manjunath and has not been paid till date for the period he worked with the landlord and the bonded labour keeper.

In Karnataka 63,886 bonded labourers are reported to have been identified and released, 57,316 bonded labourers rehabilitated as on 31 March 2006 leaving 8,570 bonded labourers for rehabilitation.

There is not much qualitative difference in the status of bonded labourers before and after rehabilitation.

Even after rehabilitation, they have large families, few earning members, wage employment is irregular and wages paid continue to be low. The average agricultural land holding ranges between half to two acres and the produce from land is not sufficient even for biological survival. This compels them to work on the land of others as agricultural labourers.

To make matters worse, there is a lot of antipathy from the land-owing community to provide employment to the freed bonded labourers.

Such antipathy is the natural outcome of criminal proceedings against erstwhile bonded labour keepers who continue to wield a lot of influence in a highly stratified social order where possession of land and access to natural resources determine the status of a person.

Statutory remedies are available for denial of minimum wage. Regretfully, the aggrieved on account of illiteracy are ignorant of the procedure for filing claims u/s 20(1) of Minimum Wages Act in the event of short payment or non-payment. No worthwhile measures have been taken by the State Government or law enforcement agencies for promoting legal literacy.

To make rehabilitation efforts meaningful and effective as also holistic, unstinted cooperation of officers of all development departments (Agriculture, Animal Husbandry and Veterinary, Education, Health, Women and Child Development) is absolutely necessary. These departments are generally indifferent and sometimes even insensitive to implementation of rehabilitation schemes in a holistic and integrated manner, defeating thereby the central objective of rehabilitation, i.e., making the beneficiaries as participants of the development process self-reliant or autonomous entities.

Jharkhand (March 2008)

No Action Plan/Perspective Plan for elimination of forced/bonded labour was put in place.

Harsh terrain and difficult agro-climatic conditions compounded by acidic character of the soil, its failure to retain water, lack of proper irrigation facilities, limited avenues of employment in agriculture, problems of maintaining livestock due to problems of growing fodder and low productivity of agriculture are some of the factors which have contributed to the phenomenon of debt bondage in most of the twenty-four districts in Jharkhand.

False notions of the poor about their own social status and taking recourse to loans/advances for ceremonial purposes also contribute to the age-old phenomenon of debt-bondage.

Absence of any worthwhile interventionist measure to address some of these factors decades after enactment of a law has further accentuated the social scourge.

VCs may have been technically constituted and may be meeting from time to time but they have not gone to the field for conducting a survey in a manner which would yield results.

There is no State-level committee to monitor and co-ordinate the functioning of VCs. The performance of VCs has not been reviewed even once by deputing a senior official from the State capital to the district headquarters.

No proper orientation has been provided to the members of VCs at the district and sub-divisional level.

A number of good and reliable NGOs committed to social action at the State, District, Sub-divisional, Block/Taluk and Panchayat level are in place. The apex court has also been repeatedly emphasising the need for involving them in elimination of BLS. Regretfully, they have seldom been approached either by the State Government or the district administration for enlisting their involvement and support in furtherance of a common objective like elimination of BLS.

A number of middlemen have been recruiting children surreptitiously and taking them out of Jharkhand by giving false promises. These promises are never kept and the children are reduced to the status of bonded labourers with long hours of work, denial of wage, physical and sexual abuse and torture. A mechanism should be put in place at the GP level to maintain 24x7 vigilance and surveillance over the movement and activity of such fly-by-night operators to recruit/traffic children for exploitation.

Teams of officers of Revenue, Labour and Police departments should be deputed by the State Government to those States where innocent children have been trafficked for exploitation, rescue, release and repatriate them back to Jharkhand for rehabilitation and re-integration.

In all, out of 218 bonded labourers identified, 206 have been rehabilitated and the whereabouts of the remaining twelve are not traceable.

There is no computerised database covering all the bonded labourers identified and released and no mechanism for tracking victims who remain untraced.

Registers required under Rule 7 of BLS (A) Rules have not been maintained and in the absence of these registers as well as a database, it is not possible to keep track of the whereabouts of freed bonded labourers.

The district and sub-divisional administration through the respective VCs have failed to maintain any contact with the rehabilitated labourers to ascertain (a) durability and stability of avenues of employment (b) extent of earnings (c) education of children of released bonded labourers (d) health and medical care of family members and themselves (e) skills which they have, new skills which they need to learn and skills which need upgradation (f) access to credit, technology and market and (g) how autonomous and self-sufficient are the beneficiaries of various anti-poverty or employment promotion programmes.

Group approach to rehabilitation of freed bonded labourers in preference to individual beneficiary-oriented approach has not yet been given a fair trial in Jharkhand.

Punjab (March 2008)

No Action Plan/Perspective Plan for elimination of BLS has yet been put in place.

Since inception of BLS (A) Act, the State Government has consistently taken a stand that (a) the problem is not as serious in Punjab as in some other States (b) there is a peculiar creditor-debtor relationship between agricultural farm houses/brick kiln establishments and labourers who have migrated from other States and who are working in these establishments.

There are over 5 lakh *seris* or attached agricultural labourers. They are working under conditions which are akin to BLS for the following reasons:

- They work in households, farmhouses and cattlesheds for an unspecified duration;
- They do not have any rest (spread-over) after specified hours, do not get weekly off (seven days wages for six days of work) and overtime wage at double the rate of ordinary wage for work in excess of scheduled working hours;
- The annual contractual wage is much less than the notified minimum wage for agriculture which is a scheduled employment;
- The adjustment process which takes place between advances paid and wages payable is not open and transparent;
- They cannot terminate the contract in the middle and go back to their village without fully liquidating the advance received.

About 75 per cent of workers employed in brick kilns of Punjab are inter-State migrant workmen hailing from UP, Rajasthan, Bihar and Haryana. Most of them have taken advances from recruiting agents to meet consumption and ceremonial needs, contingencies like family illness, paying back debt of moneylenders/landlords.

In addition to the advances, the workers keep on borrowing small amounts from their employers to defray day-to-day expenses for biological survival (after they have landed at the work site of the destination State).

The working and living conditions are poor and unsatisfactory. They live in ramshackle structures without electricity and water. They have to meet medical expenses from out of their own pocket. The nature of operations in a brick kiln (digging raw earth, sprinkling it with water to convert it to mud, carrying it to a wooden frame to make raw bricks, taking raw bricks out of the frame after water has evaporated, carrying raw bricks for drying in the hot sun, changing sides for even drying, carrying the dried bricks for burning in kilns, taking burnt bricks out for loading and transportation in trucks) being what they are, the workmen (men, women and children) are engaged perennially from six in the morning past midnight.

The wages which are payable mostly in piece-rates are calculated and adjusted against advances. If wages are to be viewed in relation to nine hours of normal work (time rate) per day, no worker in brick kiln industry can be said to have received even 50 per cent of the minimum wage of an un-skilled worker.

Inter-State migrant workmen who are recruited on payment of advances are likely to get into the status of victims of BLS (Section 2(g) of BLS (A) Act) for the following reasons:

- The wages received by them are invariably lower than notified minimum wages;
- They cannot leave the work site without fully liquidating advances, as they are told by the recruiting agents;
- In the absence of documentary evidence, they have no inkling about the wages earned by them which will eventually get adjusted

with the advances paid to them;

- The process of adjustment is neither open nor transparent.

The VCs at the district and sub-divisional level have been constituted but not in conformity with provisions of the law and guidelines issued by the apex court. They do not go to the field, do not identify pockets which are sensitive to debt bondage and do not conduct surveys to identify victims of debt bondage as is expected of them under S14(e) of BLS (A) Act.

No campaign for generating awareness of either the bonded labour keepers or the victims has been conducted about provisions of the law and judgments of Supreme Court. Consequently, a lot of doubts, misgivings and reservations continue to persist on the provisions of the law and procedure established by law.

State and District Legal Aid Authorities have been constituted for launching a dynamic and constructive legal service programme. This can help in building up Participatory Organisations of the Rural Poor (PORPs), a term coined by Prof Upendra Buxi, distinguished jurist and former VC, Delhi University.

As one travels from Chandigarh to Ludhiana to Jalandhar to Amritsar across the fertile Indo-Gangetic plain and raises queries, 'What is the status of BLS in your district?' one receives a cold and negative response, 'There is not a single bonded labourer in my district'. If one further queries, 'How do you know?', the typical response to this question is: 'We have not received any complaint from any quarter, far less from the bonded labourers themselves.'

Bonded labourers represent abject prostration of poverty; they are the poorest of the poor and weakest of the weak. They can ill afford to approach anyone to ventilate a genuine grievance, not to speak of filing a written complaint. Regretfully, 'We have not received any complaint' is the common refrain of the well-to-do, privileged and influential sections of the society who are at the peak of power, position, authority and influence. In such a milieu, where is the place for the bonded, whom Rabindranath Tagore described as 'dumb, mute and voiceless' (*Kadi and Komal*). This is the tragic reality on the ground.

Chhattisgarh (March 2008)

No Action Plan/Perspective Plan for elimination of BLS has been put in place.

Chhattisgarh has been prone to inter-State distress migration (Bilaspur, Raigad, Raipur, Rajnandgaon, Durg, Korba, Bastar, Jagdalpur, Mahasamund) and consequent misery and suffering which await them at the destination point.

While this is the ground-level reality, it is rather ironic that no precise and accurate demographic data about the trend, causes and consequences of migration have been kept at any level. There is at the same time no short or medium- or long-term strategy to minimise or prevent the incidence of distress migration which is one of the most potent factors to contribute to human bondage.

BLS in Chhattisgarh, like in MP, is known locally as *hali* and *harwah*. The State Government conducted a survey in 2003-04 but did not find a single bonded labourer.

Instead of engaging VCs to conduct survey for identification of victims of BLS, the State Government is engaging officers of Revenue, Rural Development and Social Welfare Departments. This is contrary to observations of Supreme Court in *Neerja Chaudhary Vs State of MP* judgment.

Labourers are going out of Chhattisgarh as well as coming into Chhattisgarh. Those who are going out of the State with the help of recruiting agents, do so on receipt of an advance from recruiting agents. No advance is paid without a price tag. The latter takes many vicious forms which may be termed as serious violations of human rights such as (a) unduly long hours of work (b) absence of any period of rest (spread over) (c) absence of weekly off (seven days wages for six days of work, the seventh day being a day of rest) (d) denial of overtime wages (e) non-payment or delayed payment of wage (f) unauthorised deduction from wages payable for payment of middlemen's commission in an arbitrary manner.

On a complaint from Jan Jagriti Kendra, one of the NGOs in Chhattisgardh alleging to NHRC distress migration of 200 workers to work in the brick kilns of Pulwama district in J&K, then Chairperson of the Commission, Justice S Rajendra Babu wrote to the then Chhattisgarh CM Raman Singh and J&K CM Ghulam Nabi Azad in 2009 to constitute a joint study team to undertake field visit to the site, rescue/release and repatriate the victims. Regretfully, no action was taken by either of the State governments to repatriate the labourers to their native place and the workers continued to toil under difficult and questionable conditions in the brick kilns in Pulwama for quite a number of years.

Conditions need to be created and through powerful IEC packages, people need to be told about the harrowing consequences of inter-State distress migration so that they are discouraged from taking recourse to it. No such initiative appears to have been taken by the State Government.

MGNREGA works are being taken up at odd intervals here and there with the average wage at ₹60-75 per day which is much lower than the notified minimum wage. This, however, does not generate assured employment for 100 days as originally contemplated and, therefore, has not substantially minimised or prevented the incidence of migration.

A massive orientation and sensitisation programme needs to be taken up for officers of district administration in Chhattisgarh to dispel strange mindsets such as:

- There are no bonded labourers in my district;
- All bonded labourers belonging to Chhattisgarh have been identified as such outside the State;
- They have been released on complaint and have been brought to Chhattisgarh but no formal release certificate has been issued by the district administration of the State where they were identified.

The country is one and indivisible and BLS (A) Act is applicable to the whole of India. It may be clarified that regardless of the location where people are identified as bonded labourers, i.e., whether inside or outside Chhattisgarh, they have to be released from bondage and repatriated to the source State where they have to be rehabilitated, irrespective of whether release certificates have been issued or not. In case a release certificate has not been issued by the destination State, then it should be persuaded and prevailed upon to do so. Victims of bonded labour system cannot be made to wait and suffer on account of non-issue of release certificate by the competent authority.

The central message is loud and clear. People who are victims of poverty, helplessness, migration and bondage cannot be left in the lurch. Social defence is the dire need of the hour for them.

It transpired that 586 freed bonded labourers have been awaiting rehabilitation in Chhattisgarh between 1999 and 2007. All of them belong to Bilaspur district. Seventeen were found bonded in Kanpur, sixty-nine in Rai Bareli, fifty-seven in

Unnao, fifteen in Varanasi, ninety-eight in Faizabad, ninety-five in Raisen, sixteen in Varanasi, forty-three in Kausambi, thirty-two in Sultanpur, thirty-three in Azamgarh, fourteen in Allahabad, twenty in Sagar, twenty-six in Durg and fifty-one in Hooghly. Release certificates have been issued by the competent authority but no budget provision has been made by the Government of Chhattisgarh and hence the process of rehabilitation has been delayed. Consequently, bonded labourers released from bondage have to wait for their rehabilitation assistance for one to nine years, which is frightfully long and is likely to be followed by further migration and bondage for the second time.

Bihar (April 2008)

Despite a lot of efforts, no Action Plan/Perspective Plan for elimination of BLS has yet been put in place.

There is no State-level committee for monitoring the performance of VCs and for coordination with various other departments of Government concerned with rehabilitation of freed bonded labourers. The administrative department i.e. Labour Resources does not perceive the need for such a committee for monitoring, supervision, co-ordination and activation of moribund institutions.

VCs at the district and sub-divisional levels are not being re-constituted at an interval of two years; the business transacted by the existing committees is not being monitored or evaluated; (in the absence of a State-level monitoring committee).

The administrative department does not have any clue about the methodology which needs to be adopted for identification of victims of BLS even though a number of circular letters and guidelines on the subject have been issued by both NHRC and

MoL&E. Strangely enough, the department does not perceive the need for issuing any guidelines to enable the field functionaries to effectively discharge their mandate.

Government of Bihar has not availed of any financial assistance from the centrally sponsored scheme of GoI to conduct a survey in the forty-five districts once in three years with a view to identifying bonded labourers. The procedure which is being adopted for release of bonded labourers in Bihar is rather cumbersome and long drawn-out.

In certain cases, proceedings have unnecessarily been allowed to drag out even though the landlord was prepared to give in writing that the person concerned is free to go anywhere he likes.

Release and rehabilitation are not simultaneous. Sometimes there is a gap of one year between the date of release and date of sanction of rehabilitation assistance. It is difficult to expect that the released bonded labourer will have to wait for one year to get the assistance to be rehabilitated. In all probability, he may migrate outside Bihar or in the worst eventuality may even prefer reversion to thraldom.

Even though migrant workers from North Bihar are being recruited and taken to Punjab, Haryana, Gujarat, Maharashtra and NCT of Delhi, Labour Resources Department, Government of Bihar is taking a stand that generally people move out on their own in search of a job.

Such recruitment is invariably associated with payment of advance. The documentary evidence for such advance remains with the recruiting agents and is never shared with the workers. The latter instead will all along be told, 'You cannot leave the work site until and unless the advance has been fully liquidated.'

In other words, payment of advance leads to a situation

of indebtedness and the latter to bondage but is not being acknowledged as such by the concerned department of the Bihar Government.

Recruitment of labour from rural areas (including both adults and children) takes place by malfunctional middle-men past midnight rather clandestinely and surreptitiously. Neither the village Panchayat nor the police have any clue about it.

No efforts are being made to establish an effective liaison and coordination between the originating and destination States to address problems arising out of inter-State migration, often landing the migrant workmen in a situation of bondage.

Uttar Pradesh (September 2010)

No Action Plan/Perspective Plan has yet been put in place for elimination of BLS.

The origin of BLS in UP in general and in the eastern part of the State in particular (Banda, Balia, Basti, Deoria, Azamgarh, Gorakhpur, Jaunpur, Mirzapur, Sonbhadra) may be attributed to difficult geography and topography, large size families, early age of marriage, low levels of literacy, uneven distribution of land holdings, inter-district and intra-district, inter-State and intra-State migration..

Prevalence of BLS in the stone quarries of Shankargarh taluk in Allahabad district making thousands of Kol families victims of a perverse system of lease of quarries should have been a matter of deep concern to the State Government. This is one area where all the relevant laws [Mines Act, Minimum Wages Act, Child Labour (Prohibition and Regulation) Act, BLS (A) Act and Inter-State Migrant Workmen (Regulation of Employment and Conditions of Service) Act] are being brazenly violated. The law enforcement machinery remains a mute spectator and the victims, being unorganised, are not in a position to bargain with the wily contractors for their basic entitlements.

UP has seventy-five districts while VCs have been constituted for seventy-one districts and 306 sub-divisions. There is no institutional mechanism at the State level for monitoring the performance of VCs at the district and sub-divisional level. There is no evidence that VCs have ever gone out to conduct surveys for identification of victims of BLS.

Seventy-seven cases are pending since 1996 with Executive Magistrates vested with powers of Judicial Magistrates, First or Second Class without any ostensible reason.

No summary trial is being conducted as required under S21(2) of BLS (A) Act or as emphasised by the Supreme Court and no review whatsoever has been conducted at the State level.

Fresh surveys need to be conducted by VCs under S14(e) of BLS (A) Act in all the seventy-five districts and in particular, in all the endemic pockets (brick kilns and stone quarries) by availing financial assistance (now raised from ₹2 lakh to ₹4.5 lakh per district once in three years) from the MoL&E.

While 28,946 bonded labourers have been identified and released, 668 bonded labourers are awaiting rehabilitation for several years in thirty districts of the State, the maximum number (300+) being accounted for by Muzaffarpur.

The State Government needs to be clear and specific on (a) the time since when the freed bonded labourers are awaiting rehabilitation (b) ascertain the requirement of funds for rehabilitation assistance (@ ₹1 lakh, ₹2 lakh and ₹3 lakh respectively w.e.f. 17 May 2016 under the Central scheme) (c) intimating the Ministry of Labour about the requirement of funds (d) verifying whether certificates of utilisation of funds received earlier have been sent to MoL&E or not (e) verifying whether inter-State migrant labourers who were found bonded in UP have been repatriated to their originating States or not (f) what is the current status of their rehabilitation (g) ascertaining whether labourers migrating from UP and working elsewhere under bonded conditions have been brought back to UP for rehabilitation (h) what is the current status of their rehabilitation.

Of late, there have been two positive developments. One is the collaboration between the nodal officer, AHTU, Lucknow with an NGO like Justice Ventures International (JVI) on the issue of labour trafficking in the State. A gathering of high-level government officials and local NGOs including 180 police officers from across the State organised in November 2016 was addressed by JVI on the plight and predicament of victims. Such dialogue and discussion between civil society organisations and Government (including police) with an open mind and trust and goodwill for each other with a common concern for the victim can bring refreshingly encouraging results.

The second redeeming feature is that CM of UP Yogi Adityanath has decided to focus concentrated attention towards elimination of bonded labour prevalent in brick kilns, mines and quarries. A circular letter of instruction has been issued to all seventy-five DMs to identify, rescue, release and rehabilitate victims of BLS. They must file FIR against perpetrators of the crime, have the investigations completed and ensure timely submission of charge-sheets. They must pay ₹20,000 towards immediate subsistence allowance in the wake of release prior to rehabilitation.

Question 51

What are the practical difficulties encountered by the National Human Rights Commission in providing timely justice and relief to victims?

Answer: In a set-up characterised by cooperative federalism, much of the success in the functioning of the Commission vis-a-vis provision of timely relief to the victims under BLS (A) Act would depend on the following factors:

- State governments and DMs responding to the six-week show-cause notice positively, proactively and constructively;
- Observance by the State governments/DMs of the correct procedure established by law;
- Accepting and implementing the recommendations of the Commission in letter and spirit, without ifs and buts;
- Reporting timely compliance to the Commission.

The ground level reality is, however, to the contrary. This would be evident from the following:

- Whenever a complaint or a major issue centering round victims of BLS is referred to a DM for a fact-finding enquiry report, he invariably is hard-pressed for time to personally attend to it.
- He/she, therefore, forwards the complaint either to the Labour Commissioner or to the SP of the district for enquiry and report.

Such an action on the part of the DM is not in order for the following reasons:

- Section 10 of BLS (A) Act states that such enquiries can be entrusted only to officers who are subordinate to DM and who may be authorised by the DM to exercise all or any of the powers and perform all or any of the duties so conferred or imposed;

- Officers who are subordinate to DM in ordinary parlance are (a) ADM (b) SDM (c) Executive Magistrates;
- By no stretch of imagination, Labour Commissioner or the SP of the district can be considered as subordinate to the DM; neither do they exercise the powers of the DM nor do they perform duties of the DM (as in Section 10 of BLS (A) Act);
- Past experience shows that the Labour Commissioner sub-delegates the responsibility entrusted to him either to his immediate subordinates (Deputy LC, ALC, DLO) or even to a labour inspector;
- The SP sub-delegates the responsibility entrusted to him either to Dy SP or even to the SHO in charge of a police station;
- These lower level echelons of bureaucracy who are hand- in-glove with vested interests and who have no empathy for the victims do not go to meet the latter and do not record their statements after taking them into confidence.

Instead, they go to the bonded labour keeper, make such casual enquiries as would be subserving the interests of the latter and subverting the interests of the victims, come to a rather sweeping and unreasonable conclusion that there are no bonded labourers.

The DM, without any further scrutiny and without much application of mind, mechanically forwards the enquiry report to the Commission. The Commission is left with no alternative except to reject the enquiry report and order a re-enquiry. Re-enquiry takes time and does not serve any useful purpose as in all such social investigations, time is of the essence. Delay in conducting enquiries and delay in providing relief to the victim defeats the central objective of the enquiry (as the victim may not wait indefinitely and may not be physically available to receive the relief after some time).

Besides, if the re-enquiry is conducted by the same set

of functionaries who conducted the first enquiry, it will be an infructuous exercise.

In other cases, (Aliyar Dam Case No 1242/5/2017 BL is a specific example), the DM may entrust the enquiry to his subordinate i.e. RDO (equivalent of SDM elsewhere) but the correct procedure established by law is not followed and the findings are flawed.

The findings at the end of the enquiry in respect of one household are mechanically repeated in case of enquiry in other households, reducing the enquiry to a mockery (as it happened in the Aliyar Dam case cited above).

State Governments take inordinately long time in responding to the directions of the Commission. In the above case, the directions issued by the Commission dated 30 November 2017 are pending compliance by the State Government more than two years after they were issued.

When the first enquiry was flawed, no useful purpose will be served by asking the State Government for a re-enquiry as the location, functionaries and victims are the same.

There are instances when DMs have developed cold feet when pressures are exerted by external elements to report that there are no bonded labourers in a particular area according to them. Anekal taluk in Bangalore rural district case in the 1990s is a noted example. In the above case, Jeevika/Vimukti Trust with the help of Dalit youth had got a survey conducted and identified 656 bonded labourers in the early 1990s. The DM of the district acted on the findings of the survey, albeit slowly, issued release certificates for 112 persons and sanctioned the amount for their rehabilitation. Before the funds could be released, the local MLA who has no locus-standi in BLS (A) Act took a stand that there are no bonded labourers in his constituency. The DM thereafter developed cold feet and suspended release of the sanctioned grant.

These constraints notwithstanding, the Commission has spared no pains to organise a systematic drive for elimination of BLS as would be evident from the following:

- All valid complaints are being registered and computerised;
- Instant action for getting the complaints investigated is initiated soon after their receipt and registration;
- The central objective in the entire process commencing with receipt, registration, ordering enquiry, deputing teams from the Commission in more sensitive cases having a wider jurisdiction, sitting of the full Commission (as it happened in 'bartan' system in Odisha in January 2011) to take stock of the situation has always been to provide relief to the victims in less time and cost;
- The bonded labour cell and Core group on bonded labour have been aiding and assisting the Commission in attending to all complaints relating to BLS with utmost sense of urgency and seriousness of concern;
- The Commission, ever since it was entrusted with the responsibility by the apex court w.e.f. 11 November 1997 to monitor the pace and progress of implementation of BLS (A) Act has left no stone unturned to organise field visits in different States on the one hand and to organise orientation and training workshops at the national, State and divisional/district levels for familiarisation and sensitisation of all concerned on the other.

Question 52

Can you suggest a monitoring mechanism for NHRC to keep a close watch on the pace and progress of timely, effective and meaningful rehabilitation of all freed bonded labourers?

Answer: Monitoring the pace and progress of implementation of any such rehabilitation proposal would imply the following:

- getting a periodic feedback from the State Government/DM/ implementing authority, as the case may be;
- deputing teams of officers from the Commission for an on-the-spot review of the strategy and methodology adopted for implementation of the rehabilitation scheme and the outcome/ impact thereof;
- NHRC eventually satisfied itself that (a) rehabilitation has been meaningful and effective in terms of making the freed bonded labour beneficiary truly autonomous (b) there will be no occasion for the beneficiary to further contract bonded debt (c) he/she is free from the vile influence and organised onslaughts of the erstwhile bonded labour keeper and (d) he/she is able to lead a decent and dignified human existence.

To enable the Commission to satisfy itself that all the expected outcomes of the rehabilitation process have become the actual outcomes, a questionnaire has been designed with reference to land based, non-land based and art/craft/skill based components of the rehabilitation process.

I. Land-based rehabilitation

- Whether the beneficiary at the time of release was landless or landed?
- If landless, whether steps have been taken to allot land (both homestead and agricultural)?
- Whether land allotted is free from encumbrances?
- Whether ROR (*patta*) has been prepared and handed over to the beneficiary?
- Whether physical possession of land free of encroachment has

been handed over to the beneficiary?

- Whether agricultural land allotted is fit for cultivation; if not, whether steps have been taken for making it cultivable by way of land development?
- Whether the beneficiary has been assisted in submission of an application for assistance under PM's Awas Yojana (either rural or urban) for construction of a dwelling unit?
- Whether steps have been taken to make available plough, bullocks, other agricultural implements, agro-chemicals, etc., to enable and facilitate the beneficiary to take up cultivation?
- Whether officers of Agriculture Department of the State have been given orientation and sensitised to come forward to guide and assist the beneficiary in the following:
    - testing of soil;
    - issue of soil card on the basis of the said test;
    - adoption of a cropping pattern (single or multiple crops) on the basis of (a) suitability of the soil for a particular crop (b) availability of irrigation facility, if any (flow or lift);
    - completion of formalities to avail of the benefits of crop insurance under Pradhan Mantri Fasal Beema Yojana;
    - arrangement for disposal of surplus food-grains in the nearest mandi under the Agricultural Marketing Cooperative Society (APMC);
    - Possibility of making a contribution to grain banks (one of the most effective food security institutional mechanisms) wherever such grain banks have been put in place to assist the consumers during the lean season;
    - arrangement for disposal of cash crops (cotton, sugarcane) in the local market at remunerative prices;

II. Non-land based (productive asset based) scheme

- Whether healthy productive assets (milch cows, buffalos, sheep, goats) have been procured from credible sources at reasonable prices?
- Whether steps have been taken to get the productive assets insured?
- Considering the inability of the beneficiary to bear the premium in most cases due to poverty, whether there is any scheme of the State to bear the said premium to insure the productive assets at least for the first year?
- Whether officers of the Animal Husbandry and Veterinary Deptartment concerned are sufficiently involved in giving orientation to the beneficiary on (a) yield (b) ways and means of enhancing the yield (c) is the price for the product (milk, cheese, butter, ghee) remunerative (d) whether adequate arrangements have been made to procure the products from the beneficiaries at remunerative prices (e) what are the common ailments afflicting the productive asset (f) what are the prescriptive remedies, short and long term (g) has due care been taken to familiarise the beneficiaries with both the ailments as well as the remedies (h) has the vaccination cycle been followed (i) whether the beneficiary is aware of the location of the nearest veterinary dispensary (j) maintenance of the asset during the dry period (k) source from which cattle feed and other animal feed can be obtained at reasonable prices (l) how to prevent mortality of assets (m) economics of yield, disposal of the product at remunerative prices in local market (n) how to make the beneficiary a mini animal husbandry man/woman and a barefoot doctor as in China (o) how to make the beneficiary truly autonomous/self-reliant.

III. Art/craft/skill-based schemes:

- Did the beneficiary have a background as a rural artisan (carpenter, cobbler, mason, blacksmith, painter, designer of floral motifs on walls of premises)?
- If so, does he/she possess the skill or has he/she become de-skilled after years of serfdom?
- If de-skilled, whether a complete package of providing necessary orientation to revive the old skills or to refine/sharpen/upgrade the existing skills has been put in place?
- If so, please furnish all the details (name of the trade, place where the orientation is required to be given, time schedule, simple tests to be undertaken to assess the prior skills as well as the overall proficiency possessed by the beneficiary at the end of training;
- Whether steps have been taken at the end of the training to ensure access to (a) credit (b) technology (c) raw materials at reasonable prices and (d) market;
- Whether arrangements have been put in place to assess the economics of the rehabilitation scheme at the end and to come to a conclusion that it has helped to make the beneficiary truly autonomous/self-reliant and that he/she will not have any occasion to contract and further bonded debt?

While these are the broad contours of monitoring of the content, process and impact of implementation of a rehabilitation scheme, the nitty-gritty of the operational mechanism for carrying out the actual monitoring in the office of NHRC will be as under:

- The central computer unit of the Commission will be in overall charge of monitoring. It will function under the supervision and control of the Member-in-charge of bonded labour in the Commission;

- Software for all the sub-components/activities of the main component (land based, non-land based and art/craft/skill based) will be designed by the computer unit;
- Feedback in respect of all the sub-components of each beneficiary will be required to be obtained from the State Government on a monthly basis and will be fed to the computer to build up the database;
- The feedback so received will be analysed and the outcome of the analysis will be put up to the Member for issuing further directions to the State Governments, as he may deem appropriate.

Question 53

Besides the central scheme for rehabilitation of freed bonded labourers, what are the other Central schemes which can be dovetailed to the former so that a freed bonded labourer's rehabilitation is holistic, meaningful and effective?

Answer: It is always desirable and possible to pool resources from a number of other sources and integrate them with the central scheme for rehabilitation in an imaginative and skilful manner. Some of them are:

I. Pradhan Mantri Kaushal Vikas Yojana.
II. Pradhan Mantri Awas Yojana.
III. National Rural Livelihood Mission.
IV. Pradhan Mantri Jan Dhan Yojana.
V. Balika Samruddhi Yojana.

The details of beneficiaries and benefits under these schemes are enumerated below:

I. **Pradhan Mantri Kaushal Vikas Yojana.**

Skill development is crucial to employability which precedes gainful employment.

Pradhan Mantri Kaushal Vikas Yojana (PMKVY), a flagship scheme of the Ministry of Skill Development and Entrepreneurship enables the youth to undergo industry relevant skill training that will help them in securing a better livelihood.

A potential bonded labourer or a freed bonded labourer, as the case may be, is not altogether unskilled. He/she has certain skills which may need to be refined, sharpened and upgraded. Simultaneously, he/she can imbibe and assimilate new skills.

PMKVY would help in assessing and certifying such individuals with prior skills, upgrading the existing skills and imparting new skills. The programme is self-propelled and self-driven with motivation of the potential skill learner as the key.

At the national level, we have National Skill Development Authority (NSDA), National Skill Development Corporation (NSDC), Sector Skill Councils, National Skill Development Fund and Directorate General of Training (DGT).

At the State level, we have Skill Development Missions and Skill providers.

Victims of BLS who have been freed from bondage and who are on the way to rehabilitation may be identified by the State Government on a priority basis and after completing the process of assessment and certification of skills which they are already in possession, a decision may be taken to either up-grade the existing skills or impart new skills according to aptitude, preference and interest of the potential beneficiary.

After the existing skills have been enhanced and the trainee has become employable, efforts may be made to link employability with actual employment after ascertaining the avenues which are available vis-a-vis suitability of the trained person for a particular position. Such employment may be either wage employment or self employment conforming to the endowment, aptitude, preferences and interests of the beneficiary concerned.

II. **Pradhan Mantri Awas Yojana (Urban) (PMAY-U)**
Pradhan Mantri Awas Yojana (Gramin) (PMAY-G)

- PMAY was launched in June 2015. It has two components: one for urban poor and second for rural poor.
- The PMAY-U has the following four components such as:
  - In situ slum re-development with private sector participation using land as resource;
  - Affordable housing through credit linked subsidy;
  - Affordable housing in partnership with private and public sector;
  - Beneficiary led house construction/ enhancement.
- The main features of both urban and rural housing schemes are:
  - A beneficiary can avail of a housing loan re-payable in twenty years under credit linked subsidy scheme;
  - Government will provide an interest subsidy of 6.5 per cent;
  - The houses will be constructed through a technology that is eco-friendly;
  - Preference will be given to differently abled and older persons while allotting ground floor.
  - The PMAY is converged with other schemes to ensure (a) houses have a toilet under 'Swachh Bharat' (b) electricity connection under 'Saubhagya Yojana' (c) Ujjwala Yojana for cooking gas connection (d) access to potable water and (e) Jan Dhan Yojana for banking facilities.

In the absence of a national-level survey, it is difficult to say as to how many freed bonded labour households will be eligible to receive assistance under PMAY. However, it is quite possible that most of them who are below poverty line and who do not have a roof above their head will be in need as also would qualify to receive assistance under the scheme. Like differently abled and elderly persons, they should be given preference in sanction and release of financial assistance under the scheme.

III. **National Rural Livelihood Mission**

Integrated Rural Development Programme was launched on 2 October 1980. After about two decades it was restructured as Swarnajayanti Grameen Swarojgar Yojana (SGSY) in 1999. After a decade or so, it was remodelled and a new scheme called National Rural Livelihood Mission (NRLM) was launched in 2011. It was succeeded by Deen Dayal Antyodaya Yojana on 25 September 2015.

NRLM rests on sound principles such as:

- The poor do not lack intelligence;
- They have unsuspected possibilities and potentialities;
- They have a strong desire to come out of poverty;
- They are excellent managers of assets;
- They have an essential coping mechanism to survive under difficult conditions.

The Mission, one of the world's largest initiatives to improve the livelihood of the poor, aims at enabling and facilitating BPL households to access gainful self-employment and skilled wage employment opportunities which will improve livelihoods on a sustainable basis and put an end to poverty.

The Mission works on three pillars:

- Expand livelihood options for the poor;
- Build skills for the job market outside;

- Promote and nurture entrepreneurship;

The livelihood services offered by the Mission are:

- Financial and capital services;
- Production and productivity enhancement services (which include technology, knowledge, skills and inputs, marketing linkages).

Since NRLM follows a demand driven strategy, it admirably fits into the rehabilitation programme for freed bonded labour beneficiaries where the preferences, felt needs and interests of the beneficiary are of paramount importance. It also admirably fits into a group approach to rehabilitation through participatory planning at the grass roots-level where the poor constitute the principal driving force behind all plans and programmes.

IV. **Pradhan Mantri Jan Dhan Yojana**

This is a financial inclusion programme which was launched by the PM on 15 August 2014. It aims to expand and afford financial services such as:

- Opening bank accounts;
- Facilitating remittances by the account holder;
- Easy access to credit, insurance and pension.

The scheme has the following striking features:

- The accounts opened under PMJDY do not require any minimum balance;
- Persons who do not have valid identification document can also open bank account; this type of account called 'Small Account' can be regularised within one year;
- An overdraft facility up to ₹10,000 is available after six months of opening of the account;
- In remote areas where banks do not have physical presence,

business correspondents are appointed by the Department of Financial Services, Ministry of Finance who will assist the beneficiaries to open accounts and carry out bank transactions. The former eases banking operations for unlettered persons through bio-metric based account opening.

- All Government subsidies are directly transferred to the beneficiary's account.

- As of now, nearly 35 crore bank accounts have been opened and there has been sizeable increase in the Jan Dhan accounts. Kerala and Goa have been able to provide one basic bank account to every household.
- Financial inclusion is one of the dire needs in the life of both a potential or freed bonded labourer. They are in dire need of financial literacy as well. Through PMJDY they will become financially literate, financially secure and will be able to manage their day-to-day lives. 'Mera Khata Bhagya Bidhata' which is the slogan of the scheme will usher in a fresh lease of life for the freed bonded labourer.

V. **Balika Samruddhi Yojana**

- Children of freed bonded labourers in general and girl children in particular are in need of special care and attention. As they cross the threshold of infancy and enter childhood, it is imperative that they have unhindered access to nutritious food which is a balanced combination of carbohydrate, protein, oil/fat, vitamin and trace minerals, access to regular health check-ups, access to free and compulsory education, no corporal punishment, no parental pressure and a life of freedom and spontaneity.
- The Balika Samruddhi Yojana is quite handy for the girl children of freed bonded labourers who normally do not receive such special care and attention for their children.

- The scheme has the following laudable objectives:
  - Changing family and community attitude towards the girl child at birth and towards her mother;
  - Facilitate and improve the enrolment, retention, participation and achievement of the desired levels of proficiency for all girl children in school;
  - Raise the age of marriage of girls which should not be lower than eighteen under Prohibition of Child Marriage Act, 2006;
  - Introduce girls to the world of income generating activities.
- The scheme is universal in its application (all urban and rural areas of 719 districts);
- The scheme covers girl children in all BPL families who are born on or after 15 August 1997.
- The girl children eligible under BSY will be entitled to the following benefits:

  I. A post birth grant amounting to ₹500.

  II. Every girl child born on or after the above date would be entitled to annual scholarships after she starts attending school for each successfully completed year of schooling at the following rates:
     - Class I–III ₹300 per annum for each class;
     - Class IV ₹500 per annum;
     - Class V ₹600 per annum;
     - Class VI–VII ₹700 per annum for each class;
     - Class VIII ₹800 per annum;
     - Class IX–X ₹1,000 per annum for each class;
- Benefits under BSY will be restricted to two girl children in each household born on or after 15 August 1997 irrespective of the total number of children in the household.

- In the event of the girl getting married before attaining the age of eighteen years, she will have to forego the benefit of the amount of the annual scholarship and the interest accrued thereon.
- She, however, shall stand entitled to the post-birth grant of ₹500 and the interest accrued thereon.

Modalities of implementation:

- Funds for payment of the post-birth grant and annual scholarships in rural areas will be released by the Ministry of WCD, GoI to the State Government/UT Administration.
- The latter in turn will release it to the implementing agencies to be identified by them.
- The State Governments will disburse the benefits to the girl child through ICDS scheme infrastructure in ICDS areas and through the areas which are presently implementing BSY in non-ICDS areas.
- The GPs/Municipality will be responsible for identifying the beneficiaries under BSY in their respective areas of operation. For this purpose, the services of village-level staff like AWWs, ANMs, village accountants, school teachers may be utilised.
- The GPs will also disseminate information about BSY and the procedure for availing of benefits thereunder.
- The GPs will be responsible for implementing, monitoring and following up the disbursement of benefits under different components of BSY.
- The amount under various components of BSY shall be deposited in an interest-bearing account to be opened in the name of the beneficiary girl child and an officer designated in this behalf by the State Government/UT administration in the nearest bank/ post office.

- In order to ensure that maximum possible rate of interest is earned, no premature withdrawal shall be permitted from the account.
- On the girl child attaining eighteen years and on production of a certificate from the GP/Municipality that she is unmarried on her eighteenth birthday, the implementing agency would authorise the bank or the post office concerned to allow her to withdraw the matured amount.

Question 54

What recommendations have been made by various National Commissions and Committees on elimination of BLS?

Answer: No National Commission on elimination of bonded labour has been set up as yet. To the extent, however, the various National Commissions and Committees have made recommendations on fixation, review, revision and enforcement of statutorily notified minimum wage, they have an indirect bearing on elimination of BLS.

To illustrate, the First Pay Commission of Government of India in 1947 had laid down certain principles for determination of minimum wage of unskilled labour in Government employment. These are:

- The application of the minimum wage rule must be recognised to be subject to limitations imposed by the general economic situation of the country;
- It may be applied to correct inequalities in the distribution system but not in disregard of the total production capacity of the country or without reference to the national income;
- Irrespective of the market value, the State must adopt a minimum wage, which must be the appropriate basic

remuneration for every unskilled labour.

- The Second Pay Commission (August 1957) made further additions to the concept of minimum wage by imparting the element of nutritional needs as well as the requirements of clothing, housing and other essentials for a family of three consumption units.
- The First National Commission on Labour (December 1966 to August 1969) held that 'in fixing the need based minimum wage which is in the range of lower level of fair wage, the capacity (of industry) to pay will have to be taken into account'.
- This is a clear departure from the direction given in *Crown Aluminium Works Vs their Workmen* (1958) by the Supreme Court.
- The direction of the Supreme Court in the above case was reiterated in Reptacos Brett Case (1991).
- The pith and substance of that direction is as under:

'An employer who cannot pay the minimum wage has no right to engage labour and no justification to run the industry.'

- It was, therefore, a matter beyond comprehension when the First National Commission observed, 'A national minimum wage in the sense of a uniform monetary remuneration for the country as a whole is neither feasible nor desirable'.
- It is equally a matter of regret that successive conferences of Labour Ministers in the 1980s derived inspiration and strength from the above negative recommendation of the first National Commission on Labour and opposed the idea of fixation of a uniform national minimum wage below which none can pay.
- In adopting such a negative stand, it was not visualised that disparity in notified minimum wages obtaining in different parts of the country would give rise to the incidence of distress inter-State

migration which in turn would lead to indebtedness and bondage.

- However, it is quite refreshing to note that in sharp contrast to the observation of the First National Commission of Labour, the Study Group on wages, incomes and prices set up by the Ministry of Finance under the Chairmanship of S Bhootalingam, ICS, former Finance Secretary to GoI (1978) observed, 'In our view, the real minimum wage can only be the absolute national minimum, irrespective of sectors, regions or States below which no employment would be permitted to pay'.
- In determining such a national minimum, it has to be consistent with several factors such as:
  - Per capita national income adjusted after applying the participation rate;
  - Average national consumption per consumption unit;
  - Per capita rural consumption expenditure.
- The prevailing confusion regarding the concept of minimum wage and its fixation worsened on account of these sharply conflicting views.
- The National Commission on Rural Labour (1987-91) aimed at restoration of uniformity in minimum wages throughout the country.
- However, in working out the details of such a wage, the NCRL dealt with two types of wages. One is the basic minimum wage. This has to be determined in such a manner that it becomes the minimum subsistence level wage. It must be protected from the effects of inflation. Any wage below this cannot be the minimum wage; it will become pauper or starvation level wage. The second is the statutorily notified minimum wage. This may be notified under the MW Act and will be above the subsistence level.
- According to NCRL recommendation, if the minimum

subsistence level is to be maintained, the cost of living must be fully neutralised through the mechanism of dearness allowance. It was much later (after the NCRL's recommendation) that in mid-1990s it was decided that neutralisation in the form of dearness allowance would be announced every six months. The VDA is being revised twice a year on April 1 and October 1 in the central sphere on the basis of rise in Consumer Price Index.

- The CPI on an all-India average basis is being compiled by the Labour Bureau, an attached office of MoL&E for agricultural, rural and industrial workers. Treating 1986-87 as the base year price at 100, there has been 400 per cent increase in the CPI in case of both agricultural and rural workers.
- In case of industrial workers, treating 2001 as the base year at 100, the increase has been of the order of 275 per cent.
- As against this, the rise in India's per capita income is of the order of 11.7 per cent only.
- According to a report in *Indian Express* (New Delhi) edition dated 13 January 2018, the rural wage growth has fallen to a 14-month low of 49 per cent in October 2017.
- According to an estimate prepared in 2014 by a trade union on the basis of actual average of retail prices of all components of expenditure (both food and non-food) in Delhi, Mumbai, Chennai, Kolkata, Bengaluru, Bhubaneswar and Thiruvananthapuram, the total monthly expenditure comes to ₹20,861 or ₹695 per day.
- The huge gap between income and expenditure for an average consumer leads to indebtedness of a high order and eventually to debt bondage.
- In other words, there is overwhelming justification for a substantial rise in wage income.

- The next question is what should be the quantum of a floor-level national minimum wage.
- There are certain factors and principles to be kept in view when we proceed to fix a wage. These are:

Factors

- Level of employment;
- Level of productivity;
- General level of wage;
- Price index;
- Cost of living;
- Social security benefits.

Principles

- Equality of opportunity;
- Equality of treatment in respect of every employment and occupation;
- Parity in wages between women and men.

- As far as minimum wage is concerned, price index and cost of living are relevant; other factors are not so relevant;
- The fifteenth Indian Labour Conference held in Nainital in 1957 under Chairmanship of late Gulzarilal Nanda, then Union Labour Minister had laid down the following components to be kept in view by every appropriate government while fixing minimum wage:
  - The standard working class family should be taken as one earner and three consumption units;
  - The earnings of children, adolescents and women should be disregarded;

- The minimum food requirement should be calculated on the basis of a net intake of calories as recommended by Dr Akroyd, a distinguished nutritionist;
- Clothing requirements should be estimated at per capita consumption of eighteen yards per annum which for an average worker's family of four would be a total of seventy-two yards;
- In respect of housing, the rent corresponding to the minimum area provided for under Government's industrial housing scheme should be taken into consideration;
- Fuel, lighting and other miscellaneous items of expenditure should constitute twenty per cent of the total minimum wage packages.

It did not include:

- Cost of potable water at forty gallons per head per day (for cleaning, sweeping, swabbing, cooking, bathing, gardening, drinking and flushing the toilet);
- Sanitation (including recurrent expenses for maintenance);
- Cost of textbooks, uniforms and school fees for children's education;
- Recreation;
- Medical care;
- Protection for old age.

- This omission was made good to a certain extent in the judgment of Supreme Court in Reptacos Brett Case (Civil Appeal No 4336 of 1991 arising out of SLP (C) No 15680 of 1990).
- Computed in terms of cash value of the wage, the minimum wage according to the recommendations of fifteenth Indian

Labour Conference at present would be ₹12,000 per month.

- Adding twenty-five per cent of this to the total package as directed by the apex court in Replacos Brett Case it would be ₹12,000 + 3,000 = ₹15, 000.
- Adding the cost of toilet, water and maintenance charges the minimum wage at zero inflation level would stand at ₹15,000 + 3,000 = ₹18, 000.
- Adjusting the wage to the current level of inflation at five per cent, it would be of the order of ₹18,900.
- The seventh Central Pay Commission has recommended a sum of ₹18,000 for the class IV i.e. the lowest category of employees in GoI which is slightly lower than the national floor level minimum wage as formulated above.

Question 55

Among institutions which have contributed to the elimination of BLS in India, please tell us about Lal Bahadur Shastri National Academy of Administration, Mussoorie.

Answer: In 1988, when BN Yugandhar IAS was Director, Lal Bahadur Shastri National Academy of Administration (he passed away on 13 September 2019) opened a cell at the behest of the National Commission on Unorganised Rural Labour (1987-91) headed by Dr CH Hanumanth Rao to exclusively deal with the BLS menace. It brought out on the basis of painstaking action research the following publications:

I. Study report on bonded labour Vol I- Incidence of BLS in India- Area, nature and extent- Part 1 and Part 2, November 1990.

II. Study report on bonded labour Vol II - Release and rehabilitation, November 1990.

III. Study report on bonded labour Vol III - Summary of study report and draft recommendations, November, 1990.
IV. Study report on bonded labour Vol IV - Bibliography and Directory, November, 1990.
V. Study report on bonded labour Vol V - Anthology of Act and Rules, November, 1990

The primary objective behind involvement of the Academy in efforts towards identification, rescue/release and rehabilitation of victims of BLS was to sensitise IAS probationers so that they may be able to translate what they learn in the classroom in the Academy to action as they assume the reins of district administration as DM a few years later.

With this end in view, IAS probationers in the course of their village attachment carried out surveys and helped in identification and release of victims.

From 1984 onwards, identification, rescue/release and rehabilitation of victims of BLS have been included in the curriculum of training of IAS probationers.

Question 56

How would you rate the VV Giri National Labour Institute in its contribution to elimination of bonded labour system?

Answer: The Institute came into existence in July 1974 following the recommendations of the first National Commission on Labour (December 1966 to August 1969) and Prof. Nitish Ranjan De became the first Dean and Director. Over a decade of dedicated leadership and direction, he raised it to the stature of an institute of social science and research of international repute and standing. Prof. De is internationally acclaimed for having conceptualised rural labour training camps as vibrant tools of what the author would like to term 'conscientisation of unorganised rural labour.' Such camps are unique in terms of their unconventional and unorthodox approach. They were also instrumental in identifying victims of BLS.

The idea of such camps originated from Father Paulo Freire, a radical Catholic priest from Brazil and an outstanding adult educator.

It was at Geneva that Prof. De along with Sri Debabrat Bandyopadhyay, then Joint Secretary to Ministry of Labour, had a chance meeting with Paulo Freire. This is what Paulo Freire had advised:

> Avoid the main village (in course of your visit), camp in the village school and talk to the village people in a group with no land owners around. Before this, carry out (preferably incognito) a solid economic survey of how people are living in the village. This will indicate who the possible bonded labourers are. The possible bonded labourers would be those who are working for and living in the landlord's premises and not getting any wages. Try to identify them by this method and bring them to your camp in the school. Stay with them, eat the food they eat or give them the food of their choice to eat. Stay on the floor of the building the way they sit on tattered mats. Stay with them for three days, identify yourself with them as much as you can. On the first day, nobody should speak. On the second day evening, some of them would speak and on the third day, they would open up like a sluice gate in a dam; there would be a deluge. You then start asking them about their lives, work, wages and relationship with their employers. In this manner, you will find out the number of bonded labourers and can take whatever action your law warrants you to take.

While D Bandyopadhyay used the methodology in identifying *bargadars* in West Bengal, Prof. De effectively used it for conducting rural labour training camps.

Such camps are organised primarily for landless agricultural labourers in a village. There are 20-24 participants and the camp is for five days. The groups will discover through discussion that some problems are tractable, some are not so tractable but solutions to both will necessarily have to be found out by them. The organisers who conduct the camp remain in the background as catalytic agents, promoting and facilitating a process.

Between 1974 and 1987, over forty-five such rural camps were held in quick succession.

The central message which emanates from this experiment is best put in the words of late VV Giri (former Union Labour Minister, former President of India and an outstanding trade union leader of more than five decades standing):

It is in the capacity to combine that labour has its best strength and the wherewithal of deliverance from injustice and oppression'.

Prof. De was not alone in this noble experiment. He was ably assisted by scores of colleagues such as: Dr Mahaveer Jain, Prof. Prayag Mehta, Prof. BK Srivastva, late Prof. KG Iyer, Dr Rukmini Rao, V Kulkarni, late RN Maharaj and Prof. KG Agarwal. Dr Mahaveer Jain who retired as a senior fellow of VV Giri NLI in 2010 was appointed as a Commissioner of Supreme Court in 1988 to investigate the causes which contribute to so much of poverty, deprivation, social exclusion, economic exploitation and bondage of those unfortunate sections of the society who are born as free citizens of a free, sovereign and democratic republic but who are yet to taste the nectar of that freedom which is cherished and prized by all of us. It goes to the credit of Dr Jain that he rose to the occasion to conduct this massive socio-legal investigation with a rare grit and courage to unearth the truth by using an unconventional and unorthodox methodology.

In the process, he came in touch with a large number of workers in the quarries and crushers of Faridabad who toil from dawn to dusk, who play with lethal objects of destruction of human life and limb (fuse wire, detonator and explosives) and who eventually wither away in the peak of their youth and manhood. He also came across quarry contractors, lessees, *jamadars, khatedars, munshis* and such hawks whose only pastime is to cheat, defraud, exploit and gain quick bucks through exercise of aggressively selfish control over the helpless and hapless.

The report that Dr Jain submitted to the apex court earned accolades for him from the former. What comes out of this very comprehensive investigation report is the most accurate and authentic account of the exploitation of the poor, deprived and disadvantaged sections of the society in the hands of their employers and so-called masters.

Regretfully, the gusto and tempo with which Prof. Nitish Ranjan De had conceptualised and translated into action the 'Rural Labour Training Camps' as an instrument of liberation and conscientisation of the poor, oppressed and marginalised were not sustained after he passed away in 1987.

Question 57

What according to you is the perspective in which the role of voluntary organisations/social action groups in elimination of bonded labour system in India should be perceived?

Answer: The BLS (A) Act, 1976 does not assign any direct specific role to voluntary organisations in either identification or rescue/release or rehabilitation. It simply permits an NGO to be represented as a member of the Vigilance Committee (two social workers out of ten members under S13(2)(d) and S13(3)(d)) at the district and sub-divisional level respectively). Such NGOs who have been connected with implementation of rural development programme in the district or the sub-division would also qualify to be a member of the vigilance committee.

In *Neerja Chaudhary Vs State of MP*,[56] the apex court for the first time had drawn a clear line of distinction between the roles performed by the representatives of the people [Members of the Legislative Assembly (MLA), Members of the Legislative Council (MLC) and Members of Parliament (MP)], bureaucrats like Divisional Commissioners and Collectors, local self-governing bodies vis-a-vis voluntary organisations (VOs) and had given cogent and valid reasons in according overriding preference for the latter. To quote from the judgment dated 8 May 1984 of the apex court:

> It is difficult to believe that the existence of bonded labour system can be discovered and the evil of the system can be wiped out by relying solely on the action taken by the members of the Legislative Assembly or the bureaucracy or even the panchayat though their help must certainly be sought and taken. The Commissioners and Collectors have multi-farious duties to attend and even if they are anxious to help in eradication of the vice of bonded labour system, which we are sure they are, they would not find time to make any personal enquiry or investigation but would have to rely on their sub-ordinate officers such as tehasildars and patwaris. The

56 Arising out of WP (Crl) No 1263 of 1982 (AIR 1984 SC 1099

latter at many places being either in sympathy with the exploiting class or lacking in social commitment or being indifferent to the misery and suffering of the poor and the downtrodden, the task of identification, release and rehabilitation of bonded labourers through the official machinery would be very difficult of achievement. The Panchayats, dominated as they sometimes are, by vested interests and having regard to their mode of functioning, may not be very effective in this task. We do not think that much useful purpose will be served by asking petty officials of the Revenue Department to go from house to house with a view to ascertaining whether there are any bonded labourers or not.

We had sometime back a case before us where pursuant to a direction given by the Collector as a result of an order made by this Court, the tehsildar went to the village in question and sitting on a dais with the landlords by his side, he started enquiring of the labourers whether they were bonded or not. When the labourers, obviously inhibited and terrified by the presence of the landlords said that they were not bonded but that they were working freely and voluntarily, he made a report to the Collector that there were no bonded labourers.

What is really necessary is to involve social action groups operating at the grass root level in the task of identification and release of bonded labourers. It is only through such groups that we shall be able to discover the existence of bonded labour system and shall be able to identify and release them. We would strongly urge upon the State governments to include the representatives of such social action groups in the vigilance committees and to give them full support and cooperation. These groups may appear to be un-orthodox and un-conventional and their action may be tinged with social action but they alone will be able to deliver the goods. It is high time that the State government should start taking their assistance instead of looking askance at them and distrusting them. The vested interests would undoubtedly be against such groups who are trying to organise the poor and the oppressed and would try to attack and destroy them with all the resources at their disposal including filing of false cases and even physical assaults. The State administration should not allow itself to be dominated or influenced by the vested interests and under the guise of maintenance of law and order, harass and oppress the dis-advantaged sections of the community which such social groups are trying to organise with a view to making them strong and self-reliant and capable of fighting for their rights through the process of law.'

Question 58

What according to you is the rationale behind the apex court according such overriding preference to voluntary social action groups vis-a-vis representatives of the people, the bureaucracy and the Panchayat?

Answer: The reasons for trusting non-profits are the following:

- The outreach of Government machinery to the unreached and, in particular, those who are in remote, interior and in-accessible areas to meet their genuine needs is quite limited;
- There are numerous competing claims coming from multiple channels for government agencies; the latter with limited time, energy and resources cannot fulfil them or do justice to all of them;
- Besides, the attitude and approach of the machinery remains orthodox, conventional and routinised which often is unhelpful in finding a timely correct solution to a pressing social problem;

- The VOs/social action groups live and work with the people with pulse of the people on their fingers. They easily identify themselves with the people--their joy and sorrow, laughter and tears, hopes and aspirations. The latter repose their trust and confidence in them and listen to them with patience and interest. This makes the task of mobilisation and organisation of the people and the rural poor in particular on the part of VOs much easier;
- The VOs have flexibility of structure and operations. Their internal management is simple and not hamstrung by rigid and inflexible procedures which obtain largely in government;
- The channel of communication built up by some of the VOs with the local community and the people is a two-way one which is open, natural and spontaneous. This helps to build and re-inforce the credibility of VOs with the people;
- There is a measure of transparency and accountability in the activities of some of the VOs which are pro-people, pro-poor, pro-Nature, pro-gender and pro-children which is not be found in government;
- Most of them prefer to adopt an operational strategy which is area specific, relief to the victim-oriented, people-centred, volunteer-based, time-bound, cost-effective and result-oriented.

Question 59

Name some of the voluntary organisations which have made notable contribution to eradication of BLS including, child labour and sex/labour trafficking in the past and who continue to be active even now.

Answer: Names of some of these NGOs are listed below in an alphabetic order.

1. Action Aid International
2. Adhikar
3. Aide-et-Action International
4. Antyodaya
5. Association for Human Rights and Development (AHEAD)
6. Action for Welfare and Awakening in Rural Development (AWARE)
7. Action for Cultural and Political Change
8. Bachpan Bachao Andolan (BBA)
9. Bandhua Mukti Morcha (BMM)
10. Child Rights and You (CRY)
11. Centre for Social Research
12. Centre for Constitutional Rights
13. Civil Society Forum on Human Rights (CSFHR)
14. Chhattisgarh Krishak Mazdoor Sangh
15. Diya Deva Sansthan (DSS)
16. Foundation for Sustainable Development (FSD)
17. Gandhi Peace Foundation
18. Human Rights Law Network (HRLN)
19. International Justice Mission
20. Jai Bhim Vikas Shikshan Sansthan (JBVSS)
21. Jan Sahas (JS)
22. Jan Mukti Anusthan (JMA)
23. Jivika/Vimukti Trust
24. Justice Ventures International (JVI)
25. Jan Jagruti Kendra
26. Justice and Care

27. Karnataka Rayat Sangha
28. Migration Information and Research Centre
29. MYRADA (Mysore Resettlement and Development Association)
30. National Campaign Committee for eradication of bonded labour
31. National Foundation for India
32. Navbharat Jagruti Kendra
33. Lok Drusti
34. Odisha Goti Mukti Andolan
35. Peoples' Vigilance Committee on Human Rights
36. Palli Alok Pathagar
37. Prajwala
38. Prayas Centre for Labour research and Action
39. Prerana
40. Peoples' Union for Democratic Rights (PUDR)
41. Peoples' Union for Civil Liberties (PUCL)
42. Research Academy for Rural Enrichment (RARE)
43. Shakti Vahini
44. Save the Children
45. Society for Development of Drought Prone Areas
46. Sramjeebi Sangathan
47. Santhal Pargana Antyodaya Ashram
48. Volunteers for Social Justice
49. Vidhayak Sansad
50. Vivekananda Girijan Kalyan Kendra

Question 60

Could you share some of the striking features of the operational strategy and significant achievements made by some of the

voluntary organisations as listed above?

Answer: The fifty voluntary organisations whose names have been mentioned in the list above are only illustrative and selective and certainly not exhaustive. There may be many more voluntary organisations working in remote, interior and inaccessible terrains whose performance and achievement are yet to come to public domain. Innumerable grass root level organisations have been relentlessly striving to break the shackles and fetters which make human beings un-free or bonded, to awaken the masses from their culture of silence and dependence and to conscientise them so that as free human entities they become partners of development and progress. It is not possible to count and re-count the names of all such grass roots-level organisations which may be dispersed across the length and breadth of a vast sub-continent like India. This, however, may not be construed as a reflection on their work and contribution in particular area of social action.

In terms of point of time, of the fifty names of VOs listed, the following VOs had taken a lead in the earlier years after enactment of BLS (A) Act to file WPs in Supreme Court which helped in establishing conceptual and definitional clarity on bonded debt, bonded labour, bonded labourer and bonded labour system. These are:

1. People's Union for Civil Liberties
2. People's Union for Democratic Rights
3. Bandhua Mukti Morcha
4. Bachpan Bachao Andolan
5. Bhoomi Sena
6. Centre for Tribal Conscientisation
7. Action for Cultural and Political Change

Late Justice PN Bhagwati, who wrote and delivered most of

the earlier majority judgments on bonded labour, had got a few organisations like AWARE, Hyderabad involved in the efforts towards eradication of bonded labour system.

PUCL in 1981 and BMM in 1982 were the first to knock at the doors of the Supreme Court by filing WPs 8431 and 2135. Through disposal of these by the apex court in a record time (18 September 1982 and 16 December 1983 respectively), the pace and tone of interpretation of the law i.e. BLS (A) Act was set in a substantially pro-active measure.

To illustrate, denial of minimum wage in the first was made co-terminus with forced labour as in Article 23 and the same in the second was made co-terminus with bonded labour.

As many as 21 directions were issued to the State government of Haryana by the apex court in the second which demonstrated the sense of urgency and seriousness with which the issue of bonded labour was viewed then.

The inquiry report submitted by the author to the apex court in two volumes[57] repudiated the stand of then State government that there are no bonded labourers in Haryana.

Subsequently BMM filed yet another WP[58] through which the petitioner sought issue of a writ of mandamus to direct the govt. of UP to stop employment of children in the carpet making units of Bhadoi, Varanasi and Mirzapur.

In the meanwhile, the proceedings arising out of the follow-up to WP 2135 of 1982 continued in the apex court in some form or the other (including a contempt of court petition) for almost two decades (till 16 November 1999).

---

57 Published as a book titled *Burden of Bondage* by Manak Publications, New Delhi

58 (Civil) 12125 of 1984 (with WP 11643 of 1985

President of BMM Swami Agnivesh who had filed the original WP 2135 of 1982 as also the subsequent contempt of court petition (as the 21 directions issued by the apex court were not complied with by the State Government) has continued his relentless struggle against prevalence of bonded labour system till date. Through writings, statements, debates and public discourses--both at the national and international level, he has kept the issue alive and ignited sparks in a number of likeminded individuals to work for this cause with the same passion and fervour. Simultaneously, he has given vent to his uneasiness and distress that elimination of bonded labour system has not received the prioritised attention which it deserved and instead, there is apathy, laxity and inaction alround.

This notwithstanding, BMM has been active in the field, pursuing relentlessly the cause of identification, rescue/release of the victims of bonded labour system in large number. According to the latest information available, BMM has rescued and released 1,78,000 victims of BLS since inception (1981) till date.

The constraints & challenges faced by BMM as others are two-fold. Release certificates are grudgingly issued by the Magistrate concerned even after BMM has presented full facts of the case. Even after the release certificates are reluctantly issued, the action on the rehabilitation process is not initiated making the rescue/ release rather infructuous.

To illustrate, of 632 such workmen who had migrated from Chitrakut, Banda, Mau, Bulandshahar (in UP), Satna, Sagar and Chhattarpur (in MP) who were found to be working under bonded conditions, release certificates have been issued only in respect of 205 persons but rehabilitation proposals are yet to be formulated either by the source or the destination State. The remaining 427 cases are pending for issue of RC for years.

The overall experience with the DMs of the districts concerned has been one of crippling delays which is quite frustrating.

The founder of BBA, Nobel Peace laureate Kailash Satyarthi, in his most tender, formative and impressionable age (6) was an eyewitness to the plight and predicament of working children in marginalised families. The same had cast an indelible imprint on a young mind. Even at that age, he had thought of something big and positive to bring a little cheer and laughter in the lives of those deprived children. As he grew up, the passion for the same grew and eventually led him to give up a lucrative professional career (he was a qualified electrical engineer) to work full time to bring excitement and joy to the lives of millions of poor and deprived children in India and abroad. The goal was clear, so was the iron resolve & passionate commitment to put an end to the suffering of bonded and trafficked children. In the process of liberating children from the clutches of powerful vested interests (like owners of circus esablishmens) he has suffered, fallen and bled but not given up his supreme resolve. Whether it is mobilising millions of children across continents under 'Global March' (October 1997–March 1998), playing a lead role in adoption by ILC of ILO Convention 182 on elimination of worst forms of child labour on 19 June 1999, making the ILC adopt 12 June as World Child Labour Day and issuing a clarion call for mobilising millions of youth for elimination of child labour and trafficking, Satyarthi remains like the rock of Gibraltar, unmoved, unswerving and undeterred till the goal of total elimination of these twin social evils is reached.

Bachpan Bachao Andolan, initially concentrated on rescue/release and rehabilitation of children found to be working under bonded/ slave like conditions. Over a period of nearly four decades, BBA has succeeded in rescuing and releasing over 80,000 children found to be working under bonded and slave-like conditions in some of the most hazardous occupations and processes. Subsequently it has concentrated efforts on rescue/ release and rehabilitation of trafficked children as would be evident from a series of WPs (51, 75 and 186) filed before the apex court which helped to establish clarity on the meaning, scope and content of missing children as trafficked children and involvement of police, CWC, JJB and civil society in handling cases of trafficked children.

BBA has opened a number of branches in different States and with the help of activists on the ground has been organising series of activities for conscientisation of children, to make them perceive and internalise the importance of the congruence between elimination of child labour in any form and free and compulsory universal education characterised by 100% enrolment, 100% retention, 100% participation and 100% achievement of desired levels of proficiency in mother tongue, arithmetic, sciences (physical and earth) and environment studies.

Kailash Satyarthi Educational Foundation under the stewardship of Sharad Chandra Sinha, former member NHRC who is ably assisted by a number of professionals has undertaken a series of initiatives to make achievement of the above goal possible and feasible.

Formation of Bal Panchayats is yet another significant step in the direction of carving out leadership skills amongst children with a view to making them the architects of their own destiny and taking informed and judicious decisions which are in their best interests (Article 3 of CRC of 1989).

The judgment of the Supreme Court delivered by (late) Justice Altamas Kabir, CJI on 10 June 2013 on trafficking came as a breath of fresh air by way of disposal of two WPs, namely number 75 and 186 filed by Bachpan Bachao Andolan and on account of the unremitting dedicated efforts of Bhuban Rivu in that direction.

The outcome of this splendid initiative on the part of BBA has been dealt with in response to Question 24.

In terms of point of time, it may be further mentioned that the 1980s and 1990s were devoted substantially in filing WPs for rescue/release and rehabilitation of victims of bonded labour system. While legal intervention of the courts for this purpose has continued, a significant and refreshing addition to the earlier strategy has been by way of taking up advocacy, partnership, intervention and multiple facets of involvement of civil society in innovative efforts towards rescue/release and rehabilitation of victims of bonded labour system/child labour/trafficking.

Advocacy is an act of pleading for or giving verbal support to a cause. Intervention is timely action at one end to intercede in the state of affairs prevailing at another end with a view to carrying a specific purpose to its logical close. Involvement of civil society in these efforts would mean the following:

- Opening up a dialogue and discussion with representatives of the people (MLAs, MPs, MLCs, Corporators, Panchayat bodies) to make them understand the provisions of the law, including case laws and the procedure established by law;
- This will make them better aware of the statutory provisions;
- Their awareness will help in changing mindsets of the officers vested with the responsibilities for law enforcement; it will make them more sensitive;

- Bringing representatives of the people to have an interface with victims/survivors;
- Such interface will breathe hope, faith and conviction to the lives of the victims that everything is not lost and life can be started a fresh.

Partnership implies thinking, planning and acting together. Partnership is sought as the magnitude of the problem is large and resources—human, material and financial—are limited while there is no dearth of creative talent which can be harnessed for a good cause. Harnessing the time, energy, and resources as also the best of imagination, ingenuity and creativity of the partners, makes intervention more effective, reduces the time and cost over-runs and improves the quality of implementation.

Examples of a few VOs may be cited who have effectively translated the above strategy to a more meaningful action. They are (a) International Justice Mission (IJM) (b) Jai Bhim Vikas Sikshan Sansthan (JBVSS) (c) Jan Sahas (JS) and (d) Foundation for Sustainable Development (FSD)(e) Justice Ventures International (JVI)

International Justice Mission

For IJM, partnership is the key to meaningful intervention and timely action. This is because no one individually in isolation can fight out the menace which is of very severe intensity and succeed in delivering scores of victims from the scourge of bondage and trafficking. Thinking, planning and working together with one voice, one energy and one conscience for one cause, which is worthwhile, is the only way by which the goal can be achieved. Through partnership resources—human, material and financial—

are pooled, mindsets are changed, best practices are shared, and there will be better urge, inclination and commitment to achieve the end object.

International Justice Mission, founded by Gary A Haugen, a champion of human rights against trafficking and human bondage in USA, is an international NGO with headquarters at Washington DC and with eighteen branches all over the world, including Chennai, Mumbai, Bengaluru, Delhi, Kolkata, Bhubaneswar and Patna.

IJM has been operating in over fifteen States in India for over a decade to combat sex trafficking of minors and bonded labour. It works alongside district, State and GoI officials and fellow civil society organisations to rescue/ release, repatriate, rehabilitate, and re-integrate victims of human trafficking, prosecute offenders of law and train public justice officials.

IJM has conducted training workshops for police and AHTU officials along with concerned State departments of UP, Bihar, Delhi, Odisha, and Rajasthan. It has also collaborated with National Law Universities of West Bengal, Odisha and Delhi and State Judicial Academy of West Bengal to organise judicial colloquiums. As a result of initiatives taken by IJM, elimination of bonded labour system has been included in the curriculum of the National Law University, Cuttack, Odisha and State Institute of Public Administration, Mysuru.

It has also developed resource materials in collaboration with CID of Karnataka State, Adi Dravidar and Tribal Welfare Department, Government of Tamil Nadu and Department of Labour Resources, Government of Bihar.

Along with the partners it has rescued more than 18,000 victims of bonded labour system so far. It believes in the efficacy of advocacy, partnership and collective intervention to produce desired results in less time and cost. Once the victims have been rescued, IJM implements a two-year rehabilitation programme with the consent of survivors and focusses on effective, meaningful and permanent rehabilitation and re-integration of the victim into the mainstream family, community and society.

Through this process, a half-being or a non-being is converted into a full being, his/her dignity, decency, freedom and equality are restored and he/she is resuscitated from the morass of poverty and deprivation to social and economic self-reliance. Eventually, the victim is able to assimilate himself/ herself into the realm of a civilised society to realise the dignity, beauty and worth of human existence.

Jai Bhim Vikas Sikshan Sansthan

Jai Bhim Vikas Shikshan Sansthan (JBVSS) was founded in 1993 by Tulsi Das Raj to protect and safeguard the interests of Dalit communities in Rajasthan.

Soon after being founded, JBVSS opened five schools providing free education to Dalit children and made considerable efforts for enrolment, retention, participation and achievement of desired levels of learning for the Dalit children in Jodhpur area. It continues to work in the same direction of empowerment of dalit communities through livelihood training and multiple other initiatives.

Entry of JBVSS into the arena of rescue/release of victims of bonded labour system in recent years has been a welcome initiative. Working as a partner of IJM during the last five years, JBVSS has been instrumental in rescuing/releasing a number of victims of bonded labour system from the brick kilns, first in

Rajsamand district followed by Bhilwara district in collaboration with officers of the State Government.

The victims in both the cases numbering over 150 bonded labourers happened to be inter-State migrant workmen. The refreshing outcomes in both the initiatives have been (a) a two year rehabilitation programme following rescue/release in quick succession (b) arranging release certificates in favour of the victims (c) arranging medical treatment of a victim diagnosed with TB (d) opening bank accounts for the victims (e) procuring Aadhar cards for the victims (f) arranging transportation for the victims (g) organising training for officials of AHTU, department of labour and CWC (h) filing FIR under S370 IPC (as amended) and the SC&ST (Prevention of Atrocities) Act, 1989 as amended in 2015.

It was most refreshing to listen to the survivors as to how their lives have turned a full circle due to the unstinted and unremitting efforts of JBVSS.

Jan Sahas

Jan Sahas (JS) was established in 2000 by Ashif Sheikh, primarily in response to the death of a working child and two Dalit labourers in an illegal firecracker-making facility. The activities of JS were focused on empowerment of Dalits and other socially excluded communities as also to promote, protect and preserve their inalienable human rights. In the initial years, JS was part of a noble initiative to file a PIL in the apex court for abolition of manual scavenging and rehabilitation of manual scavengers.

Formation of a lawyers' forum which is a network of 340 practising lawyers was yet another feather in the cap of the VO. One of the most significant outcomes of this initiative is training of 900 paralegals as barefoot lawyers.

The story of successful rescue/release of fifteen victims from Khargone in MP reminds one of the tragic episode of two migrant labourers from Kalahandi in Odisha on 15 December 2013 i.e., Nilambar Niyal (twenty-two), a Dalit youth and Dhangda Majhi (thirty-two), a member of the ST community whose hands were chopped off as they refused to accept their changed destination.[59] In this case too, instead of being taken to Sholapur in Maharashtra and much against their wishes, the victims landed up in Bagalkot district of Karnataka. The work in the sugarcane field (for which the labourers were illegally drafted) used to start at 4 am and went up to 6 pm (it ended only after the day's cane was loaded on trucks). Each family received only one kg of wheat flour as food provision at the end of the day.

The workers were locked up in an animal shed for the whole night, human interface was banned and their money and phones were confiscated. They suffered insufferable physical abuse. The labourers could not ventilate their grievance to anyone as they were under constant surveillance.

Two months later, one of the labourers gained access to a stranger's mobile phone, was able to establish contact with his father-in-law who could then reach out to the police. The MP Police in collaboration with the specialised unit of CID team in Karnataka and with the support of JS arrived at the sugarcane field in Bagalkot and rescued the labourers. With full police protection from Karnataka Police, the team of JS escorted the survivors back to their hearth and home at Khargone. The trafficker was arrested, FIR was filed, investigation followed and ended up with a criminal trial.

---

59 This has been dealt with at length in Chapter IV

By all accounts, this has been a truly heroic activity, justifying the name 'Sahas' which stands for courage. The same courage of conviction was demonstrated in more cases of release of brick kiln workers from Ninora in Ujjain district, rescue of two sheep rearing boys who had been trafficked to neighbouring State of Rajasthan (516 km away) under gruelling conditions of bondage. The other equally commendable activities of the VO have been (a) rescue of five child bonded labourers in Ujjain who had been trafficked to Udaipur in Rajasthan (b) organising two workshops at Harda and Ujjain on human trafficking.

Foundation for Sustainable Development

Founded in 2001, Foundation for Sustainable Development with headquarters at Vellore had promotion of tribal welfare, empowerment of indigenous people with forests and land rights as its initial principal mandate. However, the VO soon perceived and internalised the close link between tribal issues, trafficking and bonded labour. Accordingly, Dr K Krishnan, the founder who is also the Secretary General of National Adivasi Solidarity Council expanded the scope and ambit of FSD to include labour trafficking and bonded labour.

The impact of leadership of the organisation and that of the founder on the field workers has been electrifying, to say the least. This will be evident from just one example of AP Kanniappan who has been working as a State Project Coordinator for the FSD for the last fifteen years. He has visited over 1,000 villages in nineteen districts in Tamil Nadu and has assisted the government in the rescue of close to 2,800 bonded labourers.

The task of FSD in rescue/release of large number of victims of bonded labour system from the brick kiln industry in Tamil

Nadu has been greatly facilitated due to the prompt and positive response of the State Government. Being greatly encouraged by this response, FSD organised in collaboration with Sivagangai Bar Association for lawyers in December 2016 a consultation on BLS (A) Act. The consultation provided a unique opportunity to train and equip lawyers on their role in fighting the scourge of bonded labour system prevalent in brick kilns, rice mills, spinning mills, wood cutting industry, sugarcane fields, building and construction and tourism.

FSD conducted a survey in the villages within the ayacut of Aliyar dam in Pollachi revenue division of Coimbatore district and filed a complaint with NHRC in May 2017 that nearly 1,000 agricultural labourers were working with their landlords (mostly plantation owners) under bonded conditions. The NHRC asked the State Government for investigation into the complaint and report. Regretfully, the investigation conducted by a team of investigators from the Revenue Department under the guidance of RDO, Pollachi was seriously flawed and the Commission ordered on 30 November 2017 a fresh investigation after a detailed hearing of the complaint and after perusal of the investigation report. The second report from the State Government after a fresh investigation is still awaited even after expiry of more than two years.

This is a typical case where the State Government unlike in the past has been found wanting in discharge of a statutory responsibility cast on it under the BLS (A) Act. The State Labour Department reported to the Commission in December 2019 that six vigilance teams were constituted, surprise visits to the area were conducted and no case of bonded labour was found. The case was closed 2 March 2020 on the basis of the above report of the State Government with a direction to the authorities to keep a strict vigil in the area to check any violation of human rights.

In yet another case, spanning across six States and an area of approximately 2,500 sq km, twenty families and around fifty-five labourers were trafficked from Telangana to Rajasthan in December 2015. The labourers worked for long hours, had no freedom of movement and were kept under constant surveillance.

FSD team worked closely with the Government of Telangana in collaboration with JBVSS to rescue the trafficked workers but just days before the planned rescue, acting on a tip-off, the trafficker forcibly shifted the victims from out of Rajasthan to an unknown destination. Eventually with the help of technology, Telangana Police and FSD were able to seize the truck carrying the survivors and arrest the trafficker.

The eventual success of this popular rescue operation fraught with risks underlines the importance of timely collaboration between Government and VOs.

Justice Ventures International

Justice Ventures International (JVI) is committed to secure freedom, justice and rehabilitation for the poor and oppressed by collaboration for capacity building and hand holding operations. In India, JVI works with local partners and State Governments of Bihar, Delhi, UP, Mumbai and West Bengal. During 2016 alone, JVI and its local partners have (a) secured justice for over 1,700 victims through legal representation in over 180 legal cases; these include debt bondage, sex trafficking, slum dweller rights and wrongful confinement (b) conducted twenty rescue operations to secure the freedom of 290 victims of human trafficking (c) empowered the oppressed through human rights training for over 3,700 individuals including survivors, NGO leaders, government officials, police, lawyers and judges (d) promoted freedom from vulnerability of the victims by strengthening the capacity of local justice delivery system.

NGOs in Bihar in April 2016 held a consultation to learn about each other's work and vision, understand the situation of bonded labour in the State and discuss solutions for combating the issue through close partnership collaboration. JVI actively participated in this initiative.

Nine NGOs came together in May 2017 to learn about each other's work, discuss the draft Trafficking Bill and Central Scheme for rehabilitation of bonded labourers and inputs for the State level Action Plan (SAP) for elimination of bonded labour system in Bihar.

In April 2017, JVI and IJM participated as resource persons in a State level workshop jointly organised by the Labour Resource Department, Government of Bihar, JVI and IJM. The topic which was chosen for discussion was 'Laws and Procedures against Human Trafficking, Child and Bonded Labour'. The participants included AHTU nodal officers, SDOs, Labour Enforcement Officers, District Child Protection Unit officials. The author and William Christopher from IJM and Hemraj from JVI were the resource persons for this workshop.

A unique rescue operation conducted by the NHRC and JVI in 2014 involved a specific form of bonded labour through attached agricultural labour prevalent in Bihar known as Kamiya system. It is a traditional caste-based system of inter-generational bondage in which families are contractually held by landowners and exploited. In all, 164 people were rescued. The main accused in the case has been arrested and detained after a bail rejection.

The above five case studies have been presented primarily with a view to highlighting the importance of the old adage. 'United we stand and divided we fall'. i.e. the importance of understanding, communication, collaboration and partnership.

A question may be raised as to why these five were handpicked and the remaining were left out. The intention is not to exclude any successful model of thinking, planning and working together but only to highlight a few so that the primacy and centrality of the principle of collaboration for a common cause i.e. for the good of humanity is established beyond doubt and the successful experiment is further replicated elsewhere.

Each VO undoubtedly is unique in its strategy and methodology. The underlying intention is not to include any particular success story to the exclusion of another. Success stories are determined by examples of individuals and collectives working together with one goal, one mission and one dharma as also with one voice, one energy and one conscience. It is with this perspective that this entire dialectical exercise has been carried out.

Question 61

What are the gaps, omissions, ambiguities and deficiencies in the framework of BLS (A) Act? Do you have any specific suggestions for removing these gaps, omissions and deficiencies by way of amendment?

Answer: As has been repeatedly stated, BLS (A) Act, 1976 is one of the most progressive enactments in post-independent India. There are, however, two points which need to be noted here. The first: No law can be foolproof in the sense that it is not possible to anticipate all future trends. Second: If certain developments could not be anticipated at the time of enactment of the law in 1975-76, these must be taken cognisance of now and necessary changes must be effected within the framework of the law to make it relevant in the context of changing times.

Some changes visible in the current milieu are:

I. The incidence of debt bondage has declined to some extent.
II. The incidence of distress migration which has a huge potential of human bondage has, however, increased manifold. Most of the victims of such migration are reported to work under bonded conditions.
III. The incidence of trafficking for forced/bonded labour has increased substantially.
IV. While inter-State distress migration is closely related to payment of advance, trafficking is related to deceit, fraud, coercion and regimentation.
V. Children (mostly girls) are the worst victims of such trafficking.
VI. Unlike inter-State migration which is not difficult to track, there is an element of in-visibility, in-accessibility and non-accountability of perpetrators of the crime of trafficking.
VII. There are instances where forced/bonded labour situations have also given rise to trafficking for commercial sexual exploitation.

Against this backdrop, a few amendments to BLS (A) Act have been suggested as under with a view to bridging the existing gaps. These are as under:

Chapter I of BLS (A) Act

I. **Concept and definition**

- Trafficking has not been defined in 'Immoral Traffic (Prevention) Act as amended in 1978 and 1986.
- It has been defined in the UN Protocol to prevent, suppress and

punish trafficking in persons especially women and children (December 2000).

- Criminal Law (Amendment) Act, 2013 has adopted this definition.
- Since trafficking of human beings is taking place for forced/ bonded labour and vice versa, a second explanation may be inserted after the first in BLS (A) Act by which trafficking of children (boys and girls) and women can be brought within the purview of 'BLS' as defined in Section 2(g) of that Act.

II. **Chapter IV**

Implementing authorities

- Section 10 confers wide powers on the DMs. While 'shall exercise all or any of the powers and perform all or any of the duties as in Section 10 presumably includes identification, rescue/release and rehabilitation of freed bonded labourers, it may be desirable by way of abundant caution to explicitly State them within the powers and functions of DM and officers specified by DM.
- Issue of a release certificate in favour of every released bonded labourer has several plus points. It imparts a sense of identity. It precludes any possible action on the part of the erstwhile bonded labour keeper to subject the freed bonded labourer to any illegal, immoral and unethical control. It acts as the basis for formulation of a rehabilitation scheme for the released bonded labourer(s). Keeping these distinct advantages in issue of a release certificate in favour of every freed bonded labourer in view, Supreme Court in several judgments have exhorted the DMs to issue such a certificate. The same has, however, not been specifically stated anywhere in BLS (A) Act.
- Section 10 is the right place where issue of a release certificate in favour of every released bonded labourer should be included in

the powers and duties of DM and an officer specified by DM.

- Section 10 may be amended accordingly.
- DM's role and responsibility and that of the officer specified by the DM have been clearly listed in Section 11. It says '...shall, as far as possible, try to promote the welfare of the freed bonded labourer by securing and protecting the economic interests of such bonded labourers...'
- Majority of the bonded labourers belong to SC and ST and they continue to be victims of un-touchability and other caste-related atrocities which are manifestations of social exclusion and discrimination.
- It may, therefore, be appropriate to add 'social' before economic interests.
- It has been further observed that waiting period for rehabilitation of freed bonded labourers is unusually long. In such a contingency, the latter may either migrate purely for reasons of economic security to a worksite at a destination point or may lapse back to bondage under the erstwhile bonded labour keeper.
- It may, therefore, be appropriate to add after economic interests and such other measures like timely, meaningful and effective rehabilitation so that there may not be any occasion or reason for him to contract and further bonded debt.'

III. **Chapter V**

Vigilance Committees

- Experience of working with VCs, wherever constituted, has over the last forty years or so revealed the following deficiencies in their structure and functioning at the district and sub-divisional level such as:
  - The DM concerned sends the proposal to the State

Government for both constitution and re-constitution, whenever due after two years of constitution;

- Timely decisions are usually not taken to approve the proposals sent by the DM;
- Either the names proposed by the DM are dropped and new names are inserted or the composition is completely altered which is against the spirit of Section 13(2);
- In a few cases, it has been observed that as a result of such unilateral change of the proposed composition, vested interests get into the VC to the exclusion of genuine voluntary Social Action Groups whose inclusion has been emphasised in the *Neerja Chaudhary* case;
- While re-constitution of VCs gets inordinately delayed, the existing VCs do not meet at all or at regular intervals which is contrary to Rules;
- No Secretarial assistance (office space, furniture, equipment, vehicle for better mobility by way of field visits) has so far been made available for effective functioning of VCs;
- VCs have been authorised by law (Section 14 (e) of BLS (A) Act) to conduct surveys but neither the procedure, format nor resources (human, material and financial) to meet the cost of the survey has been laid down;
- VCs cannot provide for economic and social rehabilitation of freed bonded labourers as expected of them u/s 14 (b) of BLS (A) Act when they do not have any financial powers nor any budget has been exclusively placed at their disposal specifically for this purpose;
- Similarly, no funds have been placed at the disposal of VCs to defend any suit instituted against any freed bonded labourer as required u/s 14 (f).

The proposals for consideration keeping in view the above deficiencies are:

I. The DM and SDM are officers on the spot, conversant with local people, local milieu and local conditions. They have to ensure that the VCs deliver certain expected outcomes under their leadership. Their wisdom and pragmatism cannot be easily substituted by the State Government acting in discretion to accord final approval to the composition of VCs.

II. Power to constitute and re-constitute VCs both at the district and sub-divisional level may, therefore, most appropriately be delegated by the State Government to DMs of the districts concerned.

III. There may be a State-level Monitoring and Coordination Committee headed by the Chief Secretary to monitor and oversee the functioning of VCs.

IV. There may be a State-level nodal officer to look into the specific administrative and financial problems faced by VCs in their day-to-day functioning (like PWC Davidar, IAS, who functioned as the special officer of Adi Dravidar Department, Government of Tamil Nadu in 2000-2003 and imparted a new dynamism to the programmes of rescue/release and rehabilitation of bonded labourers).

V. Necessary budgetary, logistic and manpower support for VCs at both district and sub-divisional levels should be made available by the State Government. This may be provided in the Rules under the Act.

IV. **Chapter VI**

I. **Offences and Procedure for Trial**

- In the light of the judgment of the High Court of MP (Jabalpur branch) in MP 2522 of 1984 decided on 28 September 1995, judgment of the Bombay High Court in WP (Crl) 406 of 1988 decided on 25 September 1991 and judgment of the Madras High Court in WP 7650 of 2013 and MPs 1 and 2 of 2013 decided on 3 June 2014 striking down the Constitutional validity of Section 21 of BLS (A) Act, the said Section requires to be amended in the following manner:

I. The expression 'Executive Magistrate' will be replaced by 'Judicial Magistrate'.
II. '...Powers of a Judicial Magistrate of the First Class or the Second Class' to be deleted.
III. Section 21 (2) proviso relating to summary trial of all bonded labour cases may remain un-altered.
IV. All existing case records are required to be transferred by Executive Magistrates to Judicial Magistrates.

II. There is an apparent contradiction between the provisions relating to summary trial as in Section 261 and Section 262 in chapter XXI of CrPC of 1973 and sub-Section 2 of Section 21 of BLS (A) Act.

- o U/s 261 of CrPC, a case may be tried summarily which is punishable only with fine or imprisonment for a term not exceeding six months with or without fine.
- o U/s 262 of CrPC, no sentence of imprisonment for a term exceeding three months shall be passed in case of any conviction under this chapter.
- o Against these provisions, an offence u/s 16 of BLS (A) Act shall be punishable with imprisonment for a term which may extend to three years and also with fine which may extend to ₹2,000.

- o Section 3 of BLS (A) Act provides that provisions of this Act shall have effect notwithstanding anything in-consistent therewith contained in any enactment other than this Act or in any instrument having effect by virtue of any enactment other than this Act.
- o Section 5 of CrPC says that, 'nothing contained in this Code shall, in the absence of a specific provision to the contrary, affect any special or local law for the time being in force, or any special jurisdiction or power conferred, or any special form of procedure prescribed, by any other law for the time being in force.'
- o In view of these explicit provisions, it is 100 per cent possible to take up trial of all offences under BLS (A) Act by adopting the summary procedure as in Section 260 to Section 265 of CrPC, 1973.
- o However, for abundant clarity and with a view to steering clear of any further doubt, sub-Section 2 of Section 21 may be amended to read 'An offence under this Act may be tried summarily by a Judicial Magistrate under Section 21 read with Sections 16-20 of BLS (A) Act, notwithstanding provisions of Section 261 and Section 262 (2) of CrPC, 1973.

Miscellaneous

A proposal for insertion of a new provision in BLS (A) Act for award of compensation in favour of a victim of BLS in accordance with provisions of Section 357 CrPC may deserve consideration.

Section 357(1) order to pay compensation reads as under:

'When a Court imposes a sentence of fine or a sentence (including a sentence of death) of which fine forms a part, the

Court may, when passing judgment, order the whole or any part of the fine recovered to be applied:

(a) In defraying the expenses properly incurred in the prosecution;

(b) In the payment to any person of compensation for any loss or injury caused by the offence, when compensation, in the opinion of the Court, recoverable by such person in a Civil Court.

(4) An order under this Section may also be made by an appellate Court or by the High Court or Court of Sessions when exercising its powers of revision.

(5) At the time of awarding compensation in any subsequent civil suit relating to the same matter, the Court shall take into account any sum paid or recovered as compensation under this Section.

The rationale for award of such compensation to the victim may be explained as under:

- A victim of BLS suffers a lot of injuries—physical, mental, psychological and emotional in the following manner:
- Physical assault causes injury;
- These assaults are not one time but repetitive;
- Women and children of all bonded labourers are also subjected to harsh and gruelling manual labour along with parents;
- There are reported incidents of children of attached agricultural labourers (victims of BLS by all counts) being struck with red hot iron for minor lapses, which causes grievous injuries;
- Numerous indignities are hurled at the women;
- They face sexual harassment at the workplace.

Keeping the possibility of such injury being caused to the victims of BLS and the tremendous traumatic impact thereof, a specific provision for payment of compensation u/s 357(b) of CrPC by the Magistrate appointed and empowered to try cases under BLS(A) Act should be made.

Question 62

What are the problems, constraints and challenges in elimination of BLS in India?

Answer: Eradication of BLS as a social evil is not and should not be the concern only of the labour ministry at the central level and of the concerned administrative departments at the State level. It is a global concern and at the level of the State, it should be, the concern of all ministries/departments/agencies and should be viewed as a matter of national concern.

It is primarily for the facility of coordination that MoL&E has been made the nodal ministry in relation to all matters pertaining to implementation of BLS (A) Act. BLS is essentially a negation of human freedom which is the key to human development; since human development is the ultimate goal and responsibility of government which includes all ministries/departments, it is but normal and natural that all ministries/departments concerned with human development should be genuinely concerned about existence of the pernicious BLS which is anti-podal to that development.

This concern may have been expressed in black and white on a few occasions but a lot more remains to be done to translate the concern to concrete action in letter and spirit.

On 11 July 2019, due to the joint initiative of International Justice Mission (an international NGO) and Directorate General,

Labour Welfare, MoL&E in collaboration with a number of other stakeholders such as MHA, MoHRD and MSDE came together with the concerned State governments and NGOs for the common cause of elimination of BLS. NHRC also joined hands.

All of them coming together on one platform for sharing problems, concerns, achievements as also challenges, was a refreshing and extremely productive experience.

While the Central Government has enacted the law, the responsibility for enforcement of the statutory provisions has been left to the State Governments/UTs concerned. At the State level, the subject of bonded labour is being handled by different departments in different States; there are frequent changes in allocation of this subject to different departments from time to time and there is no unbroken continuity of one department handling the subject which would have been useful for acquiring experience and maintaining consistency in approach, strategy and methodology.

Regardless of this, what is important is the following:

- The administrative department or nodal department should work in close unison with other sister departments concerned with understanding, goodwill and involvement;
- There is tremendous scope for cooperation and collaboration of different departments in handling tasks relating to identification, rescue/release and rehabilitation.

To illustrate, in rescue/release, we need cooperation and support of home (police) department. In the pre-rehabilitation phase when the released victims are taken to a transit point for health check-ups, we are in need of cooperation and support of health department.

Similarly, for psychological counselling, help has to be sought from psychiatrists, clinical psychologists and psychiatric social workers who come under the health department.

For ascertaining the level of educational equivalence of the rescued/released victims, the cooperation of the education department has to be sought.

Similarly, for enrolment and retention of trafficked/bonded children (who have been rescued and released) in the formal school system, we need tacit cooperation and support of both education and WCD departments.

For ascertaining the level of skills acquired, we need the cooperation and support of skill training department.

For implementation of the programme of rehabilitation and to make the same permanent, meaningful and effective, we need the involvement of the departments of agriculture (including soil conservation, horticulture, floriculture, sericulture), animal husbandry and veterinary, forest, fisheries, irrigation (large, medium, minor and lift), skill training, rural development, housing and urban development, women and child development, food and civil supplies, SC/ST welfare, Panchayati Raj, IT and science and technology .

Since the outlay available for rehabilitation is limited (even though substantially enhanced under the new Central Scheme w.e.f. 17 May 2016), the same can be further augmented by pooling resources (human, material and financial) from a variety of sources and integrating the same imaginatively and skillfully to enhance the content, quality and impact of the programme.

While conceptually this is possible, feasible as also achievable, this has not happened in actual practice.

There are additional stumbling blocks which have inhibited

the range, sweep, content, quality and impact of the programme such as:

- The States/UTs are not prepared to acknowledge the existence of BLS;
- Most of the States, according to NHRC, are in a denial mode;
- According to them, this is a thing of the past, a one-time problem which seems to have been taken care of by enactment of a Central law;
- They disown the existence of the system without (a) constituting VCs and re-constituting them whenever due (b) getting a survey conducted by the VCs as required u/s 14 (e) of BLS(A) Act and (c) conducting instead investigation with the help of the lower echelons of bureaucracy without imagination and sensitivity and reporting nil finding.

The natural question which needs to be raised is this: 'Why are the States/UTs disowning existence of BLS? They are doing so on account of a number of mistaken notions such as:

- Acknowledging the existence of BLS in twenty-first century with all the advancements in Science and Technology will be a slur on the overall image of State Government;
- It will bring discredit to local administration.

Supreme Court had adversely commented on such a strange attitude and approach in the following words:

- The State Governments should realise that providing relief to the poor, deprived and disadvantaged does not bring a slur on Government; nor does it bring any discredit to local administration;

- Instead, such acts, by way of providing a little cheer to the cheerless faces of the deprived, excluded and dis-advantaged, will bring enormous credit to both government and local administration.

An economically prosperous State (with a very high GDP rate of economic growth) took a stand before the apex court in course of hearing WP 2135 (of 1982) that the inter-State migrant workmen may be working in the stone quarries under conditions of forced labour but they are not bonded labourers.

Even after the apex court rejected the said contention, there was no perceptible change in the mindsets of the State Government. Similarly, a very incorrect and inappropriate message has been sent out at different points of time from responsible quarters that withdrawing victims of attached agricultural labour (Kamiyas, Halis and Harwahs, Haris/Seris, Halias and Barmasias and Sagris) will sound the death knell of agriculture and agricultural economy of the State as they provide a source of cheap labour.

On the one hand, officers at the district and sub-divisional level display ignorance about the provisions of the law; on the other hand, their arrogance in refusing to issue the release certificate in a situation of genuine bondage is shocking and frustrating.

Worse still, they eventually issue the release certificate not of their own accord but only when they are driven to the wall and are directed by the NHRC to do so.

When the first complaint filed by Bagambar Patnaik of Odisha Goti Mukti Andolan (GMA) on the prevalence of *bartan* system (hereditary and caste-based bondage) in Puri district was referred by NHRC to Panchayati Raj Department, Government of Odisha in 2008-09, the PR Department without a proper examination of all the implications of the issue opined that *bartan* system was not akin to BLS.

The same department willy-nilly agreed to change its stand when the full Commission took an affirmative decision, equated bartan system to BLS in its session at Bhubaneswar (January 2011) and communicated the said decision for compliance to the State Government.

The State Government issued clear instructions to all DMs only thereafter that (a) *bartan* system tantamounts to BLS as defined in section 2(g) of BLS(A) Act; and (b) all victims of the said system should be released and rehabilitated accordingly.

Empirical studies show that persons have been nominated to the VCs on extraneous considerations and not in conformity with provisions of Section 13 of the Act.

Such members do not have the educational qualification, professional experience and expertise, far less the interest and commitment which would enable them to do justice to the mandate.

The meetings of the VCs are mostly ceremonial in character. They often meet and disperse without transacting any worthwhile or serious business, without going to the field and seldom conducting an inquiry into complaints received.

A VC undoubtedly is a very important and useful institutional mechanism u/s 13 of BLS(A) Act.

Its primary mandate is (a) to conduct a survey for identifying the victims of BLS u/s 14 (e) of BLS (A) Act (b) provide for the economic and social rehabilitation of the freed bonded labourers (c) advise the DM to ensure that the provisions of the Act or the rule made thereunder are properly implemented (d) coordinate the functions of rural banks and co-operative societies (e) keep an eye on the number of offences of which cognisance has been taken under the Act (f) defend any civil suit instituted against a freed bonded labourer or a member of his family or any person dependent on him. All these are required to be properly implemented.

Instances have been reported where a DM (in Puri district of Odisha in 2007-08) summoned the bonded labour keeper and victims of *bartan* system and attempted to work out a compromise between the parties.

Such a course of action is palpably wrong as there is no scope for compounding any offence under the law. Any such attempt at compounding the offence would amount to an abetment for commission of an offence u/s 20 of BLS(A) Act.

Section 2(g) of BLS (A) Act was amended in April 1985 and the amendment came into force on 24 December 1985. According to the explanation attached to Section 2(g) of the Act, a contract or inter-State migrant labourer would come fully within the purview of BLS, if he/she fulfils the basic ingredients of the system as defined in the Section.

Over the years, there has been a phenomenal increase in the number of contract labourers as also in the number of victims of inter-State distress migration. It is extremely difficult to estimate the number of victims of inter-State distress migration, as records and registers are not being properly maintained. In regard to contract labour, however, a country-wide survey conducted by the Associated Chambers of Commerce and Industry of India (ASSOCHAM), New Delhi under the aegis of its Social Development Foundation captioned. 'Steep rise of permanently temporary workers—India's workforce goes casual', the increase in contract labour has been as steep as amounting to 39 per cent of the total workforce. At the same time, the growth in the number of regular workers has nearly halved to 25 per cent. The disaggregated data on the presence of contract workers in different sectors are as under:

Automobiles – 56 per cent

Manufacturing – 52 per cent

Education – 55 per cent

IT/BPO jobs – 42 per cent

Hospitality and travel /tourism – 35 per cent

Pharmaceuticals- healthcare – 32 per cent

Regardless of increase in number of contract labour/ inter-State migrant labour, the working conditions and terms of employment in case of each worker need to be studied and if on the basis of such study, the status fulfils the ingredients of BLS as defined in Section 2(g) of BLS (A) Act, the same needs to be taken cognisance of and victims of BLS need to be rescued/released from bondage, repatriated to their native State and rehabilitated.

There is, however, no evidence on the part of the concerned State government to take cognisance of the presence of contract and inter-State migrant workmen working under bonded conditions.

Instead, there is evidence of strange mindsets on the part of certain State Governments such as:

- We are a prosperous and enterprising State;
- If on account of poverty, unemployment and underdevelopment, people from other States migrate to our State, they are squarely responsible for their decision and action and we cannot be faulted;
- Such people migrate entirely of their own; they will also go back of their own after the working season is over;
- We have very little to do anything with them. We are not responsible for their poverty, unemployment and backwardness.

Such a stand is regrettable on account of the following reasons:

- The country is one and indivisible;
- There are well endowed and less endowed pockets in every region/State;
- It is normal and natural for people and families below the poverty line from low endowed pockets to migrate to well-endowed pockets in pursuit of opportunities for better employment and wages;
- There is nothing wrong or objectionable in such an action which is fully supported by Article 19(d) of the Constitution;
- Additionally, the inter-State migrant workmen through their 'blood, sweat and tears' contribute substantially to the prosperity of the enterprise and GDP rate of growth of the economy.
- It will be patently unjust and unfair to dismiss them as aliens or as persons of no consequence as is evident from a description of such persons by a few destination States.

In the case of inter-State migrant workmen who have been identified, rescued/released as victims of BLS, the apex court had issued a clear direction that the preference of such labourers as to whether they would prefer to get rehabilitated at the destination point or prefer to go back to the source State should be respected and action to rehabilitate them at the preferred location and mode of rehabilitation should be initiated. There is, however, no evidence of any positive and pro-active action on the part of Governments of destination States to translate the direction of the apex court to action.

The following case which pertains to NHRC and inter-State migrant workmen who were alleged to be working under bonded conditions is gruesome:

- X number of inter-State migrant workmen were working in a brick kiln in UP under questionable conditions;
- On receipt of a complaint, NHRC deputed a team to ascertain their correct status and rescue/release them, if found working under bonded conditions;
- Before the team could reach the spot, the employer got a tip-off and bundled them into a truck like sardines and dispatched them to an unknown destination;
- Due to contact with a high tension (11 KVA) live wire, nine workers were instantly electrocuted.

In this context, it is proper to ponder over the following:

- Inter-State migrant workmen who are victims of distress migration are mostly landless, resourceless and defenceless;
- The pockets from where they migrate are mostly dry, drought-prone and deficient;
- Migration ordinarily takes place from Lakhisarai, Latehar (now in Jharkhand), Nawada and Sitamarhi in Bihar, Banda, Ballia, Basti, Deoria, Gorakhpur, Azamgarh, Mirzapur, Sonbhadra and Jaunpur in UP, Barmer, Jailsalmer, Jalore, Sikar, Jhunjhunu, Jodhpur, Bikaner and Banswada in Rajasthan, Satna, Rewa, Sidhi, Betul, Sehore, Sahadol in MP, Raigarh, Rajnandgaon, Raipur and Bilaspur in Chhattisgarh, Kalahandi, Balangir and Koraput (KBK region) in Odisha, etc;
- Conditions have not dramatically changed now from the time when families first migrated;
- The prospects of rehabilitation of these families in an effective manner in the source pockets which continue to be dry and drought-prone does not appear to be bright;
- There is every possibility that these families will continue to

migrate to well-endowed pockets until and unless there is a qualitative change in the landscape at the originating point and change in their own status of landlessness and assetlessness.

Other problems and constraints in rehabilitation of freed bonded labourers which have come to notice are:

- Notwithstanding the emphasis of the apex court on immediacy and simultaneity between identification, rescue/ release and rehabilitation, there are instances where identified bonded labourers have to wait for years for rehabilitation without there being any valid justification;
- The content, quality and impact of the rehabilitation programmes—be they land based, non-land based or art/ craft/skill based leave much to be desired for the following reasons such as:
    - o The rehabilitation schemes are not formulated in time;
    - o Whenever formulated, they are not in tune with the preferences, felt needs and interests of the beneficiaries; these are not specifically ascertained from the potential beneficiaries;
    - o There is avoidable delay in approval of the rehabilitation proposals;
    - o Even after they have been approved, they are not pressed into action in time by adoption of a coordinated, convergent and holistic approach with involvement of development functionaries of concerned departments whose involvement is vital for success of the rehabilitation effort; the rehabilitation programmes are belatedly implemented in isolation.

The following are the deficiencies of land based rehabilitation:

- Land allotted for agriculture is unfit for cultivation;
- Land development programmes are seldom put in place;
- Suitability of a particular soil for a particular species of crop on the basis of soil testing is seldom taken into account.
- There is no detailed planned exercise as to how to maximise the output from land by making available all possible inputs with forward and backward linkages;
- Desired extension effort is not forthcoming from the officers of Agriculture Department,[60] an important component of agricultural extension activity was in vogue;
- The economics of growing certain species vis-à-vis their nutritive value is not scientifically examined and communicated to the growers;

In non-land based or productive asset-based programmes, similar involvement of officers of Animal Husbandry and Veterinary Department with the following components in a sequential order is wanting, such as:

- Selection of disease-free or healthy assets;
- Involvement of the beneficiary in such selection;
- Proper up-keep and maintenance of assets;
- Orientation and training of beneficiaries.

This is absolutely necessary for maximising the yield and the incremental income generation. Instead, the ground-level reality is quite different in as much as:

- The officers of Animal Husbandry and veterinary department look upon rehabilitation of bonded labourers as a programme of some other Ministry/Department;
- They have seldom taken pains to establish a timely and proper outreach as also to have a warm and humane interface

60 As was the case earlier in 1950s and 1960s when training and visit (T&V) were in vogue

with the freed bonded labourers to orient them about the common ailments likely to affect the animals and birds, as the case may be, supplied to the beneficiaries as productive assets and prescribe remedies with a view to preventing mortality of these assets;

- They have not taken pains to design the IEC materials which are well-visualised and well-illustrated in simple and intelligible language which will help the beneficiaries to familiarise themselves with the art and technique of proper upkeep and maintenance of assets as mini-animal husbandry men or barefoot doctors (a practice obtaining in China).

Similarly, involvement of officers of Industries Department (skill training) such as District Industries Centres, Handloom and Handicraft Development Board, Development Commissioner, Small Scale Industries, Small Industries Service Institute, etc. may be ensured in the following manner;

- Undertaking a survey to find out how many rural artisans have lost their old avocation and skill and have become landless agricultural labourers;
- How many of them will be willing to undergo orientation and training for revival of their skills?
- Formulation and implementation of art/craft/skill based programmes for rehabilitation of those bonded labourers who were once rural artisans but due to sheer economic compulsion have forgotten the skills and have become de-skilled;
- Ensuring easy, uninhibited and affordable access of these ex-artisans to raw materials, credit, technology and market as part of the revival process.

Such involvement is yet to become a reality on the ground.

Question 63

What needs to be done to prevent occurrence and recurrence of BLS?

Answer: The following are some of the strategies which need to be adopted to prevent occurrence and recurrence of BLS.

I. **Easy access to credit:**

- Credit has a protective as well as a promotional and developmental role.
- Easy access to credit at affordable rates of interest is one of the surest ways of deliverance of millions of people from the clutches of landlords, moneylenders and contractors, many of whom are also creditors and bonded labour keepers in real life.
- The Jan Dhan Yojana launched by PM in 2014-15 is a very timely, positive and pro-active intervention to ensure financial inclusion.
- This has brought over thirty crore people within the purview of banking operations.[61]
- The next logical course of action in this laudable initiative would be:
  - Deposits in the accounts of passbook holders, would require to be substantially augmented;
  - This would be possible only if earnings of passbook holders go up substantially;

61 This is something which was experimented with success during 1973-75 when the author was DM, Sundargarh in Odisha State
1 A vigorous drive was launched to mobilise savings of the local population (mostly members of the ST Community) through intensive village level meetings which were persuasive and motivational
2 The results were impressive. The small savings through post offices which were of the order of ₹90lakh in 1972-73 went up to ₹400 lakh, i.e., by more than 400 per cent.
3 The then Union Minister of State, Finance, Sushila Rohatgi along with the Small Savings Commissioner, Nagpur came to Rourkela in November 1974 to accord public recognition to the district administration for this outstanding initiative

- Earnings can go up substantially only if
  - o Sufficient number of days of productive employment on a durable basis are made available;
  - o Statutorily notified minimum wages are paid in time without any deduction and principally in cash/cheque;
  - o Size of the family is brought down through planned parenthood, number of earning members in the family substantially raised through access to education and skill training, there is tacit observance of the norms of nutrition (a balanced combination of carbohydrate, protein, oil/fat, trace minerals and vitamins) as also restraint in spending on *beedi*, tobacco, alcohol and drugs. Ensuring stability of the price of foodgrains and other commodities which are essential for living on the one hand and ensuring stability in the purchasing power of the local currency on the other; this is a major responsibility to be discharged both by GoI and State governments together.
  - o This will be possible by a sustained drive against hoarding, black marketing and smuggling including application of preventive detention law against those who indulge in activities which are prejudicial to maintenance of supplies and services essential to the lives of the people and the community.
  - o Simultaneous efforts will have to be made to increase the number of thrift and credit groups or self-help groups particularly those formed by women so that Jan Dhan Yojana and SHGs together can provide a fillip to small savings and strengthen the foundation of individual and collective self-reliance of the poor.

II. **Vigorous enforcement of land reforms:**

A vigorous programme of land reforms should be viewed as a tool of removing inequality in distribution and possession of land, inequality in access to means of production and removal of impediments in terms of reaping usufructs from land.

There are undoubtedly severe legislative, administrative and judicial constraints in carrying the process of land reforms to a logical conclusion.

This notwithstanding, recourse may be taken to the following:

- A new law should be enacted by every State Government to ban purchase of land belonging to members of SC/ST/OBC by persons who do not belong to these communities;
- Such a law exists in many States for members of ST only (Odisha, Maharashtra and Andhra Pradesh being three examples); this needs to be vigorously enforced;
- The proposed law should cover, in addition to land allotted by Government, land otherwise owned by a member of SC/ST/OBC;
- Three categories of land, i.e., ceiling surplus land, Government land (including forest land) and private land owned by temples, *mutts*[62] and other trusts should be considered for the purpose of allotment of house site and agricultural land;
- Any relaxation in ceiling surplus law should be sparingly considered and invariably not agreed to;

62 A *mutt* is a religious trust or organisation meant for propagating certain faiths and beliefs while carrying out a number of welfare programmes for the poor and the deprived

- All lands owned by Central or State Governments or any other public authority which is not required ostensibly for any public purpose should be available for distribution among the landless agricultural labourers on high priority;
- In the wake of Scheduled Tribe and Other Traditional Forest Dwellers (Recognition of Forest Rights) Act, 2006 and notification of Rules, survey in forest areas should be undertaken and land cultivated/encroached by the forest dwellers should be identified, demarcated and settled with the dwellers at the earliest;
- In States like Andhra Pradesh, Odisha, Maharashtra where there is Tribal Land Alienation Prevention Regulation, a systematically planned drive should be launched by every State Government to restore land to the possession of members of SC/ST whose land has been taken away/usurped by way of lease or transfer or sale by members of non-SC/ST/OBC;
- Every unit of land allotted and given possession should be developed to its full productive capacity;
- Wherever ground water resources are available, irrigation wells should be provided;
- Where rainfall is less and ground water has been depleted, other ways and means of improving water table through integrated watershed planning, management and development should be explored on the Ralegaon Siddhi model developed by noted social activist Anna Hazare. This will be the most effective answer to the problem of drought, migration, poverty, indebtedness and bondage.

III. Access to full, freely chosen, productive and remunerative employment (ILO Convention 122 of 1964 which India has ratified on 17 November 1998):

The root cause of debt bondage may be traced to:

- Inequity in access to employment opportunity for all able-bodied adults;
- Non-remunerative character of that employment.

The inequity in access to employment opportunity arises on account of the following:

- Wide disparities in levels of literacy and education;
- Fads and prejudices based on sex (responsible for the low rate of female participation in economic activities);
- Non-availability of skill training institutions and providers to impart skills/endowments suiting a particular occupation (technical skills, shop skills, computer literacy skills, quality management skills, entrepreneurial, managerial and supervisory skills).

The current employment scenario in rural areas which has considerable bearing on the pernicious system of debt bondage is characterised by the following:

- Lack of stable and durable avenues of employment caused by excessive seasonality of employment;
- The number of small, marginal and landless agricultural labourers is continuously on the increase;
- A number of agricultural labourers is simultaneously getting displaced from land (oral and informal tenants in particular);
- Such displacement is invariably accompanied by poor quality of employment that is unsafe, insecure and exploitative;

Non-remunerative character of employment arises on account of the following:

- Wage periods are not fixed and wages are not ordinarily paid between seventh to tenth day of the month succeeding the month to which the wages relate;
- Minimum wages are not paid principally by cash/cheque;
- Deduction takes place from minimum wages (sometimes for payment of commission to middle-men) which is not authorised under the Payment of Wages Act;
- Computation of cash value of wages, wherever the same are being paid in kind, is fraught with problems of under-weighment and poor quality of food grains; happily for us, the provision of payment of wages in kind has been removed in the Wage Code;
- Weekly day of rest is not observed;
- Workers being made to work on the weekly day of rest are not given compensatory off and not being paid OT wages at double the rate of ordinary wages;
- In various seasonal operations as in brick kilns, there is no co-relation between wage rates (which are piece rate) and long duration of work (going beyond sixteen hours) which works against the interests of workmen.

IV. **Access to skill training for both skill formation and up-gradation:**

Skill training is an integral part of the total process of human resource development. The process is directed towards imparting new skills which are need based while making simultaneous efforts to refine, sharpen and upgrade existing skills to make them more market relevant.

In terms of process and institutional mechanism, we had TRYSEM in the 1970s, DWCRA in 1980s and PM's Kaushal Vikas Yojana since July 2015. A new skill training policy has been enunciated and announced by GoI on 15 July 2015. Institutional mechanisms like Skill Development Council, Skill Development Corporation and Skill Development Fund have been set up at the national level.

Employment and Skill Development Missions have been launched at the State level. Rural livelihood missions (Ajeevika) have also been launched. As far as skill training for released bonded labourers is concerned, there are certain inherent limitations which need to be kept in view while designing a skill training programme for them.

The limitations are:

- The level of functional literacy and numeracy of these persons will be quite low;
- The ability to imbibe, assimilate and absorb reading, writing and calculation skills in daily life is also quite limited;
- The level of awareness, agility and alertness of human mind to handle crisis situations is considerably low.

It is imperative that these weaknesses are taken care of first before embarking on any skill training programme. Additionally, the following measures are suggested for consideration:

- Majority of the freed bonded labourers would come from the background of agriculture;
- Agriculture is currently in crisis and the possibility of having a reasonably appreciable income from agriculture is bleak;
- The moot question will be to what extent we can think of shifting all freed bonded labourers from farm to non-farm activities in the secondary and tertiary sector;

- If there is possibility for such a shift, this will have to be backed by adequate planning and preparation before requisite skills relevant to the non-farm activity in question are imparted;
- In any case, a detailed exercise will have to be undertaken to identify the potential for imparting training to the beneficiaries in a particular skill/trade, keeping in view the level of their literacy and numeracy and match the two before the programme of skill training is taken up;
- In formulating such programmes, preferences and interests of the beneficiaries should always be kept in view;
- Institutional arrangements for supply of raw materials, provision of credit and technology and easy and hassle-free access to the market should be ensured so that freed bonded labourers may have necessary physical and financial wherewithal to start producing, selling what they produce at remunerative prices and earning soon after skill training.

V. **Enforcement of the law on minimum wage.**

Long-term measures:

The practice of fixing and notifying minimum wage in respect of employments notified as scheduled employment only should be dispensed with by an amendment of MW Act (this has since been provided in the Wage Code, 2019).

Minimum wage should be universal for workers in all employments. Minimum wage should be fixed and notified preferably by the direct notification method which is less time consuming than the Committee method which is expensive and often ends up rather inconclusively.

- Payment of notified minimum wage in MGNREGA works has been a contentious issue.

- Despite a number of Supreme Court judgments that no Government, no employer, and no contractor/sub-contractor has any moral and ethical right to deny a worker his/her entitlement to statutory minimum wages and despite two judgments of Andhra Pradesh and Karnataka High Courts striking down Section 6 of MGNREGA Act, the Ministry of Rural Development has taken a contrary stand not to pay minimum wages for MGNREGA work and has taken the issue to Supreme Court. The same stand has also been reiterated in the Section 66 of the Wage Code.
- In view of this, all freed bonded labourers, most of whom are likely to be beneficiaries of MGNREGA works, at the initial stage, after their release from bondage will have to wait till the day this contentious issue gets conclusively resolved in the apex court.
- In the Wage Code which has come into force w.e.f. 9 September 2019, no period as to when the claim adjudicating authority will dispose of a claim petition has been laid down. This should be done and it should be as short a period (say six months) as possible in the interest of labour.
  - There is no guarantee that an erring/recalcitrant employer will agree to pay the wages as determined by the claim adjudicating authority; in such a contingency, a requisition will have to be sent to Collector/DM for issue of a certificate under the Public Demands Recovery Act. Such a case, however, may drag on for years heightening the predicament of the aggrieved employee/worker.
- Keeping the above limitations in view as also keeping in view the fact that (a) minimum wage constitutes the rock bottom below which no employer can go but nothing prevents the employer to pay higher than minimum wages (b) millions of workers in

the subsistence sectors of the economy are being deprived of this rock bottom for no fault of theirs, the Code on Wages which has recently come into force w.e.f. 9 September 2019 may provide by way of amendment for a Labour Tribunal which should have powers to (a) entertain claims (b) adjudicate claims within the period fixed by law and (c) have power of enforcing its decisions, i.e., to direct the employer concerned to make the payment within the prescribed time limit.

VI. **Strengthening the Public Distribution System:**

- The National Food Security Act, 2013 declared entitlements of citizens of India to food grains every month at subsidised prices.
- Every person in a priority household will be entitled to five kg of food grains, every Antyodaya household to thirty-five kg, every pregnant or lactating mother to a daily free meal during pregnancy and six months after child birth plus ₹6,000, every child under six years to a daily free meal, every child between six to fourteen years to a free mid-day meal and in case of non-supply of food grains or meals to a food security allowance.
- It was intended to cover, if necessary, up to seventy-five per cent of rural population and up to fifty per cent of urban population.
- A State Commission would oversee the implementation of the Act in each State.
- This was a bold, ambitious and expensive intervention.
- Six years have passed since the Food Security Act was enacted and enforced in 2013 (w.e.f. 5 July 2013).
- Regretfully India's rank among 119 countries in 2017 is 100 with an index score of 31.4.
- The number of hungry people in the world was estimated at 842 million in 2011-13 by Global Hunger Index (GHI).

- In the eighth report submitted to the Supreme Court, NC Saxena, Commissioner and Harsh Mander, Special Commissioner had said, 'In the dark shadows of this land, the silent tragedy plays out, millions of women and men, boys and girls who sleep hungry'.
- According to GHI, India is home to a quarter of the world's hungry.
- From an independent evaluation study conducted by a UN official, 36 per cent of the food grains are being siphoned off and do not reach the intended beneficiaries.
- According to a report of the sixty-sixth round of survey conducted by NSSO, the nutritional intake measured in terms of kilo calorie declined from 2,153 kilo calories per person per day in 1993-94 to 2,020 in 2009-10 in rural areas and from 2,071 to 1,946 kilo calories in urban areas.
- Against such a disquieting scenario, the existing PDS needs to be revamped and a number of simultaneous and related measures including strengthening ICDS, mid-day meal scheme, national maternity benefit scheme with supplementary initiatives for bettering access to livelihood and employment, credit, national family benefit scheme, pension scheme, etc., should be undertaken.
- The scope and ambit of PDS should be enlarged to include those food grains which constitute the preferred choice for consumption by members of the ST community (*jower, bajra* and *ragi*) in addition to rice, wheat, soyabean, sugar and pulses which are available to an ordinary consumer and card holder.
- In case PDS is not able to cater to the preferred items of consumption for members of the ST Community, grain banks for storage of food grains which are consumed by the latter

should be opened by way of contribution of food grains from ST members and Government in an equal measure or such measure as may be agreed upon. Such grain banks should be opened in required number in pockets of concentration of tribal population.

VII. **Alleviating the plight and predicament of victims of distress migration (inter-State)**

- Item 81 of the Union List in the Seventh Schedule of the Constitution of India—Article 246 (1)—relates to inter-State migration.
- The responsibility of the Union Government in the matter of regulating inter-State migration is three-fold:
  - Enact a law and formulate a policy and programme of action;
  - Bring the originating and destination States to a common table for a dialogue and discussion on all outstanding issues centering round inter-State distress migration with a view to resolving the same;
  - Organise joint study teams to inspect worksites, interact with inter-State migrants, identify if they are working under conditions akin to BLS and provide the desired relief to the victims if the findings are affirmative by way of rescue/ release, repatriation and rehabilitation.
- The Union Government has enacted a law in 1979 which came into force from 2 October 1980 but the same is not fool-proof; it requires extensive amendments to remove gaps, omissions and ambiguities.
- The Union Government also needs to take an initiative in the last two items as suggested above.

Further Suggestions

- The originating State should provide access to information to potential migrants about existing avenues of employment which they should seek/avail of at the source point.
- A special drive should be launched for enforcement of statutorily notified minimum wage;
- Minimum wage should be linked with food security and the Food Security Act, 2013 should be enforced;
- Bank accounts for all potential migrant labourers should be opened under Jan Dhan Yojana at the originating point prior to their migration;
- The destination State Governments should be persuaded to open similar bank accounts for all migrant labourers after they have migrated and landed at the destination point;
- A special drive should be launched for allotment of homestead and agricultural land in favour of all BPL families at the originating point;
- Similar drive should be simultaneously launched to ensure provision of a roof above the head by making available assistance under PM's Awas Yojana;
- Food grain banks on the model obtaining in Odisha and Maharashtra in all tribal areas should be set up;
- An appropriately worded IEC package should be designed which should inform and make people intensely aware that while there may be some temporary gains, the damage on account of involuntary or induced migration and, in particular, deceptively alluring migration through middlemen without a careful consideration of all the implications thereof is severe, permanent and often not easily remediable on account of laxity and inaction on the part of the

originating State and indifference of the destination State.

Additional statutory responsibilities

- Licensing u/s 8 of ISMW (ROE&COS) Act of all recruiting agents must be rigorously enforced.
- All sources of recruitment must be effectively tapped.
- Local self-governing bodies must be fully involved in the entire exercise to keep a tap on all persons/families entering a village / ward/mohalla and going out of the same.
- The process of exercise of vigilance and surveillance over such movement must extend to making an entry in a register of movement of all recruiting agents entering the village and going out as also movement of all intending migrants.
- The checks and controls to be exercised over the recruiting agents must be fool-proof; it must instil a sense of accountability in them for all their activities.
- Each recruitment should be reduced to a contract in black and white, incorporating the nature, characteristics and conditions of employment at the destination point.
- A copy of the contract should be shared with the intending migrant workmen who are being recruited.
- The terms and conditions as spelt out in the contract should be properly explained to all intending migrant workers, many of whom may be unlettered.
- Soon after arrival at the worksite of the destination point, an account should be opened in the name of the recruited migrant workman in a bank adjacent to the worksite.
- All payments—journey allowance, displacement allowance and wages during the journey period including advances paid during the currency of employment—should be deposited in the name

of the migrant workman.

- This will hopefully put an end to the era of deceit and fraud being taken recourse to by middle-men.

Obligation of the destination State Governments

- The destination State should ensure that all principal employers of establishments recruiting inter-State migrant workmen apply for and obtain registration certificate u/s 4 of ISMW (ROE&COS) Act as without such registration certificate, recruitment of inter-State migrant workmen will be illegal.
- The destination State should own the inter-State migrant workmen as dearly as they own their land and building.
- It should make provision of all welfare facilities and amenities at the worksite for the inter-State migrant workmen (residential accommodation, crèche, washing facilities, latrines and urinals, canteen, rest rooms, drinking water) as have been provided in Rule 45, 44, 43, 42, 41, 40 and 39 respectively of ISMW (ROE&COS) Rules, 1980.
- The destination State Government must enable and facilitate visit of Inspectors from the originating State to visit and inspect any establishment(s) in the destination State where inter-State migrant workmen are employed and extend full cooperation for such inspections as required u/s 20 (3) of ISMW (ROE&COS) Act.
- If an inter-State migrant workman meets with an accident in course of and arising out of his/her employment, succumbs to injuries or gets incapacitated, the destination State Government may transfer the case records of the proceedings relating to employee's compensation on an application from the legal heirs

of the deceased/disabled workman to the Court of the Employees' Compensation Commissioner of the originating State.

- The destination State should create a computerised database for all inter-State migrant workmen and their family members, if any, accompanying them; the data should be shared with the labour law enforcement machinery of the originating State.
- It should also organise orientation programmes for officers of its enforcement machinery to familiarise them about the provisions of the laws which are applicable to the inter-State migrant workmen.
- Surprise inspections should be conducted by officers of the enforcement machinery of the destination State on the working and living conditions of the workmen.
- If in course of such inspection it is found that the workmen are working under oppressive conditions, the same should be brought to the notice of DM concerned for action u/s 10, 11 and 12 of BLS (A) Act.

Question 64

What do you think about Wage Code that came into effect on 9 September 2019 vis-a-vis the Provisions of BLS (Abolition) Act?

Answer: It indicates an honest desire of the Government to simplify and rationalise all laws relating to wages by amalgamation of existing wage-related laws into one consolidated legislative framework; it also demonstrates the political will, commitment and determination to give a push to labour law reform. So far, so good.

The Wage Code, 2019 however, suffers from two major anomalies or contradictions as far as the provisions of BLS (A) Act are concerned. These provisions are:

I. Section 2(g)(1)

Denial of wage or even nominal wage is one of the four consequences of creditor-debtor relationship which ends up in BLS.

Nominal wage has been defined in Section 2(g)(1) of BLS (A) Act as under:

- The minimum wage fixed by the Government, in relation to the same or similar labour, under any law for the time being in force; and
- Where no such minimum wage has been fixed in relation to any form of labour, the wages that are normally paid for the same or similar labour, to the labourers working in the same locality.

- Exclusion of MGNREGA works from the purview of the Code as in Section 66 is discriminatory, patently unjust and violative of the provision of Section 2(g)(1) of the BLS (A) Act for the reasons as would appear from the subsequent paragraphs.
- The arguments used for such exclusion are:
  - MGNREGA is a national programme being implemented by the Ministry of Rural Development;
  - There is no employer-employee relationship in MGNREGA works;
  - Government does not have enough resources to pay minimum wages and back wages.
- These arguments are without any rationale or force for the following reasons:
  - I. Minimum wage has universal application under the Code after removal of the earlier conditionality of scheduled employment in Section 3(1A) of MW Act;
  - II. It is immaterial whether the Government through a particular Ministry or Department is the controlling authority of MGNREGA works.

III. In *Dharangdhara Chemical Works Vs Dharangdhra Municipality* SC of India,[63] Supreme Court laid down a ruling that even the barest element of supervision would be sufficient proof of an employer-employee relationship.

Such an element of supervision has to be there in every work/employment including MGNREGA works.

Supreme Court in the Crown Aluminium Works judgment (1958) had observed:

> If an employer cannot maintain his enterprise without cutting down the wages of his employees below even a bare subsistence or minimum wage, he would have no right to conduct his enterprise on such terms.

IV. The language used by Justice Kuldip Singh who wrote the majority judgment in *Workmen of the Reptaco Brett Co Vs Management* (1992 LLJ 340) is even sharper and far more emphatic than the one used in Crown Aluminium Works:

> The concept of minimum wage is no longer the same as it was in 1936. Even 1957 is way behind. A worker's wage is no longer a contract between the employer and an employee. It has the force of collective bargaining under the labour laws. Each category of wage has to be tested at the anvil of social justice which is the life fibre of our society today.

The spirit of the above two judgments has been reiterated in the following other judgments such as:

- Asiad Workers' case, 18 September 1982;
- Bandhua Mukti Morcha case, 16 December 1983;
- Sanjit Bunkir Roy case, 20 January 1983;

---

63 1959 AIR 1271 1960 SCR (I)388

- Labourers Working on Salal Hydro-Electric Project case, 25 April 1984;
- Mukesh Advani case, 2 May 1985.

The judgment of the apex court is the law of the land and is binding on all subordinate courts (Article 141). Denial of minimum wage tantamounts to forced labour as in Article 23, so said the judgment in Asiad Workers' case (18 September 1982).

Denial of minimum wage tantamounts to BLS—so said the judgement in the Bandhua Mukti Morcha case (16 December 1983).

Therefore, the stand of GoI as reflected in Section 66 of the Code regarding denial of notified minimum wage to MGNREGA workers is clearly violative of Section 2(g)(1) of BLS(A) Act and is not sustainable.

II. **Section 4(2)**

Section 18(f) of the Code speaks of deduction of advances of whatever nature. This is not in order as it contravenes Section 4(2) of the BLS (A) Act which reads as under:

- After the commencement of BLS (A) Act, no person shall make any advance under or in pursuance of BLS.

Section 6(1) of BLS (A) Act makes it abundantly clear that such bonded debt stands extinguished. How then can an advance of whatever nature be recovered as in S18(f) of the Wage Code? In other words, Section 18(f) is clearly violative of Section 4(2) of BLS (A) Act and is not sustainable.

Question 65

How would you react to the proposal for a self-contained, comprehensive and integrated law covering trafficking, other

forms of forced labour including bonded labour and child labour?

Answer: The normal and natural reaction to such a proposal is positive and affirmative for the following reasons:

- Article 23 of the Constitution is a composite provision encompassing offences like trafficking in human beings, *begar* and other similar forms of forced labour;
- All these are offences punishable under the law and have been prohibited under Article 23;
- Article 35(a)(ii) vests power in the Parliament alone to enact such a law, as soon as may be, after commencement of the Constitution;
- Even though BLS (A) Act was enacted twenty-seven years after commencement of the Constitution and is one of the most progressive legislations in post- independent India, it does not cover the following:
  - o *Begar*;
  - o Trafficking in human beings;
  - o Other similar forms of forced labour.
- Other similar forms of forced labour are the following by way of illustration:
  - o Pledging of children by parents;
  - o Child begging (where the begging child is part of a ring);
  - o Child camel jockeying (children are trafficked and forced into it);
  - o Forced adoption;
  - o Forced marriage;
  - o Forced domestic help;
  - o Forced transfer of organs;
  - o Commercial sexual exploitation.

- As far as pledging of children by parents to contractors/ middle-men is concerned, there is The Children (Pledging of Labour) Act, 1933. The punishment for such pledging is negligible and does not serve any useful purpose;
- As far as other offences are concerned, there are no laws except Transfer of Organs Act, 1994 and Criminal Law (Amendment) Act, 2013;
- Since Article 23 speaks of a composite offence, we should have an integrated, comprehensive and omnibus law to deal with all the offences mentioned in Article 23;
- This, however, has not been the case as would be evident from the following:
    - o Prevention of Immoral Trafficking Act was enacted in 1956; this has undergone two major amendments in 1978 and 1986;
    - o This, however, cannot be called a law to qualify to deal with the offence of trafficking in human beings under Article 23 as it deals with prevention, regulation and control of prostitution;
    - o This is not a law to deal with prevention and suppression of traffic in human beings in all its dimensions;
    - o Section 370 of IPC dealing with slavery and slave-like practices was amended by the Criminal Law (Amendment) Act on 2 April 2013 to introduce trafficking in human beings for:

i. Forced/bonded labour, slavery and slave-like practices, servitude.

ii. Commercial sexual exploitation;

iii. Forced transfer of organs.

It does not explicitly include the following:

- o Domestic labour;
- o Industrial labour;
- o Agricultural labour;
- o Begging;
- o Circus;
- o Camel jockeying;
- o Marriage;
- o Adoption;
- o Missing children.

While it makes trafficking in human beings a cognisable and non-bailable offence and provides for stringent punishment going up to life imprisonment, it does not provide for the following:

- Rescue/release of victims;
- Repatriation of victims;
- Restoration of victims to the custody of parents if they are children and others to the family, if they are adolescents and adults;
- Rehabilitation of victims--physical, economic, emotional and psychological;
- Re-integration of the victims into the mainstream family, community and society.

Currently we have multiplicity of laws dealing with victims in various age groups in a variety of situations. The laws are:

I. The Children (Pledging of Labour) Act, 1933.

II. The Child and Adolescent Labour (Prohibition and Regulation) Act, 1986 as amended in 2016.

III. Bonded Labour System (Abolition) Act, 1976.

IV. The Prevention of Immoral Trafficking Act, 1956 as amended in 1978 and 1986.

V. Criminal Law (Amendment) Act, 2013.

VI. The Inter-State Migrant Workmen (Regulation of Employment and Conditions of Service) Act, 1979.

VII. The Contract Labour (Regulation and Abolition) Act, 1970.

VIII. The SC&ST (Prevention of Atrocities) Act, 1989 as amended in 2015.

No useful purpose is served by having multiplicity of laws enacted at different points of time to deal with perpetrators and victims of forced/bonded/child/migrant/contract/trafficked labour.

Ministry of Women and Child Development made one such sincere effort to introduce a comprehensive law captioned. Trafficking of Persons (Prevention, Protection and Rehabilitation) Bill first in 2016 and again in 2018 but did not succeed in getting it passed by both Houses of Parliament. The Bill has since lapsed.

It may be appropriate as also in the larger interest of millions of human beings who are victims of child labour, bonded labour and trafficking to think of re-introducing the same Bill with changes as deemed appropriate to incorporate all forms of forced/bonded labour including child and migrant bonded labour and trafficked human beings with comprehensive measures for rescue/release, repatriation, rehabilitation and re-integration of all victims (children, adolescents and adults) along with measures for prevention and dealing with offenders of the law in the most stringent manner.

Question 66

Could you give some practical tips as to what is required to be done for a potential bonded labourer to secure his/her release and rehabilitation?

Answer: This is a difficult question as (a) a person who is working under bonded or slave-like conditions and who is a potential bonded labourer is not aware of the fact that he/she is bonded (b) he/she is not aware of the meaning and implications of rescue/release and rehabilitation vis-a-vis provisions of BLS (A) Act (c) he/she does not have the freedom to leave the work site and seek redress outside by ventilating his/her grievance (he/she will be caught and brought back); he/she may not also muster enough courage and strength to lodge a formal complaint against the bonded labour keeper before the DM for fear of reprisal from the former. There is, therefore, urgent and imperative need for intervention of an external agency—say an NGO or voluntary social action group.

This is absolutely necessary as (a) VCs who are statutorily mandated to conduct survey for identification of victims of BLS have miserably failed to discharge this responsibility (b) Supreme Court in *Neerja Chaudhary Vs State of MP and Others* has categorically emphasised the role of such NGOs and Social Action Groups and the need for enlisting their involvement and support.

With the involvement of such NGOs or Social Action Groups, a survey can be conducted, victims of BLS can be identified and the identified bonded labourers may be enabled to file an application before the competent authority i.e. the DM for their release and rehabilitation.

Jeevika/Vimukti Trust has been playing an active and interventionist role since 1990 when it was formed. It has formed teams of seven to eight activists per taluk in seventeen taluks in Karnataka State. These activists have been regularly identifying potential bonded labourers in their respective areas after the Ugadi festival in April-May. The identified bonded labourers are enabled by the activists to file applications for their release and rehabilitation to the Deputy Commissioner of the district or the Assistant Commissioner in charge of a sub-division or being an Executive Magistrate.

During the interregnum, before the release certificate is issued by the Deputy Commissioner/Assistant Commissioner, as the case may be, the identified labourers are brought together to village-level union *samiti* of the Central Union called Okkuta (Karnataka Jeeta Dalu Mattu Krashikarmakara Okkuta) which means 'Union of bonded labourers and agricultural workers' which was registered as a trade union under the Trade Union Act, 1926 (as amended in 2001-02). Other agricultural labourers are also made to join them. This is basically a phase which is utilised in raising awareness of labourers about various avenues of employment, livelihood, wages payable and how to pre-empt the possibility of getting into bondage in future due to pressing need.

The author believes that the release certificate should act and be treated as an identity card (since there is no specific provision for issue of an I-card in BLS(A) Act as it obtains in section 13 of B&OCW (ROE&COS) Act, 1996). Using the release certificate as a basis, job card, Aadhar card, voter ID, caste certificate, ration card and health card can be prepared and delivered to the victim/beneficiary. This may also constitute a valid basis for allotment of homestead land, agricultural land and a roof above the head under PM's Awas Yojana-G or U, as the case may be. Using this as the basis, a bank account can also be opened.

Additionally, an International NGO like IJM undertakes the following activities for a released bonded labourer such as:

- An exercise in needs assessment is undertaken to know what the particular survivor's family might immediately require;

- This process also facilitates mapping the medium- and long-term needs of the family.
- After the needs assessment exercise, a further one in freedom training is undertaken; this focuses on empowering the survivors towards community inclusive rehabilitation practices. The six components of freedom training are:
  - o Safety;
  - o Mental well-being;
  - o Economic empowerment/education;
  - o Physical well-being;
  - o Social support;
  - o Legal protection.
- A family development plan is worked out to maintain basic family information and priorities for the family;
- After assessing the needs of the families, they are enabled to plan for a few short and long term goals and guided as to how to achieve the same;
- At the end of the two-year rehabilitation programme, the survivors celebrate their lives through what is known as celebration of freedom.

In case of Jeevika/Vimukti Sangathan Trust, the NGO has entrusted multiple tasks to its activists in the phase following release and preceding rehabilitation. These are:

- Constant interaction with, motivation of beneficiaries and nurturing group efforts;
- Building up individual confidence;
- Making the victims/beneficiaries aware of different legal provisions, social issues and imparting skills of communication and leadership;

- Helping the beneficiaries to secure their various rights under various poverty alleviation and employment promotion programmes such as:
  - o Allotment of housesite;
  - o Allotment of agricultural land for cultivation;
  - o Allotment of housing grant under PM's Awas Yojana-G or U, as the case may be;
  - o Toilets;
  - o Other housing accessories;
  - o Ration cards;
  - o Caste and income certificate;
  - o Old age monthly pension;
  - o Widow and disability pension;
  - o Job card for MGNREGA works;
  - o Various loans, subsidies and training for self-employment;
  - o Scholarships for children of bonded labourers;
  - o Health and medical care;
  - o Community facilities like drinking water (Potable), community halls, drainage, street light, village roads, grave yards and anganwadi centres.

The teams of activists at the taluk/district level are given professional orientation on awareness generation through street theatres on the following topics:

- Elimination of bonded and child labour;
- Protection and conservation of environment;
- Gender justice;
- Promotion of rational, secular and scientific temper;
- Role of panchayati raj institutions.

Public awareness on elimination of BLS through role plays is generated on specific dates such as:

- Bonded Labour Day on 26 January;
- International Labour Day on 1 May;
- Child Labour Day on 12 June;
- BLS Elimination Awareness Day on 25 October;
- International Women's Day on 8 March.

Question 67

What are the constraints and limitations in conducting an effective social investigation? How should the social investigator proceed to deal with them? Do you have any personal experiential perceptions about the same?

Answer: Every social investigation is fraught with severe limitations. The first and foremost is the language barrier. The social investigator and the persons (including victims) to be interrogated may be hailing from different parts of the country with a different socio-cultural background and may be speaking different languages/dialects. Even if the investigator avails of the services of a language interpreter, local idioms are often untranslatable. Besides, translation on the spot may reduce the spontaneity and natural rhythm of an effective communication process which has to be two-way.

Secondly, the gap in the socio-economic-cultural background between the social investigator and the persons to be interrogated leaves a lot of doubts in the minds of the latter. They may be harbouring an impression that the investigator is either a detective or an espionage agent or a representative of the enforcement machinery and has come to take something away from them and not to give anything in return. It is precisely for this reason that they may have reservations to accept the role of the investigator on the surface and may not be willing to respond to the latter's queries. It may take quite some time before the social investigator is able to establish his/her own credibility and win the trust and confidence of the persons to be interrogated.

Thirdly, the hawk-like presence of the employer/contractor/ sub-contractor and close surveillance exercised by the latter over the movement of the persons to be interrogated makes interrogation at the work site extremely difficult. Even if the employer's permission is obtained prior to interrogation (which is rather doubtful), interrogation in the presence of the employer (which is also not desirable) may be a laboured or superficial exercise over which not much credibility can be attached.

The author was appointed as a socio-legal investigator by the Supreme Court in the final order of 16 December 1983 while disposing of the WP 2135 filed by President, BMM in February 1982. He was directed to visit all the stone quarries and crushers in Faridabad in Haryana State, interrogate over 10,000 workers, record the impressions and findings arising out of such interrogation and submit a detailed report. He was given three months from the date of the order to complete his assignment.

At the relevant point of time, the author was DG(LW)/JS in the MoL&E. A request for providing transport to visit the quarries/ crushers at Faridabad made to MoL&E did not yield any positive response. He had to hire a taxi at considerable expense, leave home early morning at 6 am, be at the quarries/ crushers till midnight, return to his residence at 1 am, have barely a sleep of 2-3 hours before getting ready at 6 am to leave for the quarries once again. Such routine continued for almost a month without break. He was entirely on his own while conducting this massive social investigation.

When, on the first day, he reached a quarry (Gadarpur) and made an earnest effort to establish a rapport with the quarry workers, he did not succeed. He was a rank outsider for all workers, most of whom were inter-State migrant workmen from UP, Bihar and Rajasthan. It was a herculean task to carry conviction to them that the author has been appointed by the apex court so that if there was anything wrong, necessary corrective measures could be taken.

The author had to repeat this exercise of confidence building for almost a week at each quarry and crusher. Eventually, they shared everything with him starting from their source or origin, who were the recruiting agents who approached them and paid advances to enable them to liquidate the loans taken from village moneylenders/landlords and the various other promises and allurements offered by them to lure them to the site. They were subjected to a process of ruthless exploitation. The duration of work both at the quarry and the crushers was 16-18 hours and the nature of work was such as posed grave risks to their life and limb. They were unskilled workers, totally illiterate, were required to convert rocks to boulders/stones with the help of detonator and fuse-wire. Carrying out such dangerous operations without any formal training meant risk of injuries which turned fatal in a number of cases. Such accidents were never reported by the mining lessees and contractors and, therefore, no formal cases got registered with the Commissioner, Workmens' Compensation.

Since during daytime the workmen were under the hawk-like surveillance of *sardars, jamadars, khatedars* and *munshis*, the author could only take rounds of the quarries and crushers, mentally observe and record the extremely hazardous working conditions in a surrounding laden with dust and the real interrogation could take place only at night.

The author used to sit with the workmen and their family members after their evening meal between 8 pm until midnight in a circle, discuss all that happened during day time while recording their statements in response to specific questions put by him with reference to the questionnaire which he had designed in advance. As he observed, the response to the questions put by him was honest, straight and candid; there was no exaggeration, far less any colouration in any of the statements. This is what greatly helped the author to come to the conclusion about their status–free or unfree.

The report was submitted by the author in two volumes to the Court a fortnight before the deadline. While the first volume dealt with free or unfree status of the quarry and the crusher workers, the second volume dealt with issues relating to occupational health and safety. The report was approved in toto by a division bench comprising Justices PN Bhagwati, Amarendranth Sen and RS Pathak.

There were a number of attempts on his life and life of the workmen being interrogated. As they sat in a circle discussing various issues, a truck would come in a brazen attempt to run over them. Their reflex action saved them even though the pots, in which women members of the families of workers had stored water after collecting them with difficulty from long distances, would be smashed to pieces in a split second. Such attempts were repeated thrice without any success.

The author developed arthritis and viral pneumonia and life-long problems of breathlessness.

There was an attempt to break open the office at dead of night on 1 March 1984 to steal copies of the report prepared by the author, being unaware of the fact that sufficient number of copies of the report loaded in fifteen trunks had been handed over by the author personally to the Registry of the Supreme Court one day in advance. This was a misadventure which resulted in loss of over 300 valuable files of the labour welfare division of the MoL&E which could not be later retrieved; they had to be re-constructed with considerable efforts.

Question 68
What would be the most effective solution to this long persisting human malady?

Answer: A permanent solution can be found only when:

- The victims are made intensely aware of their disadvantage, factors which contribute to such disadvantage and the wherewithal of their deliverance;
- A realisation or critical consciousness dawns on the victims that their deliverance from the culture of silence and helpless dependence lies in their being organised into self-help groups, cooperatives, trade unions, NGOs or voluntary social action groups or such other forms of organisation as are in their best interest and as they deem expedient and appropriate;
- Once the victims are organised, a number of economic or income generating activities can be built into and started around the organisation;
- The victims will be both beneficiaries and participants in such economic activity; they will be initially employed as workers in the activity but over a period of time, they will be progressively transformed into managers, supervisors and owners;

- They will eventually emerge as the architects of their own destiny; there will be no exploiters and no exploited;
- This process of generation of critical awareness or consciousness was coined as 'conscientisation' by Paulo Freirie, an outstanding Brazilian adult educator in 1967-68 when he wrote his seminal work *Pedagogy of the Oppressed.*

The following are the distinct advantages of conscientisation for the victims of BLS:

- They will be enabled to perceive and internalise the forces - both internal and external which are inimical to their existence and interest;
- Through a correct understanding of the provisions of the law, directions of the Supreme Court and High Courts and those of NHRC as also with the solid strength and support of their organisations behind them they can grapple with and overcome these forces;
- They will be made aware of their own strengths and weaknesses vis-à-vis the strength and weaknesses of their adversaries;
- They would acquire a social conscience for eradication of some of the age old pernicious practices like untouchability, caste-based division and discrimination, addiction to alcohol, lavish and irresponsible spending on festivities associated with birth, death and other ceremonies, which lead to land alienation, indebtedness and bondage;
- They would be empowered to de-mystify and de-mythologise aura of the false consciousness surrounding their lives and develop a new consciousness which is rational, secular and scientific.

While these are general objectives, there could be specific objectives for a few specific categories of victims of BLS such as:

- Landless agricultural labourers;
- Victims of inter-State distress migration;
- Fisher women and men;
- Paddy growers;
- Rice mill workers;
- Handloom/powerloom workers;
- *Beedi* rollers, labellers and packers;
- Handicraft women and men;
- Collectors of raw hides and skins
- Leather workers (tanners and flayers);
- Garment makers;
- Salt manufacturing workers;
- Workers in brick kilns;
- Workers in stone quarries/crushers;
- Scavengers;
- Collectors of minor agricultural and forest products;
- Loaders and unloaders;
- Rickshaw pullers;
- Sewer workers;
- Domestic help;
- Working/Trafficked children.

The specific objectives for these numerous categories and sub-categories of workers (many of whom are potential bonded labourers working under bonded conditions but have not been identified as such) can be worked out, keeping in view their peculiarities and complexities.

I. **How do we bring about the critical awareness/ consciousness?**

This is a sequential process; the two stages in the process are:

- We need to identify the broad categories of un-free labour or victims of BLS;
- We need to design a recipe or IEC package for each category.

The victims of BLS may be broadly divided into the following categories:

- Potential bonded labourers;
- Bonded labourers who have been identified as such and awaiting their release;
- Released bonded labourers who are awaiting their rehabilitation;
- Released bonded labourers who have been rehabilitated under land, non-land and art/craft/skill based activities;
- Rehabilitated bonded labourers who in terms of income have not become fully autonomous and may need a second dose of assistance;
- Rehabilitated bonded labourers who have lapsed back to bondage or have migrated to a work site at a destination point as their rehabilitation was a failure and did not make the beneficiary autonomous or self-reliant;
- Inter-State migrant workmen who have been working under bonded conditions and are awaiting release, repatriation and rehabilitation at the source point.

The IEC package for each category should take cognisance of the peculiarities and complexities of their socio-cultural background, occupation, working and living conditions and if properly designed and administered should enable them to think, reflect, critically analyse the causes and contributory factors for their disadvantage and the wherewithal of their deliverance.

II. **Who brings about the much-needed critical awareness/ consciousness?**

Conscientisation is essentially an educational process. The person/ agency who has been made responsible to conduct the process is expected to impart and instil the following into the mind and psyche of every bonded labourer—potential or real, such as:

- He/she represents a human being, the finest and best in the scheme of evolution, endowed with reason and rationality and entitled to lead an autonomous existence which is decent and dignified; he/she is also entitled to be treated with dignity and decency;
- Although some of these have been lost, by virtue of being bonded to somebody else for a specified or unspecified period, everything in life has not been lost;
- With freedom from bondage, life can be started afresh, equipped with knowledge, information and skills (life skills, communication skills, survival skills, entrepreneurial and leadership skills), she/she can be made free from the culture of silence and helpless dependence and can be entirely on his/her own instead of looking up to someone for guidance and support as before;
- There is, therefore, no cause for despair or giving up the attempt to live with freedom, dignity and self-esteem;

Such a process can be initiated and carried to a logical conclusion by people who are first-rate human beings, effective social communicators, totally committed to social action, who are both altruistic and optimistic, who have no craving for loaves and fishes of office, no expectation of any award, reward or recognition.

Such persons may be called human rights defenders as in the lexicon of NHRC, animators in the phraseology of the Council of Advancement of People's Action and Rural Technology (CAPART) or teacher/trainer/motivator in the lexicon of MHRD.

Regardless of differences in nomenclature, the primary task of these persons is social communication and carrying conviction to a set of people who represent the abject prostration of poverty, deprivation, exclusion and exploitation.

Such persons are not confined to any particular place or territory; they can be found anywhere and everywhere. A dedicated search for such human resource should begin by every educational institution, institute of social science research, NGO or voluntary social action group in the respective area of its operation and after the search has been successful, the names and full particulars of such persons need to be documented as a Directory of Resource Persons exactly the way CAPART did in 1994-95.

Such persons after being identified should be given orientation about their mandate and how to go about the same by a team of resource persons who will have to be found from multiple sources (universities, research and training institutes, NGOs, etc). In view of shortage of such resources, a cascading approach to training will have to be adopted so that trainees of today become trainers of tomorrow.

The entire exercise will have to be converted to an action plan with time and cost implications so that the same can be implemented in a planned, coordinated, concerted and time-bound manner.

Question 69

Would you like to support your contention that such conscientisation is possible, feasible and achievable with the help of a real-life illustration?

Answer: Tajmira Khatun (17) belongs to Sandeshkhali village of Sarberia Agarhati GP of North 24 Parganas district in West Bengal. She was born in a large family with a few earning members and steeped in poverty, fads and superstitions. When she turned seventeen, her parents wanted to give her away in marriage.

Tajmira had perceived the lethal consequences of child marriage. She, therefore, reached out to a group called Ajker Surya (Today's Sun) that had been working for some time to put an end to child marriage, child labour and child trafficking. Together they approached Sarberia Agarhati GP to seek justice. The members of the GP collectively carried conviction to Ajmira's parents to drop the marriage proposal.

This happened in 2015. Four years later (2019) Tajmira is now an active member of Ajker Surya. In October 2019, Sarberia Agarhati became one of the 22 GPs (out of a total of 2.5 lakh GPs in the country) to win the Union Ministry of Panchayati Raj's coveted Child Friendly Panchayat Award for 2019.

Ajker Surya group was formed in 2004 in an area which was notorious for trafficking in human beings; the incidence of child marriage was also quite high. According to Sheikh Sahajahan, the head of the GP, children were trafficked and taken to different parts of the country such as NCT of Delhi, Haryana and Maharashtra to be sold as domestic help to work under oppressive and inhuman conditions.

Organisations like Ajker Surya which have emerged and grown from the grass-root level have faced and continue to face enormous operational hurdles and challenges. They not only survive but grow from stature to stature and strength to strength as they comprise women of sterling character and unmistakable commitment to a cherished cause and supreme resolve.

It is a happy augury that fourteen such groups like Ajker Surya have taken shape, each group having 15-20 children 14-18 years of age. They maintain 24x7 vigil over people entering the village and the purpose of their visit. They have a network of children who inform the group about families planning to marry off their daughters before the permissible age, the incidence of school drop-outs and the reasons thereof. They also identify children who appear to have gone missing. They visit the concerned household to make enquiries and directly report to the GP or to the Dhagariya Social Welfare Society (DSWS), a partner of NGO Save the Children.

On the basis of reports given by members of these groups, out-of-school children have been given training so that they can be re-admitted to age-appropriate classes.

Over the years, the groups have been harbingers of a refreshingly welcome social change. The incidence of child marriage, child labour and child trafficking has come down to zero or reduced substantially.

Question 70

Would you recommend an appropriate mechanism and procedure for ventilation and redressal of grievances of the victims of trafficking and bondage?

Answer: In a landmark judgement popularly known as Asiad workers' case,[64] Supreme Court Justices PN Bhagwati and

64 AIR 1982 SC 1473 1982 Lab IC 1646 WP No 8143 of 1981 PUCL vs Union of India and Others–date of judgement 18 September 1982

Baharul Islam had very candidly observed: 'National government should ensure that provisions of labour laws which are meant for the health, safety and well-being of workers are strictly observed. It should not wait for any complaint to be received from the aggrieved workers in regard to non-observance of such provisions.'

As Rabindranath Tagore wrote in *Kadi and Komal*:

Into the mouths of these
Dumb, pale and meek
We have to infuse the language of the soul
Into the hearts of these
Weary and worn, withered and forlorn
We have to minstrel the language of humanity...

Ventilation and redressal of grievances of those who are genuinely aggrieved and victimised will have to be viewed in the larger context of where they are placed in a situation characterised by

- 'their own poverty, illiteracy, social and economic backwardness';
- a rigid, inflexible, archaic and moth-eaten administrative/ bureaucratic framework;
- tyranny of law;
- rigidity and soullessness of the legal process.

In such a situation, they have eyes to see, ears to hear but no tongue to speak. It is evident that on their own they will not be able to muster enough courage to ventilate their anguish either orally or in writing.

How do we, therefore, ensure that their wailing does not die down in wilderness since it does not naturally surface? There are two ways by which this should be possible.

- Members of the VCs at the district and sub-divisional level, if properly constituted and re-constituted with women and men of character, integrity, empathy and sensitivity should, in course of their field visits in general and to pockets which are sensitive to prevalence of BLS should interact with workers, record their grievances and bring them to the notice of the DM/SDM;
- The other and more important source of information about complaints/grievances could be good, conscientious, non-political or a-political NGOs who are deeply committed to social action. Government and local administration could take them to confidence, enlist their involvement in the process of collection of such information bordering on deprivation/exploitation of the workmen and get accurate and authentic feedbacks on what is happening on the ground.

The following procedure should be adopted for redressal of such grievances

I. All such grievances–oral or written or collected through VCs or NGOs or any other reliable source should be registered and acknowledged.

II. Prompt action for redressal of all such grievances should be initiated and deadlines for redressal by way of providing the much-needed relief to the aggrieved should be fixed for the person/authority, as the case may be, who is competent to dispose of the complaint/grievance by issue of a speaking order.

III. A formal communication to the aggrieved/victimised should follow both by way of acknowledgement of receipt as well as at the expiry of the deadline conveying regret in the event of avoidable delay.

IV. The final communication on the outcome by way of redressal of the grievance should be sent direct either to the aggrieved or through the same channel which helped to bring the complaint/grievance to surface.

V. The DM at the district level or an officer to be authorised by him and SDO (civil)/RDO at the sub-divisional level should earmark one day in a week for personal hearing of all such grievances which involve complexities in interpretation of law and ruling in the matter of administration of statutory relief like (minimum wages, employees' compensation)

VI. When a law or ruling is capable of being differently interpreted, it should always be interpreted in a manner which makes the law or ruling beneficial for those for whom they have been enacted. This golden principle should always be in the back of the mind of the authority interpreting a law or ruling.

Section III
ENDNOTE

In Retrospect and Prospects

I

LAW IS MERELY a framework, an inanimate object with certain guiding principles which are sought to be translated to action and carried to a logical conclusion by individuals and institutions within a prescribed time-frame and in a given environment. Every law is the product of a particular time and, with certain seminal messages, acquires certain primacy and centrality when backed by political will, commitment and resolve. The entire machinery of the State revolves round the process of dissemination of those seminal messages underlying every law and ensuring that the laudable objectives contained in the 'Statement of Objects and Reasons' of the legislative framework are brought to a logical close.

This was exactly the case with the BLS (A) Act whose enactment was preceded by promulgation of an Ordinance by the President of India on 25 October 1975, the day on which BLS (A) Act became enforceable.

It can be safely said that the ebullience which had characterised implementation of the Twenty Point Programme in the first few years after it was launched were no longer visible on the horizon. The Supreme Court no doubt kept the torch of human freedom alive by pronouncing as many as twenty-six judgments (from 1981 onwards) and giving a broad, liberal and expansive interpretation of the law without changing it. It is a happy augury that 1990s also represented a period when maximum number of positive and pro-active directions of the apex court on Article 21, i.e., right to life and liberty were pronounced. The NHRC on whom the mantle of monitoring the enforcement of the provisions of the law fell w.e.f. 11 November 1997 has also kept it going till date with full vigour.

What could be the factors which contributed to the ebb tide as far as the enforcement of the law relating to complete abolition of BLS is concerned? Is it lack of political will and commitment? Is it on account of any change in policy to change the order of prioritisation? Is it on account of change in the basic perception relating to BLS or mindsets?

It is difficult to come to any single, precise and authoritative conclusion as to what could have led to a decline both in interest and commitment as far as implementation of this programme as a torch-bearer of human freedom and dignity is concerned.

- An objective and dispassionate analysis would lay bare some of the general misperceptions and strange mindsets obtaining among the so called literate and educated sections of society emanating from the author's field visits as Special Rapporteur, NHRC (2006-2011) and Senior Advisor, ILO (2000-2003) to some of the State governments as well as institutes of social scierce research. Some of these are: The law of abolition of bonded labour is silent on factors of social production;

- BLS is largely a thing of the past. Literacy rates have improved, people have become more aware and vigilant; they cannot be easily duped and far less get bonded;
- People tend to run to traditional moneylenders in preference to banks and other credit institutions as the former are easily accessible and people find them more convenient;
- Migrant workers send a lot of remittances to their poor families at the source point (of migration) and, therefore, there is nothing wrong or objectionable about migration *per se*;
- Media and NGOs sensationalise and romanticise the problem and blow it out of proportion for their own selfish motives.

Nothing could be farther from truth than such ill-perceived notions which are not supported by any logic, far less any ground level reality. To put the entire issue in a proper perspective, it is necessary to lay bare the facts as they are:

- As would be evident from a bare reading of the 'Statement of Objects and Reason', BLS (A) Act provides for complete abolition of BLS with a view to preventing economic and physical exploitation of the weaker sections of the society as also because the system implies infringement of basic human rights and destruction of the dignity of human labour. It is not mandated to deal with factors of social production;
- The literacy rates have undoubtedly improved but the dire need to take recourse to loan/debt/advance for personal consumption, ceremonial and development purposes has also increased manifold. The persons/families in such need

will continue to knock at the doors of non-institutional forms of moneylending such as landlords and moneylenders who are easily accessible at usurious rates of interest; the situation will not undergo any change for them until and unless they learn to moderate their need. High rate of literacy does not necessarily dampen the urge to obtain loan/advance to defray certain items of unavoidable expenditure in day-to-day life for which there is no adequate earning;

- Easy access to traditional moneylenders is one thing but the consequences of such access are too harrowing to be imagined. The prospective loanee or debtor may not be aware of the usurious rates of interest which will be charged and which he/she in his/her lifetime would find it difficult to liquidate; the tendency to run to traditional moneylender to obtain loan/advance at a disadvantage, therefore, needs to be discouraged as the same is fraught with grave risk;
- Assuming but not conceding the fact that migrant labourers send remittances to their homes, it does not necessarily follow that their exploitation at the work site of the destination point gets mitigated by such remittances. Such labourers who are recruited on receipt of advances from the recruiting agent will all along be told that 'they cannot leave until/unless the advances taken by them are fully liquidated'. Such advances cannot be easily liquidated as (a) the rate of interest will be quite high, (b) the documentary evidence will always remain with the creditor, (c) the terms of repayment will never be discussed with the debtor and (d) the quixotic logic of usury accentuated by manipulative accounting will make the loan assume astronomical proportions without ever showing any sign of reduction;

- Media and NGOS have rendered a yeoman service to bring abuse of human rights to the surface with grit, courage and determination notwithstanding heavy odds. They cannot, therefore, be accused of either sensationalisation or romanticisation.

On child bonded labour, some of the typical and equally strange mindsets are:

- Parents send their children to work so that limited parental income can be supplemented;
- Girls in Bengaluru (rural) engaged in sericulture cannot be the victims of bondage and sexual assault as the owner of such firms are Muslims and workers are Hindus.

Such myths need to be demystified in the following manner:

- Childhood is the most tender, formative and impressionable stage of human development. Education being a potent tool of such development, all children from six years of age are supposed to be at school and not at the workplace. Secondly, working children do not receive the same wages as their adult parents and other adults doing the same or similar nature of work; instead, what they receive for their long hours of work is a pittance. The question of children supplementing the limited income of poor parents, therefore, is a myth. As a matter of fact, if a balance sheet of pushing children involuntarily to work is drawn up, the damage caused to the health, psyche and wellbeing of children would far outweigh the temporary gains, if any. Parents, therefore, are not justified in pushing their children to work. By such insensitive acts of parents, all the excitement and joy associated with that childhood will be lost forever; the children additionally would become the worst victims of educational deprivation;

- Merely because owners of sericulture units in Bengaluru (rural) are Muslims and workers are Hindus, it does not necessarily follow that the girls who are employed in sericulture will not be subjected to sexual exploitation. The framers of the law at the time of enactment of POCSO in 2013 did not consider religion as a factor not to contribute to sexual exploitation.

Elimination of BLS is not the task or responsibility of one Ministry or Department or Agency; it is a national responsibility. It may be that purely for administrative reasons of monitoring, supervision and co-ordination, the subject has been assigned to a particular Ministry or Department. The urge, inclination and commitment to deal with the task or mandate must naturally and spontaneously emanate from the hearts and minds of the functionaries of both the administrative Ministry/Department as also other supporting Ministries/Departments. It hardly needs to be emphasised that human development and human freedom go together. It is, however, a pity that they also suffer from strange mindsets, do not come forward to pour out their very best to the accomplishment of the sacred mandate entrusted to them and had to be reminded by the Supreme Court again and again to discharge their assigned responsibility.

Some of the strange perceptions/mindsets of Government functionaries are:

- Administration is saddled with numerous responsibilities relating to the maintenance of law and order (including public order), handling collection of land revenue, cess (on account of irrigation, forest, minor minerals) and taxes, handling public distribution system, discharge of quasi-judicial functions, survey/census, investigations into routine complaints including complaints forwarded by NHRC/SHRC, NCPCR/SCPCR, as also other Courts which are imposed on administration regardless of its capacity to handle them;

- While more and more laws such as BLS (A) Act, CL (P&R) Act, ISMW (ROE&COS) Act, CL (A&R) Act, B&OCW (ROE&COS) Act, POCSO Act, Prevention of Sexual Harassment at the Work Place (Prevention, Prohibition and Redressal) Act, SC&ST (Prevention of Atrocities) Act, Prevention of Dowry Act, Prevention of Domestic Violence Act, etc., keep on getting added to the statute book year after year, widening thereby the ambit of enforcement responsibility of administration; the number of functionaries remains virtually the same for years with numerous other constraints (communication, mobility vs large jurisdiction, limited support staff);
- On account of continued and unwarranted interference from a number of quarters, administration gets confused, develops cold feet, loses interest as well as balance. In that state where it is saddled with too many responsibilities, it is likely to commit errors in the decision-making process.

Such mindsets can be easily demystified in the following manner:

- Administration should ponder over as to why complaints are filed. They are filed as right things are not done at the right time in the right manner. They are filed on account of negligence, inefficiency, unresponsiveness/callousness, indecisiveness and insensitivity of administration. They are also filed on account of inordinate delay in taking decisions which cause grave injustice, loss, misery and suffering to the poor, deprived, displaced and dis-advantaged;

- Administration should, therefore, gracefully accept the recommendations of statutory bodies like NHRC/SHRC, NCPCR/SCPCR which are meant for providing relief to the poor and helpless victims; they should honestly and sincerely implement them instead of viewing them as intrusion or interference in their functioning;
- Enactment of a new law and its addition to the Statute Book arises out of a genuine need perceived by representatives of the people and Government; this should be construed as a normal process in a democracy and not as imposition of a burden. It is true that the process of law enforcement gets inhibited due to vast jurisdiction, constraints of mobility and shortage of good quality human resources. While these constraints need no doubt be addressed, they cannot be excuses for not carrying out legitimate statutory functions. Nor can they be postponed to a future date on such alibis/ excuses as the cost of such postponement will be quite heavy;
- NHRC is a quasi-judicial authority created under Protection of Human Rights Act, 1993. It is mandated to promote, protect and safeguard individual and collective rights arising from Constitutional and legal provisions. Violation of such provisions poses a threat to the life and limb, dignity, decency, equality and freedom of individuals which are sacrosanct and non-negotiable. NHRC's role involves unearthing crimes

committed under BLS (A) Act while simultaneously giving a fresh lease of life to victims of BLS which has been assigned to it by the Supreme Court w.e.f. 11 November 1997; this should not be viewed as an unwarranted interference with the due process of law or procedure established by law but as that of a legally constituted national-level authority for protecting and safeguarding human freedom and dignity. The situation caused by violation of human rights which are galore would have been far worse without NHRC/SHRC.

It is against this background that the apex court had to issue a series of directions from time to time contained in twenty-six judgments delivered between 1981 and 2012. These were necessitated as law enforcement authorities as well as employers of enterprises often evade and circumvent provisions of the law with a number of alibis and pretexts. In *PUCL and Others Vs State of Tamil Nadu and Others*,[1] the Court lamented that nearly two decades after the enactment of the BLS (A) Act, no significant progress has been made by the authorities concerned and that there is not much change in the attitude of the latter. The apex court nevertheless pinned hope that alike in the lives of institutions so in the lives of individuals, there is always scope for correction and improvement and with that robust optimism had issued the following directions:

1. Officers who are posted at different levels to deal with the problem of bonded labour should be properly trained and sensitised so that they may develop a sense of involvement with the misery and suffering of the poor.

---

1 WP 3922/85 1994- SC(2)-GJX-0516-SC with equivalent citation 1994-(005)-SCC-0116-SC delivered on 13 May 1994

2. Every officer who is placed in charge of identification, rescue/release and rehabilitation of bonded labourers should be made fully conscious of his/her responsibilities. He/she should be imbued with a sense of purpose and dedication which is necessary if this important task is to be accomplished successfully.
3. There should be constant check and supervision over the activities of the officers charged with the task of securing identification, release and rehabilitation of freed bonded labourers.
4. Officers who are socially committed, naturally motivated, inspired by idealism, unafraid of all kinds of pulls and pressures and are prepared to brave opposition should be encouraged to put in their very best despite limitations and constraints and their efforts should be appreciated/ commended by way of suitable public recognition so that they may become exemplary models for other officers.

II

It may be appropriate to conclude this dialectical exercise by referring to a true story which is without parallel in terms of the immensity of human tragedy which occurred on 15 December 2013, vitally affecting lives of two innocent and hapless labourers of South Odisha.

The story reads like this. Twelve workers of Jaipatna Block of Kalahandi district in south-western Odisha are paid *dadan* (advance) with the false promise of getting jobs in Raipur. They leave their hearth and home behind to take up their jobs that promised them the illusory El Dorado.

Half-way to their destination, they realised they had been duped and were being taken to the brick kilns at Rangareddy in Andhra Pradesh (and not Raipur in Chhattisgarh). Ten of the twelve labourers managed to escape while two members of the team (Nilambar Niyal, a 22-year-old unlettered and landless Dalit youth from Pipalguda village and Dhangda Majhi, a 32-year-old tribal from the same village) were left in the firm grip of the hawk-like middle-men. The two hapless victims had to bear the brunt of the middle-mens' wrath by having their right hands chopped off deep inside a forest in Belpada in Balangir district. The labour contractor and his accomplices dragged them to the forest and committed the heinous act of wanton cruelty after asking them which of their limbs they would prefer to lose: a leg or an arm. Reactions over such a gruesome and barbaric act have ranged over a period of time from disbelief to outrage and disquiet. The questions which had to be raised in the wake of such a macabre tragedy are:

1. Can we restore for such innocent, guileless and defenceless human beings what they have lost? (Nilambar died while Dhangda Majhi, though alive, is spending his days in utter misery).
2. Can we ensure that the penalty under the law against the offenders of such a heinous crime is sufficiently stringent and deterrent so that there will be no occurrence or re-currence of such a brutal act in future?

There are perhaps no straight and simple answers. The cause for our disquiet is not one but many.

The first: A law like BLS (A) Act enacted with the best of intentions is not, cannot and has not so far been a panacea for all social evils. This is what Dr BR Ambedkar had said with a lot of anguish way back in the late forties.

The second: When a law is capable of diverse interpretation, we tend to interpret it in a manner which makes it the enemy of those for whom the law has been enacted.

The third: The human appetite for cruelty is beyond imagination, beyond description and beyond comprehension. It is indeed inexplicable as to why one set of human beings derive such sadistic pleasure from the torture of other living creatures–human and non-human alike.

The fourth: It is equally inexplicable as to why public memory of such wanton cruelty is so short. When public memory is so short, it becomes the best defence for the crime, for the brazen acts of criminals and a shield for flagrant violation of human rights. It keeps justice at bay or makes the struggle for justice long-winded.

A bonded labour specialist who has conducted over 300 rescue operations for the release of victims across Tamil Nadu, Karnataka and Andhra Pradesh has written:

> It's the first time that the case of bonded labour is causing such nationwide stir but the fact is that such cases are not at all an exception. In one case, the head of a family was tied to a pole and beaten to death. The owner was wealthy and influential and he made sure that the post-mortem report read suicide by consumption of poison as the root cause of the mishap. But all the workers in the facility knew the truth. In another case, a young mother was savagely raped by the owner and when she resisted, her hands were burnt.

Stringent Punitive Action is the Need of the Hour

Most bonded labour crimes emerge from a misplaced sense of

power, a power that makes the bonded labour keeper think and believe that he owns the workers under him (analogous to slavery). To get to the root of the problem, the owners need to be divested of that power by a law that criminalises their actions.

Regretfully—and this is a sad reflection on the functioning of the contemporary justice delivery mechanism—conviction rates for human rights violations in matters relating to bonded labour are abysmally low and are not at all proportionate to the judicial severity of the crime. The proceedings are also protracted, entailing huge waste of time, energy and money and what comes out at the end is a travesty of justice.

III

Kalahandi (literally meaning black pot) which had supplied rice to West Bengal during the 1943 famine and which today is worse than TS Eliot's 'Wasteland' is not the only source point of distress migration. As many as forty-five such dry and drought-prone pockets across the length and breadth of the country have been identified. Notable among them are Banda, Ballia, Basti, Deoria, Gorakhpur, Azamgarh, Jaunpur, Mirzapur and Sonbhadra (in Uttar Pradesh), Nawada, Lakhisarai, Sitamarhi and Nalanda in Bihar, Palamau, Chatra, Pakur and Deoghar (in Jharkhand), Sehore, Sahadol, Betul, Raisen and Vidisha (in Madhya Pradesh), Durg, Rajnandgaon, Raigarh, Raipur, Bilaspur, Mahasamund (in Chhattisgarh), Barmer, Jaisalmer, Jalore, Sikar, Jhunjhunu, Jodhpur, Bikaner and Banswada (in Rajasthan). With sweeping changes in the labour market, many more new pockets may have been added to this list by now. These are mostly examples of distress migration when people migrate on receipt of advances which put them in the category of full-fledged victims of BLS.

All such source points of distress migration which are dry and drought-prone need to be identified, ways and means like intensification of public works with enforcement of minimum wage and Food Security Act (2013) and stringent enforcement of ISMW (ROE&COS) need to be put in place to prevent and minimise the incidence of such distress migration.

Concluding Remarks

The Bonded Labour System will not end without an intensely sensitive and proactive attitude and approach of law enforcement agencies on the one hand and planned, co-ordinated, concerted and time-bound holistic efforts from both the Centre and States/UTs to promote human development which is just, fair, equitable, holistic and integrated based on un-diluted human freedom on the other. A long-term State-level Action Plan with components of massive advocacy for generation of mass critical awareness of all sections of the civil society, stringent and deterrent punishment of bonded labour keepers, built-in institutional mechanisms (like VCs) with year-round vigilance and surveillance and collection of accurate intelligence on the prevalence of the social scourge in all sensitive pockets, timely action for rescue/release, repatriation, restoration and rehabilitation–cum–re-integration of all freed bonded labourers are some of the undisputed needs of the hour which deserve prioritised attention.

Such a massive programme needs to be supplemented and complemented by good, reliable NGOs committed to social action who can be productively involved in all rescue/release operations and HRD (orientation and training of all stake-holders) initiatives. Simultaneous dialogue is urgently called for between the originating and destination States with the goal of minimising the incidence of distress migration and redressing the grievances of victims of inter-State distress migration, most of whom are locked up in a situation of debt bondage at the work sites of the destination point.

The negative mindset of the destination State Governments and those of local administration therein also need to be replaced by a positive, proactive and supportive one. This is on account of fact that (a) the country is one and indivisible and (b) it is but normal and natural that people and families will always migrate from backward pockets to well-endowed pockets in search of better jobs, better wages and better standard of living. Besides, inter-State migrant workmen through their 'blood, sweat and tears' make immense contribution to the prosperity of the enterprise and GDP rate of the growth in the economy of the State. It will be difficult to easily measure the extent and quality of this contribution and the destination States have every reason to be grateful to these workers for their contribution.

Media and communication agencies which have all along played a positive and supportive role in unearthing abuse and violation of human rights need to continue to play the same pro-active role as far as elimination of BLS and trafficking is concerned. They deserve to be given all encouragement and support for this cause.

Judicial activism, which has been the dominant feature in the functioning of the apex court and which has breathed hope, faith and conviction to the vulnerable as well as the victims, should percolate to the functionaries of all subordinate courts.

The legislature, executive and judiciary at all levels must acknowledge that elimination of BLS and trafficking represent the worst violation of human rights. They must regard programmes related to elimination of boned labour system and trafficking as their own and demonstrate their commitment to this cause in letter and spirit at all times and in all conceivable situations.

Simultaneously and finally, if delivery of justice is to be ensured to those who are in need of the same most i.e. the poor, deprived, disadvantaged, oppressed and marginalised, the legislature, executive and judiciary will have to function in close unison with each other.

The implications of this are as under:

- The legislature cannot implement laws passed by it;
- This task is left to the executive in as much as interpretation of the law is left to the judiciary;
- Judiciary cannot entirely execute all its orders; it needs the tacit understanding and support of the executive for this purpose;
- Similarly within the judiciary, the courts will not be able to carry the judicial process to its logical close unless the lawyers professionally conduct themselves to present their cases, assist & fully cooperate with the Courts in arriving at just, fair & equitable conclusions;
- It is this interdependence between the bench and bar on the one hand and between legislature, executive & judiciary on the other which holds the key to delivery of justice, execution of judicial orders and eventual justice to the aggrieved.

References

1. Bhaduri, Amit – *Analysis of Semi-Feudalism in East Indian Agricultural Frontier Calcutta*, 29 September 1973.
2. *A Fistful of Dry Rice – Land, Equity and Democracy – Essays in Honour of Debabrat Bandopadhyay*, edited by KB Saxena, Manoranjan Mohauty and Sumet Chakravarty.
3. Freire, Paulo – *Pedagogy of the Oppressed*, England, Penguin Books (1972).
4. Markham, Edwin – *The* Man with the Hoe and other poems*, (2004), MT, Kessinger Publishing.
5. Mishra, Lakshmidhar — *Burden of Bondage: Report of Investigation into Working and Living Conditions of Quarry Workers of Faridabad* (1984), Manak Publications, Delhi.
6. Mishra, Lakshmidhar: 'Will the voice of sanity and reason wake up to the call against human bondage', *Mainstream*, New Delhi, Volume L II No 9, February 22, 2014.
7. Mishra, Lakshmidhar: *Child Labour in India* (1999)
8. Mishra, Lakshmidhar: *Human Bondage – Tracing its Roots in India* (2011)
9. Mishra, Lakshmidhar: *Discovery of Truth—Nothing but Truth—Memoirs of a Civil Servant* (2017
10. *National Survey on the incidence of BLS* – a preliminary report

submitted by MoL&E in March 1979 by Gandhi Peace Foundation and National Labour Institute, New Delhi.

11. *Organising Unorganised Rural Labour for Social Justice–Strategy and Methodology*–Proceedings of a National Seminar held at Viswa Yuvak Kendra, Chanakyapuri, New Delhi (05.01.84 to 08.01.84), published by MoL&E in 1986.
12. Siralkar, Ajit 'The Joy of Freedom'.
13. Sen, Amartya (1999), *Development as Freedom*, Oxford University Press, New York.
14. Tagore, Rabindranath – 'Pran', in the anthology of poems *Kadi and Komal.*
15. Report of the First National Commission on Labour (December 1966 to August 1969), published by MoL&E.
16. Report of the Study Group on Wages, Incomes, and Prices, May 1978.
17. Report of Survey conducted by the Associate Chamber of Commerce and Industry of India (ASSOCHAM) captioned, 'Steep rise of permanently temporary workers – India's workforce goes casual), 2013.
18. *Right to Food*, published by Human Rights Law Network (HRLN), pages 215-325.
19. *Global Slavery Index,* Walk Free Foundation, (2013).
20. Yunus, Muhammad, Nobel Peace Laureate (2006) "A World of Three Zeros: The New Economics of Zero Poverty, Zero Unemployment, and Zero Net Carbon Emissions"
21. *Trafficking in Women and Children–India*, Orient and Longman – a publication of NHRC (2005-06).
22. TS Eliot, *Wasteland* (Originally published in 1922 by Liveright Publishing Corporation, New York.)

Abbreviations

ADM	Additional District Magistrate
AHEAD	Association for Human Rights and Development
AHTU	Anti-Human Trafficking Unit
AIDS	Acquired Immuno Deficiency Syndrome
AIR	All India Reporter
ALC	Assistant Labour Commissioner
ANM	Auxiliary Mid-wife and Nurse
AP	Andhra Pradesh
APMCS	Agricultural Marketing Cooperative Society
ASSOCHAM	Associated Chambers of Commerce and Industry
ATR	Action Taken Report
AWARE	Action for Welfare and Awakening of Rural Development
AWW	Anganwadi Worker
B&OCW (ROE & COS) Act	Building and other Construction Workers (Regulation of Employment and Conditions of Service) Act, 1996.
BBA	Bachpan Bachao Andolan

BLS (A) Act	Bonded Labour Sysytem (Abolition) Act
BMM	Bandhua Mukti Morcha
BPO	Business Process Outsourcing
BPR&D	Bureau of Police Research and Development
BSY	Balika Samruddhi Yojana
CAPART	Council for Advancement of People's Action and Rural Technology
CAREBOLA	Campaign for the Abolition and Rehabilitation of Bonded Labour
CBWE	Central Board of Workers Education
CID	Criminal Investigation Department
CIF&B	Chief Inspector of Factories and Boilers
CJI	Chief Justice of India
CJM	Chief Judicial Magistrate
CL (R&A) Act	Contract Labour (Regulation and Abolition) Act
CM	Chief Minister
CPI	Consumer Price Index
CRC	Convention on the Rights of the Child
Crl	Criminal
CrPC	Criminal Procedure Code
CRY	Child Rights and You
CSE	Commercial Sexual Exploitation
CSFHR	Civil Society Forum on Human Rights
CWC	Child Welfare Committee
DG (LW)/JS	Director General (Labour Welfare)/ Joint Secretary
DGFASLI	Director General, Factory Advice and Service and Labour Institutes
DGMS	Director General, Mines Safety

DGT	Director General of Training
DIG	Deputy Inspector General
DLO	District Labour Officer
DM	District Magistrate
DSS	Divya Seva Sansthan
DSWS	Dhagaria Social Welfare Society
DWCRA	Development of Women and Children in Rural Areas
Dy SP	Deputy Superintendent of Police
ECS	Electronic Clearance Service
ERRP	Economic Rehabilitation of Rural Poor
EVM	Electronic Voting Machine
FIR	First Information Report
FSD	Foundation for Sustainable Development
GMA	Goti Mukti Andolan
GOI	Government of India
GP	Gram Panchayat
HIV	Human Immuno-deficiency Virus
HRLN	Human Rights Law Network
IAS	Indian Administrative Service
ICDS	Integrated Child Development Service
ICF	Indian Circus Federation
ICS	Indian Civil Service
ICT	Information and Communication Technology
IEC	Information, Education & Communication
IJM	International Justice Mission
ILO	International Labour Organisation
IPC	Indian Penal Code
IPD	In Patients' Department

IRDP	Integrated Rural Development Programme
ISMW (ROE&COS) Act	Inter-State Migrant Workmen (Regulation of Employment and Conditions of Service) Act, 1979
IT	Information Technology
ITPA	Prevention of Immoral Trafficking Act, 1956 (as amended in 1978 & 1986)
JBVSS	Jai Bhim Vikas Sikshan Sansthan
JJ	Juvenile Justice
JJB	Juvenile Justice Board
JMA	Jan Mukti Anusthan
JPC	Joint Parliamentary Committee
JS	Jan Sahas
JVI	Justice Ventures International
LAMP	Large Agricultural Multi-Purpose Co-operative Societies
LC	Labour Commissioner
LPG	Liquified Petroleum Gas
MEA	Ministry of External Affairs
MGNREGA	Mahatma Gandhi National Rural Employment Guarantee Act
MHA	Ministry of Home Affairs
MHRD	Ministry of Human Resource Development
MLA	Member of Legislative Assembly
MLC	Member of Legislative Council
MoL&E	Ministry of Labour and Employment
MoRD	Ministry of Rural Development
MP	Madhya Pradesh
MP	Member of Parliament
MSDE	Ministry of Small and Medium Enterprises

MW Act	Minimum Wages Act
NALSA	National Legal Services Authority
NCLP	National Child Labour Project
NCPCR	National Commission for Protection of Child Rights
NCRB	National Crime Records Bureau
NCRL	National Commission on Rural Labour
NCT	National Capital Territory
NGO	Non-Governmental Organisation
NHRC	National Human Rights Commission
NIA	National Investigation Agency
NLI	National Labour Institute
NRLM	National Rural Livelihood Mission
NSDA	National Skill Development Authority
NSDC	National Skill Development Corporation
NSSO	National Sample Survey Organisation
OBC	Other Backward Caste
OT Wage	Over-time Wage
PDS	Public Distribution System
PIL	Public Interest Litigation
PMAY	Pradhan Mantri Awas Yojana
PMJDY	Pradhan Mantri Jan Dhan Yojana
PMKVY	Pradhan Mantri Kaushal Vikas Yojana
POCSO	Protection of Children from Sexual Offences Act, 2012
PORP	Participating Organisations of Rural Poor
PUCL	Peoples' Union for Civil Liberties
PUDR	Peoples' Union for Democratic Rights
RARE	Research Academy for Rural Enrichment
RBC	Red Blood Corpuscles

RDO	Revenue Divisional Officer
RTE	Right to Free and Compulsory Education
RTMIS	Real Time Management Information System
SC	Scheduled Caste
SC	Supreme Court
SCC	Supreme Court Case
SCPCR	State Commission for Protection of Child Rights
SDM	Sub-Divisional Magistrate
SHG	Self-Help Group
SHO	Station House Officer
SITA	Suppression of Immoral Trafficking
SLP	Special Leave Petition
SOP	Standard Operating Procedure
SP	Superintendent of Police
SSP	Senior Superintendent of Police
ST	Scheduled Tribe
T&V	Training and Visit
TDCC	Tribal Development Co-operative Corporation
TOT	Training of Trainers
TRYSEM	Training Scheme for Employment of Rural Youth
U/S	Under Section
UNIFEM	United Nations Development Fund for Women
UNESCO	United Nations Educational Scientific and Cultural Organisation
UNODC	United Nations Office on Drugs and Crime

UP	Uttar Pradesh
USA	United States of America
USAID	United States Agency for International Development
UT	Union Territory
VC	Vigilance Committee
VDA	Variable Dearness Allowance
VO	Voluntary Organisation
VV Giri	Varaha Giri Venkat Giri
WB	West Bengal
WBC	White Blood Corpuscles
WCD	Women and Child Development
WHD	Women Help Desk
WHO	World Health Organisation
WP	Writ Petition

Index

C

J

K

L

M

N

T

Lakshmidhar Mishra joined the Indian Administrative Service in 1964. He holds a doctorate in educational planning from Inter-Cultural Open University, Amsterdam. He held important positions in the Government of Odisha (1964-78 and 1994-95) and Central Government (1979-2000), during which time was also appointed by the Supreme Court as Socio-legal Investigating Commissioner into bonded labour. In 2000, he took voluntary retirement to join ILO as Senior Advisor. A prolific writer, he has twenty books and about 350 articles to his credit, as well as seven prestigious awards, including the Mother Teresa International Award for outstanding contribution to promotion of human rights.